Solving Writing Problems

Holt, Rinehart and Winston

New York
Chicago
San Francisco
Atlanta
Dallas
Montreal
Toronto

Louise P. Clara
South Georgia College

Betty P. Nelson
Volunteer State Community College

Solving Writing Problems
A Self-Paced Workbook

**Library of Congress Cataloging in
Publication Data**

Clara, Louise P.
  Solving writing problems.

  Includes index.
    1. English language—Rhetoric.   2. English
language—Rhetoric—Problems, exercises, etc.
I. Nelson, Betty P., joint author. II. Title.
PE1408.C482   808'.042   78–11147

ISBN: 0-03-042986-2

Published by Holt, Rinehart and Winston

To the Instructor

Solving Writing Problems: A Self-Paced Workbook meets the need in classrooms and writing labs for a brief, easy-to-understand, basic review of English usage and for practice that can be both individualized and self-paced. This book addresses these two needs through its three parts:

1. Handbook for review and reference
2. Workbook for self-paced, individualized instruction
3. Writing Assignments for application of new learning by the student and further diagnosis of student progress by the instructor

The handbook, Part 1, is a text easily read and understood. It contains explanations, examples, and illustrations of the basic terms and principles of traditional English grammar. The workbook, Part 2, is provided for individualized, self-paced instruction in either the laboratory or the classroom. The handbook and the workbook are complementary in organization and content so that students working on workbook units can extend their instruction through use of the handbook. Extensive cross-references simplify coordination of these two parts. Part 3 gives short writing assignments to help students apply what they have learned to their own writing and to show the instructor what the next step should be.

A unique feature of *Solving Writing Problems* is the problem-solution format of the workbook. Problems are defined in a writing context so that students can learn to reason about mistakes even as they correct them. The problems not only reflect an analysis of the frequency of student errors made in more than four thousand papers; they also reflect an analysis of why the errors were made. For example, instruction deals separately with different causes of fragments so that students can learn why their own particular fragments fail to communicate. There is also specific instruction in how to correct each kind of fragment. The premise of this book is the same as Mina B. Shaughnessy's in *Errors and Expectations*: "errors carry messages." Side-headings, running headings, and an index with complete, itemized listings help students to find specific problems for reference or review.

Another feature of the format that will benefit both instructor and student is the design for self-paced mastery of each error unit. After each short step of instruction, a formative, or teaching, test lets students assess their understanding to that point as they check their own answers. Reinforcement of learning is thus attained without an instructor's help. At the end of the error unit, the instructor can check the post-test, or summative test, and, using it, readily give corrective feedback to the student. This material is fully suited to the kind of mastery-learning strategy discussed in Benjamin S. Bloom's *Human Characteristics and School Learning*. Because the material is designed for flexibility of use, it can be used in an individualized, self-paced writing lab or classroom. Specific assignments can be made and accounted for through the workbook assignment sheet, or students may begin with the first unit and pretest into or out of it, continuing to the next at their own pace. The book may also be used in the traditional classroom for in-class assignments and/or homework, or in conjunction with a lecture/demonstration method.

The last part of *Solving Writing Problems* contains writing assignments that can be easily understood and followed individually by students whenever each shows readiness to apply recent learning. With sentence-writing assignments, they can demonstrate understanding of the problem they have been studying. The paragraphs and essay assignments provide exercises to demonstrate mastery of writing problems, but their directions also instruct in ordering and development.

This book came into existence because of the authors' own acute need for low-readability, error-specific, and individualized instruction. The students who most need to study an English handbook need one that is easy to read. These students also need to study their specific errors at their own pace and to review charts, examples, and explanations of usage constantly as they write. Material to facilitate all of this should be under one cover, and now it is, in *Solving Writing Problems: A Self-Paced Workbook*.

Since we began this task, we have had the support and active encouragement both of many of our colleagues and of the administrators of our two colleges. At Volunteer State Community College, we are both especially indebted to Dr. Hal R. Ramer, President, and to Dr. Donald R. Goss, Chairman of Humanities, and, at South Georgia College, our thanks go to Dr. Christian Sizemore, Academic Dean.

In the preparation of the manuscript, we are grateful for the help of Jean Robnett and Sherry Lawler and for the advice of Professor Richard S. Beal.

L.P.C.
B.P.N.

Douglas, Georgia
Gallatin, Tennessee
November 1978

To the Student

The English language is hard to write. Here are some reasons that it is.

Languages are not logical. Ways of saying things become accepted because most people say them in those ways. So, if you figure out a logical way to say something, it still may not be the accepted way.

Language that is acceptable in everyday life sometimes is not acceptable for college or job writing. So you have to learn written English as different from the kind of English you use in talking.

Writing is harder than talking for another reason, too. When we speak, we change our voices to help say what we mean. But we cannot do this in writing. So you have to learn signals like punctuation to do what your voice does in talking.

And, finally, writing is a skill learned by practice. Most of us talk much more than we write; so, of course, we talk better than we write.

This book will try to make the difficult problems of learning written English as simple as possible. Your instructors will help when the book fails. And, perhaps the most helpful thing is that you will get much practice.

Contents

RELATIONSHIPS WITHIN A SENTENCE   111

PUNCTUATION   219

MECHANICS   289

SPELLING   299

PART 3 WRITING ASSIGNMENTS 353

HANDBOOK

INSTRUCTIONS FOR USE

PART

The first section of this text, the handbook, gives some necessary information about English usage. You can use it to study things that you do not know, to review things that you do know, or to refer to something you are not sure of. To find something quickly, use the Index at the back of the book and the headings at the side and top of each page.

Grammar

A GRAMMAR VOCABULARY

1 Sentence Parts

As a student writer, you need to understand the terms of grammar that describe your language. You will be able to deal with grammatical relationship within a sentence if you know how words function. This vocabulary of grammar explains terms and describes functions and relationships. Use it for close study, for review of specific areas, or for quick reference when working in the Manual or when writing.

SENTENCE A sentence is an independent unit of thought that has a subject and a predicate or verb. It makes sense by itself.

> *Sentence*: My <u>dog</u> <u>is reading</u> a paper.
>
>   subject   predicate (verb)
>
> My <u>dog</u> <u>is</u> Lassie.
>   subject   predicate (verb)

Subject The subject answers the question, "Who or what is the thought about?" It is about a *dog*.

Predicate The predicate answers the question, "What does the subject do?" It can also state that the subject *is* something.

> The dog <u>is reading</u>. The dog <u>is</u>.

Compound Subject A compound subject occurs when two or more words form the subject and share the same predicate (verb).

> The <u>dog</u> and her <u>owner</u> <u>are reading</u> the paper.
>   subject   subject   predicate (verb)

3

Compound Predicate (Verb) A compound predicate occurs when two or more words form the predicate. Each of these words is a separate action.

The <u>dog</u> <u>is</u> reading a paper and <u>smoking</u> a pipe.
subject   predicate

The Sentence Fragment An error in sentence structure occurs when a thought which is not independent is used as a sentence. It does not make sense by itself. It is only a part of a sentence—a fragment.

Wrong: I laughed. Because <u>he</u> <u>was</u> funny.

a fragment

Correct: I laughed because he was funny.

a sentence

The fragment has a subject (<u>he</u>) and a predicate (<u>was</u>), but, without the sentence that comes before it (I laughed), it does not have a complete meaning. It is *not* independent of another unit of thought.

Fused Thoughts Independent thoughts must be separated from each other by strong end-punctuation (periods or semicolons).

Wrong: I laughed he was funny.

fused thoughts

Right: I laughed. He was funny.

Comma Splice Independent thoughts cannot be separated with weak punctuation (commas).

Wrong: I laughed, he was funny.

a comma splice

Right: I laughed. He was funny.

2 Parts of Speech

There are only eight kinds of words in the English language. These kinds of words are called parts of speech, and they open the door of language use. Every word in the dictionary falls into at least one of these eight kinds. A word may fit into more than one kind, depending on its use in a sentence.

THE NOUN Nouns are the words used most often. They are used to identify someone or something. They are labels, or name words, naming a person, a place, a thing, or an idea.

Persons: teacher, Chris Columbus, woman, child, Lucy
Places: Denver, Africa, house, store
Things: car, Christmas, day, sandwich
Ideas: peace, religion, love, freedom

Common Nouns and Proper Nouns There are two kinds of nouns, *proper nouns* and *common nouns*. A proper noun names a particular person, place, or thing. It is always capitalized. A common noun names any one of a group of persons, places, or things. A common noun is not capitalized.

Common Nouns	Proper Nouns
teacher	Socrates, Jane Addams
city, town	New York, Norwich
business	Sears-Roebuck, Hy's Plumbing
month	May, September, August
movies	*Jaws, Blazing Saddles*

Compound Nouns When two or more words are used as a single noun, they are *compound nouns*. A compound noun may be written as one word or as two or more words, or it may be hyphenated. Some examples of compound nouns are *playmate, city-state, master builder, track star*. A dictionary will give the correct form for a compound noun.

THE PRONOUN A pronoun is used to substitute for a noun after the noun has been identified. Once a noun has been used within a sentence, a pronoun can take its place within that sentence or in a following sentence.

Jim rides his motorcycle and likes it.

After the noun *motorcycle* has been used, the pronoun *it* can take its place in the sentence.

I called Jim and learned that he had wrecked his Honda and that he had been hurt. (The pronouns *he* and *his* substitute for *Jim*.)

Jim said the insurance company had told him that they would cover the cost but that he would have to file a report with them. (The pronouns *they* and *them* take the place of *company*.)

Antecedent of the Pronoun Pronouns almost always take the place of a noun that is mentioned earlier in the sentence or in a preceding sentence. The noun on which the pronoun depends for its meaning is called the *antecedent*, or "something that goes before." In the following examples, the arrows connect the antecedents with the pronouns.

Country music is popular all over the world
because *it* speaks to common feelings.

Ernie Ford took a country music group to
Russia, and *they* were received enthusiastically.

When the *group* returned, the governor
welcomed *them*.

Personal Pronouns   Personal pronouns show in what person the speaker is speaking. For example, they show that someone is speaking about herself (first person), about the person to whom she is speaking (second person), or about another person or thing that may or may not be present (third person). The chart below explains personal pronouns further.

	Singular	Plural
First Person (the person speaking)	I, my, mine, me	We, our, ours
Second Person (the person spoken to)	you, your, yours	you, your, yours
Third Person (Another person or thing)	he, his, him, she, hers, her, it, its	they, their, theirs, them

You will also use the following kinds of pronouns:

Reflexive Pronouns   *Reflexive pronouns* are the *-self, -selves* forms of the personal pronouns.

Singular	Plural
(I) myself (you) yourself (he, him, it) himself, herself, itself oneself	(we) ourselves (you) yourselves (they) themselves

Hisself, theirself, and *theirselves* are not correct forms.

Relative Pronouns   *Relative pronouns* are used to introduce adjective clauses. These pronouns relate two ideas to each other. A relative pronoun substitutes in one idea for a noun or pronoun in the other idea.

These are the relative pronouns:

> who, whom, whose
>
> which
>
> that

Harold Robbins, *who* has written several best-selling novels, wrote *The Betsey*.
>   (*who* substitutes for *Harold Robbins*)

The movie, *which* is based on the book, is not good.
>   (*which* substitutes for *movie*)

Laurence Olivier is the only actor *who* or *that* performs well in the movie.
>   (either *who* or *that* may substitute for *actor*)

Interrogative Pronouns   *Interrogative pronouns* are used in questions.

Who?   Whose?   What?   Whom?   Which?
Who are you?

Demonstrative Pronouns   *Demonstrative pronouns* are used to point out a specific person or thing.

this   that   these   those
That is a lie.
I asked for *those* first.

Indefinite Pronouns   *Indefinite pronouns* do not refer to a definite person or thing. They are often used without antecedents. Study the following list of indefinite pronouns.

all	either	more	one
another	everybody	most	other
any	everyone	much	several
anybody	everything	neither	some
anyone	few	nobody	somebody
anything	fewer	none	someone
both	fewest	no one	something
each	many		

Reciprocal Pronouns   *Reciprocal pronouns* are pronoun pairs. Although they refer to two persons, they are also singular.

each other   one another
each other's   one another's

They smiled at *each other*.

THE ADJECTIVE   The adjective in a sentence relates directly to a noun or a pronoun. The adjective describes or modifies the noun or pronoun to make the meaning of the noun or pronoun clearer. An adjective modifies a noun or a pronoun by answering one of these questions: what kind? which one? how many? In the examples below, the underlined adjectives modify by answering these questions:

What kind?	Which one?	How many?
bright dress	*that* book	*four* books
educated fool	*next* year	*few* excuses
small return	the *third* one	*many* reasons
happy birthday	the *oldest* man	*few* days

In the phrases in the last two columns above, *that, third, few,* and *many* are adjectives, not pronouns. They are adjectives because they are modifying the nouns in these phrases, not taking the place of the nouns. If the word modifies a noun, it is an adjective. If it takes the place of a noun, it is a pronoun.

> I prefer *these* apples to *those*.
>
>   (adj.)   (pro.)
>
> I want the *third* one, not the *second*.
>
>   (adj.)   (pro.)

Adjectives versus Possessive Pronouns   The possessive forms of personal pronouns (*my, your, his, her, its, our,* and *their*) are called "possessive" because they show ownership. Although they are pronouns in form, they modify nouns in a sentence. Consequently, they act as adjectives.

Comparison of Adjectives   Adjectives can be changed to show degrees of comparison. This means that when two or more nouns are modified by the same adjective, the adjective can be changed to show which noun it applies more to or most to. There are three ways of changing adjectives to use them in comparison.

For short words (words of one syllable and most words of two syllables), add *-er* for comparing two.

Jane is *smarter* than Jean. (comparing two)

For short words, add *-est* for comparing more than two.

Edna is *smartest* of the group. (comparing more than two)

For longer words (some words of two syllables and all words of three or more syllables), use *more* for comparing two.

Mr. Sims is *more experienced* than Mr. Titus. (comparing two)

For longer words comparing more than two, use *most*.

Mr. Roberts is the *most experienced* painter I know. (comparing more than two)

A few adjectives change their whole form to show degrees of comparison.

Used without comparing	Used to compare two	Used to compare more than two
good	better	best
bad	worse	worst
many	more	most
much	more	most
little	less, lesser	least

Jack is a *good* driver. (no comparison)
Earnest is a *better* driver than Jack. (comparing two)
Susan is the *best* driver in her class. (comparing more than two)

To compare the degree to which an adjective does *not* apply to the word it describes, always use *less* and *least*.

gladdest	gladder	glad	less glad	least glad
most happy	more happy	happy	less happy	least happy
worst	worse	bad	less bad	least bad

Adjectives as Articles   Three adjectives (*a*, *an*, and *the*) are called articles. *A* and *an* are *indefinite articles*, referring to one of a general group. *The* refers to someone or something particular and is called a *definite article*.

An apply a day is my advice.
We arranged for *an* hour of time.
The weather is getting colder.

Use of a/an   *A* is used before words beginning with a consonant sound. *An* is used before words beginning with a vowel sound. In the second example above, *an* is used before a noun beginning with the consonant *h* because the *h* in *hour* is silent. *Hour* is pronounced as if it began with a vowel (like *our*). the sound of the word, not the spelling, determines which indefinite article will be used. The sound of an initial (the name of a letter of the alphabet) may differ from the sound that the same letter makes when it is pronounced. For instance, the letter *m* makes the humming sound *mmm*. But the initial *m* sounds as if it begins with an *e: em*. If an initial begins with a vowel sound, use *an* before it. If it begins with a consonant sound, use *a* before it.

She is *an* RN. (*r* begins with an *a* sound)
She is *a* registered nurse. (*registered* begins with an *r* sound)

Position of the Adjective An adjective is usually placed before the noun it modifies.

> He liked *fast* horses.
> *Gray, damp* fog drifted before us.

Sometimes, adjectives may follow the words they modify:

> The fog, *gray* and *damp*, drifted before us.

An adjective may be separated from the noun or pronoun it modifies by other words.

> You look *lost*. (*lost* modifies *you*)
>
> Bill was very *grieved*. (*grieved* modifies *Bill*)
>
> *Looking at him lovingly,* she picked up her change.
>
> (entire phrase used as an adjective)

Identifying Adjectives When you are trying to decide if a word is an adjective, ask yourself these questions: Does it modify a noun or pronoun? Does it tell what kind, which one, or how many? If the answer to these questions is "yes," the word is an adjective.

THE VERB A verb either names an action by the subject or asserts something about the subject. Words such as *run, do, see*, and *write* are action verbs. They name an action that can be seen. Sometimes action words name an action that cannot be seen: for example, *feel, believe, know, think, understand, smell*. Other verbs do not name actions. They assert something about the subject's state of being: for example, *is, are, was, were, been*.

Transitive Verbs There are two classes of action verbs: the transitive verbs and the intransitive verbs. A verb is *transitive* when the action it expresses is directed toward a person or thing named in the sentence.

> The actor won an award. (The action of the verb *won* is directed toward *award*. The verb is transitive.)
>
> The child finally washed her face. (The action of the verb *washed* is directed toward *face*. The verb is transitive.)

In these examples, the action passes from the doer (the subject) to the receiver of the action. Words that receive the action of a transitive verb are called objects—either *direct* objects or *indirect* objects. The object names the person or thing that receives the action of the action verb.

Intransitive Verbs A verb is *intransitive* when no action is passed to a receiver. Linking verbs are intransitive verbs because they do not pass an action to a receiver. Action verbs are intransitive when their action is not directed to anything in the sentence. The following sentences contain intransitive verbs:

The pilot <u>was</u> | tired. (linking)

He <u>arrived</u> | out of breath. (action)

Our ship <u>sails</u> | on Wednesday. (action)

Both Transitive and Intransitive Verbs The same verb may be transitive in one sentence and intransitive in another. A verb that can take an object is often intransitive when the emphasis in the sentence is placed on the action rather than on the person or thing affected by the action. When the action, rather than the person affected by it, is the important thing, the verb is usually intransitive.

The soldier <u>saluted</u> the flag.   (transitive action passes)

The soldier <u>saluted</u> | quickly.   (intransitive action stops)

I <u>met</u> my friend at the airport.   (transitive action passes)

I <u>met</u> | with my friend today.   (intransitive action stops)

Linking Verbs (to be form) Linking verbs are intransitive verbs that do not express an action but have a linking function. They join a subject to another word in the sentence that completes the meaning of the subject. The most commonly used linking verbs are the forms of *to be* listed below. You should become thoroughly familiar with them.

be	shall be	should be
being	will be	would be
am	has been	can be
is	have been	could be
are	had been	should have been
was	shall have been	would have been
were	will have been	could have been

Other Linking Verbs These linking verbs are also used frequently.

appear	get	remain	stay
become	grow	seem	taste
equal	look	smell	turn
feel	mean	sound	

How the Linking Verb Links To be a linking verb, a verb must link the subject of a sentence with a word that identifies, classifies, or describes it. The word that follows the linking verb does two things: (1) it fills out or completes the meaning of the verb and (2) it refers to the word preceding the verb.

Tom is an actor.

Tom is talented.

Sometimes the same verb may be used as either a linking verb or an action verb.

John proved capable.   (linking)

John proved his point.   (active)

Helping Verbs or Auxiliary Verbs   Forms of the verb *to be* can be used as helping verbs, too. (auxiliary verbs). These forms are listed above. Other helping verbs include the following:

has	can	might
have	may	must
had	should	do
shall	would	did
will	could	does

Helping Verbs with Main Verbs (Verb Phrases)   These helping verbs work with main verbs to make a unit called a *verb phrase*. The helping verbs are underlined in the verb phrases below.

is leaving	may become	might have remained
had seemed	should move	must have thought
shall be going	could jump	does sing

Interrupted Verb Phrase   Sometimes the parts of a verb phrase are separated from each other by other parts of speech.

You may not have been responsible.   (separated by *not*)
We will surely hear something soon.   (separated by *surely*)

Verb Phrases in Questions   Parts of verb phrases are often separated from each other in questions.

Will you call her tomorrow?
Did he make the team?
Have they met Jerry yet?

THE ADVERB   Adverbs, like adjectives, are modifiers. They modify verbs, adjectives, or other adverbs. An adverb usually modifies a verb. The adverbs italicized below modify verbs by answering one of these questions: where? when? how? to what extent (how long or how much)?

Where?	When?
I moved *there*.	I moved *immediately*.
Sit *down*.	Call *later*.
Do you live *here*?	Do you go *daily*?

How?	To what extent?
I *quickly* declined.	She *hardly* noticed.
Sleep *well*.	He did *not* sleep.
Did you go *quietly*?	Did you go *far*?

Adverbs Ask Questions   Adverbs may come before or after the verbs they modify. They may interrupt the parts of a verb phrase. And they may introduce questions.

> *How* will we *ever* finish our work on time?
> (The adverb *how* modifies the verb phrase *will finish*. The adverb *ever* interrupts the verb phrase and also modifies it.)

Adverbs Modify Adjectives   Sometimes an adverb modifies an adjective.

> Martha is a very beautiful woman.
> (The adjective *beautiful* modifies the noun *woman*.
> The adverb *very*, telling how beautiful, modifies *beautiful*.)

Adverbs Modify Adverbs   Sometimes an adverb modifies another adverb. In the first column below, each underlined adverb modifies a verb or an adjective. In the second column, each underlined adverb modifies another adverb.

> Allen is never still.
>   (adj.)
>
> He wrote me recently.
>   (verb)

> Allen is almost never still.
>   (adv.)
>
> He wrote fairly recently.
>   (adv.)

Comparison of Adverbs   Adverbs are changed to show degree of comparison. When they describe two or more words and apply to the words to a greater or lesser extent, their forms show the extent or degree of comparison. The forms of adverbs change in three ways to show degrees of comparison.

For short adverbs, *-er* is added to compare two things.

> He drove faster than his competitors. (comparing two things)

To compare more than two things described by a short adverb, add *-est* to the adverb.

> He drove fastest on the last race of the three.
> (comparing more than two things)

Many adverbs are made up of an adjective plus *-ly*. For instance, the adjective *glad* becomes the adverb *gladly* and the adjective *easy* becomes the adverb *easily*. As a result, most adverbs are two or more syllables long. Like longer adjectives, longer adverbs use *more* and *most* to compare.

Ella sang more sweetly than Ruth. (comparing two)
Beatrice sang most sweetly of all. (comparing more than two)

A few common adverbs change their form entirely to show degrees of comparison.

Used without comparing	Used to compare two	Used to compare more than two
well	better	best
badly	worse	worst
little	less	least

Ann cooks badly. (no comparison)
Herman cooks worse than Ann. (comparing two)
Jane cooks worst of all. (comparing more than two)

All adverbs use *less* and *least* to show the degree to which an adverb does *not* apply to the word it modifies.

I wanted to go less badly than Jerry. (comparing two)
Sue wanted to go least badly of us all. (comparing more than two)

Identifying Adverbs   When trying to identify a word as an adverb, ask yourself: Does this word modify a verb, an adjective, or another adverb? Does it tell when, where, how, or to what extent? If the answer to each question is "yes," the word is an adverb.

THE PREPOSITION   Prepositions connect or relate nouns and pronouns to other nouns and pronouns, to verbs, or to modifiers. A preposition is a word that shows the relationship of a noun or pronoun to another word in the sentence.

The relation shown by prepositions is an important one. In the examples below, the way the italicized prepositions relate *car* to *ran* and *him* to *book* makes a great difference in meaning.

I ran *to* the car.   The book *by* him is missing.
I ran *around* the car.   The book *about* him is missing.
I ran *toward* the car.   The book *for* him is missing.

Common Prepositions   The following words are commonly used as prepositions. Study the list carefully so that you will learn to recognize the words in sentences.

aboard	after	around	below	between
about	against	at	beneath	beyond
above	along	before	beside	but
across	among	behind	besides	by
concerning	inside	on	throughout	until

down	into	out	till	up
during	like	over	to	upon
except	near	past	toward	with
for	of	since	under	within
from	off	through	underneath	without
in				

Prepositions versus Adverbs Many of the words in this list of prepositions can be adverbs. To be a preposition, a word must relate a following noun or pronoun to a word that comes before it. Compare the following:

> Walk *around*. (adverb)
> Walk *around* the square. (preposition)

Compound prepositions Compound prepositions are prepositions made up of more than one word. Here are some frequently used compound prepositions.

according to	in addition to	on account of
as to	in front of	out of
aside from	in place of	owing to
because of	in spite of	prior to
by means of	instead	

The Prepositional Phrase The noun or pronoun that follows the preposition is called the object of the preposition. Together, the noun or pronoun and the preposition make up a *prepositional phrase*.

> around the corner   by   him
> (prep.)   (noun)   (prep.) (pronoun)
>   (object of prep.)   (object of prep.)

THE CONJUNCTION A conjunction is a word that joins words or groups of words. There are three kinds of conjunctions: coordinating conjunctions, correlative conjunctions, and subordinating conjunctions.

The Coordinating Conjunction Coordinating conjunctions may join *single* words or *groups* of words. They always connect items of *the same kind*.

> food *and* drink (two nouns)
> at home *or* at the store (two prepositional phrases)
> I know she has arrived, *for* I saw her in the hotel.
> (two complete ideas)

The following words are sometimes used as coordinating conjunctions:

and	nor	yet
but	for	so
or		

No other English words may be used as coordinating conjunctions, but some of these conjunctions may be used for other purposes.

For as a Conjunction   *For* is a conjunction only when it means "because." Otherwise, it is a preposition:

> We waited a long time, *for* the taxi was late.
> (*For* means "because.")
>
> He waited a long time *for* the taxi. (*For* is a preposition.)

The Correlative Conjunction   Correlative conjunctions also connect items of the same kind. Unlike coordinating conjunctions, correlative conjunctions are always used in pairs. These are correlative conjunctions:

> both .... and
> not only .... but also
> either .... or
> neither .... nor

Notice that the correlative conjunctions always include one of the coordinating conjunctions *and, but, or,* or *nor.*

> Both Bobbie Joe and Roy entertained the group. (two nouns)
> Jerry asked not only for a holiday but also for a raise.
> Either you must study, or you will not be allowed to enter the program.

The Subordinating Conjunction   A subordinating conjunction connects a subordinate (dependent) clause to the rest of the sentence. Subordinate clauses have a subject (noun or pronoun) and a predicate (verb), but they cannot exist alone as sentences. You must be able to recognize the subordinating conjunctions that mark the introduction of subordinate clauses because punctuation is involved.

> I will tell you when he arrives. (The subordinating conjunction *when* in the middle of the sentence begins the subordinate clause. No comma is needed between the clauses because the subordinate clause comes after the main clause.)

> When he arrives, I will tell you. (The subordinating conjunction *when* comes at the beginning of the sentence. A comma is needed after the subordinate clause because it comes before the main clause.)

Study the following list of subordinating conjunctions. The italicized conjunctions are the ones most often used.

after	*before*	*since*	until
although	even if	so (that)	*when*

as	even though	so that	whenever
as if	except	than	where
as long as	*if*	that	wherever
as soon as	in order that	*though*	whether
as though	provided	till	*while*
because	provided that	unless	

THE INTERJECTION An interjection is a word expressing an emotion that has no meaningful relation to the rest of the sentence. Such words are unrelated grammatically to other words in the sentence. They are set off from the rest of the sentence by punctuation. They are usually followed by an exclamation point. However, when the emotion is mild, the interjection may be followed by a comma.

My! You are original!
Ouch! You're too close.

Oh, all right.
Well, then we left.

3 Sentence Core

The basic unit of communication is the sentence. A sentence, as you have learned, is an independent thought punctuated at the end with a period, a question mark, or an exclamation point.

You will also need to learn the three main elements of a sentence: subject, verb, and complement.

PARTS OF THE SENTENCE

Subject The subject of the sentence is a noun or a part of speech that substitutes for a noun (pronoun, gerund, infinitive, noun clause). The subject, which may be either simple or complete, is the thing the sentence tells about.

simple subject The simple subject is the subject standing by itself:

Hopeful <u>Horace</u> brought roses to his Gertrude.
(*Horace* is the simple subject.)

complete subject The complete subject is the simple subject (Horace) and any other words that relate to it (Hopeful Horace).

<u>Waiting for the doctor</u> makes me nervous.
(*Waiting* is the simple subject. *Waiting for the doctor* is the complete subject because the phrase *for the doctor* modifies *waiting*.)

compound subject A sentence may have a compound subject. A compound subject is made up of two or more subjects joined by a conjunction and sharing the same verb.

The grasshopper played all summer.
(*Grasshopper* is the simple subject.)

The grasshopper and the ant did not agree about the use of time.
(*Grasshopper* and *ant* are compound subjects.)

Verb In the sentence, the function of the verb is to assert something about its subject. Every verb in a sentence must have a subject, either expressed or understood.

The subject *you* is sometimes understood:

Stop! (You stop!)

You is the only subject that is understood without being expressed.

The verb asserts by showing the subject's action or state of being.

The pitcher walked the first man.
(action—an action verb)

The pitcher is unusual.
(state of being—a linking verb)

verb forms The verb has different forms like *walk, walks, walked, walking*.

I walk.   He walks.
I am walking.   She had walked.
I walked.

main verb The verb may be one word or more than one word.

Mark met President Ford.
   main verb

Ellen turned off the light.
   main verb

auxiliary verb (helping verb) The President was asking him questions.

(The auxiliary or helping verb *was* helps the main verb *asking*.)

simple predicate The main verb and its auxiliaries make up the simple predicate of a sentence.

Edward was asking for you.   I shall be going soon.
(*was asking* is the   (*shall be going* is the
simple predicate)   simple predicate)

compound predicate Two or more simple predicates sharing the same simple subject are called a *compound predicate* (verb).

The men weighed anchor and came in to the dock.

(Weighed and came, the compound predicate, share the subject men.)

complete predicate The complete predicate of a sentence is everything that is asserted about the subject. It is the verb, its complements, and its modifiers.

> He swam across the lake.
>   main verb
>   complete predicate

Complements (Completers) Complements are words or phrases that follow the verb and complete its meaning. They answer the question *what* or *whom* after the verb.

direct objects as completers Complements can be direct objects. A direct object receives the action of an action verb.

> Napoleon sent a letter to the Duke.
> subject   verb   direct object

The complement *letter* receives the action of the verb *sent*. It answers the question *what*. The direct object may also answer the question *whom*.

> Napoleon sent a messenger to the front lines.
> subject   verb   direct object

indirect objects as completers An indirect object of the verb is a noun or pronoun that comes before the direct object and tells *to whom* or *for whom* the action is done. It may also tell *to what* or *for what*.

> I   told   John   a   lie.
> subject verb   indirect   direct object
>   object
>   (to whom)

In order to work with a completer that can receive action (indirect or direct object), a verb must be an action verb. In other words, it must be able to pass action from the subject to the receiver of the action.

objective complements as completers In a few sentences, a word follows the direct object and tells *what* or *whom*. This is called an objective complement because it completes a direct object.

> We named Ted   president.
>   direct   objective
>   object   complement

(We named whom? *Ted*, so *Ted* is the direct object. We named Ted what? *President*, so *president* is the objective complement.)

The candidate made Smedley his campaign manager.

   subject   verb direct object   objective complement

Notice that the objective complement always comes after the direct object.

transitive verbs and complements

A verb that carries action to a direct object is called a transitive verb.

The candidate mailed letters to voters.

  subject verb   direct object

The candidate mailed voters   letters.

  subject   verb   indirect direct
                   object object

Notice that the indirect object comes before the object and that it cannot receive action from the verb unless it is in this position.

intransitive verbs as linking verbs

Some completers follow intransitive verbs. Intransitive verbs cannot carry action from the subject to the object. These verbs link or join the subject to a completer rather than expressing an action that goes from subject to completer. Because of their function in the sentence, they are called *linking verbs*.

predicate nouns and predicate adjectives

Completers that follow linking verbs may be nouns or adjectives. They are called predicate nouns (p.n.) or predicate adjectives (p.a.). A predicate noun asserts that it is the same thing as the subject.

Elizabeth Ray was a staff member.

  subject   linking verb   predicate noun

(*Member* refers to *Elizabeth Ray*, helping to complete the meaning of the subject.)

A predicate adjective describes or modifies the subject.

She   was fatal to her employer's career.

Subject verb predicate adjective

(*Fatal* describes the subject *she*.)

SENTENCE CORE: WORD ORDER

The typical order of words in the sentence core is one of these:

SUBJECT—VERB:

John threw.

  (s.)   (v.)

SUBJECT—VERB—OBJECT:

John threw a pass.

  (s.)   (v.) (obj.)

SUBJECT—VERB—OBJECT—OBJECTIVE COMPLEMENT:
John made Jim receiver.

   (s.) (v.) (o.) (oc.)

SUBJECT—VERB—INDIRECT OBJECT—DIRECT OBJECT:
John threw Jim a pass.

   (s.) (v.) (io.) (do.)

SUBJECT—LINKING VERB—COMPLEMENT (PN or PA):
John is a runner.

   (s.) (lv.) (pn.)

John is hard-working.

   (s.) (lv.) (pa.)

Finding the Sentence Core The sentence core is made up of the main parts of the sentence.

> Subject — verb — complement.

first, the verb To find the sentence core, locate the verb first. The verb shows action or being. So ask yourself, "What word is an action word, or shows existence?"

Aladdin rubbed the magic lamp.
(What is an action word? *Rubbed*, which is the verb.)

second, the subject Then ask yourself "who" or "what" (in relation to the verb), and you will have the subject.

Aladdin rubbed the magic lamp.
(Who or what rubbed? *Aladdin*, who is the subject.)

third, the complement (action verb) or The complement is the third part of the core. To find it, ask yourself if a word after the verb shows the receiver of the action that has been expressed through the actor (subject) and the action (verb).

Aladdin rubbed the magic lamp.
(Aladdin rubbed what? *Lamp*, which is the direct object.)

third, the complement (linking verb) Remember that the linking verb will complete its sentence core relationship with the subject and the complement by renaming or describing the subject. To find it, ask if a word after the verb is renaming or describing the subject.

Aladdin is a fictional character.
Aladdin is friendly.

error to avoid Be sure that your subject is free to join the sentence core. A noun that is part of a phrase cannot do this.

One of the reasons is a secret.

(The subject cannot be *reasons* because it is part of the prepositional phrase *of the reasons*.)

Unusual Word Order in the Sentence Core Sometimes the typical word order of sentence elements is reversed. This happens with questions or exclamations.

Have you seen the morning paper?

the question This question begins with the helping verb *have*. Questions may also begin with a main verb or with word such as *what, when, where, how,* or *why*. In any case, the subject in a question usually follows the main verb or helping verb.

In questions that begin with a helping verb, the subject always comes between the helper and the main verb.

Have   you   seen   him?
(helping (subject)   (main verb)
verb)

In questions that begin with *what, when, where, how,* or *why,* the subject follows both this word and the helping verb.

When   did   you   see   him?
      (helping verb) (subject) (main verb)

finding the subject in a question You can also find the subject in a question by turning the question into a statement. Then follow the steps above.

Did   John   go?
(helping (subject) (main verb)
verb)

John   did go.
(subject)   verb)

adverb pointers The words *there* or *here* at the beginning of a sentence can point to a place. If they do this, the order for the sentence core is reversed.

There   is   the   entrance.

adverb   verb   subject
pointer

Here   are   the   answers.

adverb   verb   subject
pointer

There and *here* tell where. They are adverbs, not subjects. The subject is the thing that the sentence is about. In these sentences the subjects are *entrance* and *answers*.

the expletive The word *there* also begins sentences when it is not pointing to any particular place but
there means "in the world," or "in existence." It is used as an expletive (or filler) to start the sentence which asserts that something does exist. The expletive is not a subject. It fills the starting place of the sentence until the subject is named after a linking verb.

> *There*   are many   reasons.
> expletive verb   subject
>
> *There*   is no hope.
> expletive verb   subject

SECONDARY A sentence has secondary elements as well as main elements. Some secondary sentence
SENTENCE elements are modifiers. These elements may be words, phrases, or clauses. Word mod-
ELEMENTS ifiers are usually related to parts of the sentence core through word order.

Adjectives Adjectives usually can be found before the nouns they modify.

> The *silent* crowd waited.
> adjective noun

Of course, if the adjective is a predicate adjective, it comes after a linking verb.

> Sharon is *pretty*.
> noun   adjective

Adverbs An adverb is usually found next to the verb that it modifies. But an adverb modifying a verb may be in other places in the sentence.

> The spirit floated *slowly* downstairs.
>   verb adverb
>
> *Slowly* the spirit floated downstairs.
> adverb   verb
>
> The spirit floated downstairs *slowly*.
>   verb   adverb

An adverb that modifies an adjective or another adverb is found before the adjective or adverb that it modifies.

> Sharon is *really* pretty.
>   adverb adjective
>
> He ran *very* slowly.
>   adverb adverb

Appositives   Appositives are nouns that identify or explain other nouns and follow them closely in sentences. They rename, with another noun or a noun phrase, the noun to which they are in apposition.

> I'm watching my favorite *show, The Jeffersons*.
> (*The Jeffersons* is an appositive explaining *show*.)

Verbals   Participles, gerunds, and infinitives are verbals. Verbals do the work of two parts of speech. They have a verb form and may do some of the things that verbs do, like have an object. (By themselves they *cannot* be the predicate of a sentence core.) But they also do the work of adjectives, adverbs, or nouns.

Participles   A participle is a verb form that is used as an adjective. A participle usually ends in *-ing*, *-ed*, *-t*, or *-en*.

> *Exhausted* players are not reliable.
> *Purring* softly, the tiger advanced.
> *Driven* by flies, the heifer leaped wildly.
> *Left* alone, they went to sleep.

Gerunds   A gerund is a verb form that ends in *-ing* and is used as a noun. It occurs in any sentence position that a noun can fill.

> *Walking* is healthful. (subject)
> She hates *walking*. (direct object)
> She keeps her weight stable by *walking*. (object of preposition)
> Her favorite exercise is *walking*. (complement—predicate noun)

Because a gerund is used as a noun, a pronoun coming just before it and telling about it must be possessive. See 8 on possessive pronouns acting like adjectives.

> She works at *her walking*.

Infinitives   Infinitives are verb forms that begin with *to*. They can be used in three ways—as a noun, an adjective, or an adverb.

> *To read* is her delight. (noun)
> She can show you the way *to read*. (adjective)
> She is always ready *to read*. (adverb)

PARTS OF SPEECH CHART

Part of Speech	Description	Use	Example
NOUN	Naming word. Names a person, place or thing.	names	*John* hates *peanuts*.
PRONOUN	Substitutes for a noun.	substitutes	*He* and *I* will do *this* for *you*.

Part of Speech	Description	Use	Example
ADJECTIVE	Modifies a noun or a pronoun.	modifies	Asters are *blue* flowers.
VERB	Asserts action or being.	asserts	We *talked*. She *is* willing.
ADVERB	Modifies a verb, an adjective, or another adverb.	modifies	We left *afterwards*. She is *extremely* upset. She dropped *it very* quickly.
PREPOSITION	Relates a noun or a pronoun to some other word in the sentence.	relates	We planted it *on* the terrace.
CONJUNCTION	Joins words or groups of words.	joins	The town *and* the countryside are much alike.
INTERJECTION	Expresses emotion or surprise.	exclaims	Wow! Really!
PARTICIPLE	Usually ends in *-ing* or *-ed* or *-en*. Looks like a verb; acts like an adjective.	adjective	The *playing* field was wet.
GERUND	Ends in *-ing*. Looks like a verb; acts like a noun.	noun	*Playing* is my career.
INFINITIVE	Begins with *to*. Looks like a verb; acts like a noun, an adjective, or an adverb.	noun adjective adverb	*To leave* you is hard This is the way *to act*. He went home early *to rest*.

PARTS OF SPEECH AND SENTENCE CONTEXT

Some words can be used as more than one part of speech. The way they are used in a sentence determines what parts of speech these words are.

The *truck* passed me. (noun)
They *truck* fruit to market. (verb)
The *truck* firm is successful. (adjective)

To find out what part of speech a word is, you must read a sentence carefully, studying the way the word is used in the sentence.

SENTENCE STRUCTURE

Words in a language work together as groups in order to communicate something. The group that communicates a complete meaning is a sentence. It makes sense by itself because it communicates a complete thought. All the word and groups of words in a sentence are related to each other. And these relations make the sentence idea complete.

4 The Phrase

The phrase is a unit within a sentence. It is a group of words that does not contain a subject and a predicate. It always does the job of one of the parts of speech.

The Noun Phrase   A phrase may work within the sentence as a noun. It can work, as a noun does, as subject, object, or complement. If it does the work of a noun, it is a noun phrase.

> That *sport* is fun. (*Sport* is a noun used as a subject.)
>
> *Swimming underwater* is fun. (The italicized phrase is used as a noun, for the subject.)
>
> *To swim underwater* is fun. (The italicized phrase is used as a noun, for the subject.)

The Adjective Phrase   A phrase may also work as an adjective. An adjective modifies a noun or pronoun. It points to it or describes it, tells how many it is, or limits it. When a phrase does the same things, it is an adjective phrase.

> The *blonde* girl is the one to meet. (*Blonde* is an adjective modifying *girl*.)
>
> The girl *with blonde hair* is the one to meet.
> (The italicized phrase is used as an adjective modifying *girl*.)
>
> The girl *to meet* is the one with blonde hair.
> (The italicized phrase is used as an adjective modifying *girl*.)
>
> The girl *meeting the tall boy* is his sister.
> (The italicized phrase is used as an adjective modifying *girl*.)

The Adverb Phrase   A phrase may work as an adverb to tell more about a verb, adjective, or another adverb. It tells how, when, where, why, or to what extent. A phrase doing this is an adverb phrase.

> He drove *carefully*. (*Carefully* is an adverb modifying *drove*, telling how.)
>
> He drove *on the wrong side*. (The italicized phrase is used as an adverb modifying *drove*, telling where.)
>
> He drove *to forget his worries*. (The italicized phrase is used as an adverb modifying *drove*, telling why.)

5 The Clause

A clause is a group of related words that includes a subject and a predicate.

Independent Clause If the clause makes sense by itself, it is an independent clause.

Dependent Clause If the clause depends on another clause to make sense, it is a dependent clause. All the words in a dependent clause work together to do the job of some other part of speech. Like phrases, dependent clauses may work as nouns, adjectives, or adverbs. The whole clause is one *unit* in the sentence.

dependent clauses as nouns A dependent clause may do the work of a single noun in a sentence. It may be a subject, object, or predicate noun. When it does the work of one of these, it is a noun clause.

Her *speed* amazed me. (*Speed* is the subject in this sentence, so it is a noun.)

That he said no amazed me. (The italicized dependent clause is used as the subject, so it is used as a noun. It names the *thing* that amazed me.)

He said *that I should go*. (The italicized clause is used as the object. It names the *thing* that he said, so it is used as a noun.)

The car was *what I had wanted*. (The italicized dependent clause is used as a predicate noun renaming car. It is used as a noun.)

dependent clauses as adjectives The dependent clause may be used to modify a noun or pronoun. It may point out, describe, tell how many, or limit a noun or pronoun. When it does any of these, it is being used as an adjective. Adjective clauses begin with a word substituting for the word that the adjective clause tells about. These words (relative pronouns) are *who, whom, whose, which*, and *that*. Occasionally, *when* and *where* are used as relative pronouns.

The *vanilla* ice cream is gone. (*Vanilla* is used as an adjective to modify *ice cream*.)

The ice cream *that I like* is gone. (The italicized dependent clause is used as an adjective to modify *ice cream*.)

The ice cream, *which was vanilla*, was good. (The italicized dependent clause is used as an adjective to modify *ice cream*.)

My brother, *who likes most ice cream*, hates vanilla. (The italicized dependent clause is used as an adjective to modify *brother*.)

dependent clauses as adverbs The dependent clause may be used as an adverb. Adverbs modify verbs, adjectives, or other adverbs. They tell how, when, where, why, or to what extent. A dependent clause may tell any of these. The word that introduces it says that it tells one of these. Some of these words (subordinate conjunctions) are *when, because, if, although, unless*, and *where*. See 2 for a more complete list. If a clause modifies a verb, adjective, or adverb, it is an adverb clause.

Later, he went home. (*Later* is an adverb modifying *went*, telling when he went.)

When he had finished talking with his friend, he went home. (The italicized dependent clause is used as an adverb modifying the verb *went*, telling when he went.)

He was gone longer *than he meant to be.* (The italicized dependent clause is used as an adverb modifying the adverb *longer*, telling to what extent *longer* applies.)

She was guilty *as much as her friend was.* (The italicized dependent clause is used as an adverb modifying the adjective *guilty*, telling to what extent *guilty* is so.)

6 The Sentence

A sentence is a complete statement. Its basic parts are presented in **3**. But, as the sections above show, a phrase or clause may be used for one of these parts, and complete statements may be put together to make one sentence.

Independent Clauses   An independent clause is also a group of related words that contains a subject and a predicate. But it makes sense alone. It does not depend on any other word or group of words to make sense. It does not do the job of just one part of speech.

> EVERY SENTENCE MUST CONTAIN AT LEAST ONE INDEPENDENT CLAUSE.

independent clauses as simple sentences   A single independent clause may be a sentence by itself. A single independent clause that is a sentence is called a *simple sentence.*

He flies. (*He* is the subject, the naming word; *flies* is the predicate, the acting word. This group of words is a clause. Because it makes sense by itself, it is an independent clause. So, it can be a sentence all by itself.)

independent clauses in compound sentences   Two or more independent clauses may be joined into one sentence by a semicolon (;) or by conjunctions that show the clauses are equal. The conjunctions that show equality are *and, but, or, nor, for, so,* and *yet.*

He flies; *he also races boats.*

He flies, and *he also races boats.* (The italicized clause, like *He flies,* is an independent clause, so it, too, *could* be a simple sentence. But, since two independent clauses are in the same sentence, it is a compound sentence.)

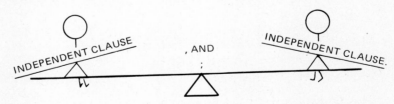

Two or more independent clauses joined by a semicolon (;) or by *and, but, or, nor, for, so,* or *yet* make a compound sentence.

independent and dependent clauses in complex sentences An independent clause can stand alone as a sentence. A dependent clause *cannot*, although it, too, has a subject and verb. This means that every dependent clause must be in a sentence with an independent clause. A sentence containing both kinds of clauses is called a complex sentence.

> He flies *because that makes him feel free.* (The italicized dependent clause cannot make sense by itself, so it must be joined with the independent clause.)

Words that join dependent clauses to independent clauses do *not* make the clauses equal. They show that the dependent clause works in the sentence as a part (a noun, an adjective, or an adverb) of the independent clause. Some of these joining words (conjunctions) are *where, when, because, if, although*, and *unless*. They mark a dependent adverb clause. Relative pronouns are the joining words for dependent adjective clauses. The most common of these are *who, whom, which*, and *that*. Some common joining words for dependent noun clauses are *that, what, whatever, whomever*, or *whoever*.

A dependent clause joined to an independent clause makes a complex sentence.

independent and dependent clauses in compound-complex sentences One or more dependent clauses may be added to a compound sentence (two or more independent clauses). This is a compound-complex sentence. A sentence containing a dependent clause will always be complex or compound-complex.

> (1) *He flies* and (2) *he races boats* (3) *because that makes him feel free.* (1) is an independent clause, (2) is an independent clause, and (3) is a dependent clause. The sentence is compound because it contains two independent clauses. It is complex because it contains a dependent clause. It is compound-complex.

See lessons and exercises in **23–26** about sentence construction and in **37–47** about punctuating phrases and clauses.

RELATIONSHIPS WITHIN THE SENTENCE

7 Subject-Verb Agreement

The subject of a sentence tells what the sentence is about. The verb asserts something about the subject. The relation of these two makes the core of the sentence. The subject and the verb must agree in number. The form of some verbs shows this agreement.

In sentences about things that are happening right now (the present time), most verbs have two possible forms. The forms show agreement in number between subject and verb.

The boy <u>sleeps</u>.
The boys <u>sleep</u>.

In sentences about past time, a few helping verbs (was/were, has/have) change form to show agreement with their subjects.

He <u>was</u> tired.
They <u>were</u> tired.
The girl <u>has</u> gone.
The girls <u>have gone</u>.

Other verbs do not change form to show agreement.

Agreement with or without s If the subject means only one thing, the present-time verb or the verb *was* ends in *s*. If the subject means more than one thing, the verb does not have an *s* added to the end.

The <u>candle</u> (one thing) <u>burns</u> (*s* added).
The <u>candles</u> (more than one) <u>burn</u> (no added *s*).

Agreement with or without es If the verb already ends in *s* or an *s* sound, add *es* instead of *s* alone to make the verb agree with a subject meaning only one.

They <u>miss</u> but he <u>misses</u>.

Agreement with Hard-to-Pronounce Verbs Even if the pronunciation of a word makes it hard for us to hear an *s* at the end, there should be an *s* if the subject means only one thing.

They <u>rest</u> but he <u>rests</u>.

Agreement with Irregular Verbs The four verb pairs that give the most trouble with subject-verb agreement are irregular. This means that they change more than the others in spelling and pronunciation.

> But even for these irregular verbs, the verb form that agrees with a subject meaning one does have an *s* at the end. The verb form agreeing with a subject meaning more than one does not.

These are the irregular verbs:

Verbs agreeing with one	Verbs agreeing with more then one
is	
was	are
has	were
does	have
	do

He (one) is going.   They (more) are going.

He (one) was going.   They (more) were going.

He (one) has gone.   They (more) have gone.

He (one) does go.   They (more) do go.

Agreement with Compound Subject A subject is usually a single word that means one or more than one. But a sentence may use two words as subjects for the same verb. This is called a compound subject. If these two subjects are joined by *and*, the subject means more than one, so the verb does not end in added *s*.

The girls go.   Mary and Ann go.

(one *and* one are more than one)

If the compound subject is joined by *or*, *nor*, or *but*, only one of the words can be the real subject of the sentence. The verb must agree in number with the subject closest to the verb. Do not make the verb agree with all subjects. Cover up all the subjects except the one closest to the verb.

Mary or Jane (one) goes.   Mary or her sisters (more) go.

one *or* one is one.

more *or* more are more.

one *or* more are more.

more *or* one is one.

Agreement with Separated Subject and Verb In many sentences, verbs do not come immediately after their subjects. Other words may come between a subject and its verb. These separating words may seem to be subjects, but they are not. Some of the following are ways in which subject and verb may be separated.

Separation by a single word:
He (always) goes.

Separation by a phrase:
He (along with his friends) goes.

He (calling out her name) leaps over the cliff.

He (of all my brothers) is the tallest.

Separation by a clause:
   He (who wants to learn) has a chance.

Separation by another verb and its complements:
   He (writes foolish letters and) mails them immediately.

If words come between a subject and its verb, do not pay attention to the separating words when you choose the correct verb. Find the subject and ask yourself what verb goes with *it*.

Agreement with the Verb before the Subject   English sentences usually put the subject first, the verb next, and then any complements. But sometimes the verb or part of the verb comes before the subject. This happens in questions.

   Is he going?

It also happens with *there*, *here*, *next*, *then*, and some other words.

   There are three.
        (verb) (subject)

   Next is lunch.
        (verb) (subject)

It also happens with phrases.

   In the box was a surprise.
   (phrase)   (verb)   (subject)

When the verb comes before the subject, it is necessary to read past the first part of the sentence to find the real subject (what the sentence is about). The verb must agree with this subject. See **3**, Unusual Word Order, for more about this.

Agreement with Indefinite Pronouns as Subjects   Indefinite pronouns do not substitute for specific persons or things that have been named before the pronouns. There are three types of indefinite pronouns.

The first type always means more than one:	
both	few
several	fewer
many	fewest

The verb for these indefinite pronoun subjects should not end in *s*:

   Many go.

The second type always means only one, though sometimes it may seem to mean more than one. This type includes:

another	everybody	none
anybody	everyone	neither
anyone	everything	one
anything	no one	somebody
each	nobody	someone
either	nothing	something

The verb form for these indefinite pronouns should end in *-s*.

<u>Everybody</u> <u>goes</u>.

The third type of indefinite pronoun sometimes means only one and sometimes means more than one. It means only one when it talks about things that we do not count but think of as total amount, or mass, like flour. It means more than one when it talks about things that are counted, like haystacks.

<u>Some</u> of the flour <u>was</u> used.

<u>Some</u> of the haystacks <u>were</u> used.

These are pronouns of *the third type*:

any	most
more	some

When you choose the verb to agree with these pronouns, ask whether they mean something counted (more than one thing) or something thought of as one amount, or a mass (one thing).

Agreement with Relative Pronouns as Subjects

A relative pronoun relates two statements to each other by substituting in one statement for a word that is in both statements.

He hit the ball + the ball flew over the fence =

He hit the ball, *which* flew over the fence.
(*Which* is a relative pronoun substituting for *ball*, the word used in both statements.)

The relative pronouns used as subjects are *who, which*, and *that*. Because the relative pronoun substitutes for some other word in the sentence, you must look at that word and decide how many it means. If you make the verb agree with that word, the verb will agree with the relative pronoun.

The boy (one) <u>who</u> <u>goes</u> is Tom.

The boys (more) <u>who</u> <u>go</u> are Tom and Jim.

Agreement with *I* as Subject   There are three rules to follow in making verbs agree with the pronoun *I* when it is a subject.

> Rule 1: In using the verb *be* in the present time, the word *I* takes *am*, never *is* or *are*: I am tired.
>
> Rule 2: In using the verb *be* in the past time, the word *I* takes *was*, not *were*: I was tired.
>
> Rule 3: In using all other verbs, the word *I* takes the form without an added *s*: I tire easily.

Agreement with Singular Subjects Ending in *s*   Not all subjects ending in *s* mean more than one. The names of many of the things you study in school, for instance, end in *s* but mean only one.

Mathematics <u>is</u> hard for me.

Similarly, many words naming abstract qualities end in *ness* or *ence* or some other *s* sound. But they mean only one quality in spite of the *s* sound at the end.

Patience <u>is</u> his best quality.

Agreement with Titles   The title of a book, movie, play, television program, poem, song or other musical composition, painting, or any such creation names one thing, so it means only one and agrees with a present-time verb ending in *s*:

<u>Jaws</u> <u>is</u> a realistic movie.

See lessons and exercises about subject-verb agreement in **27–32**.

8 Verb Tense Forms

Tense means time. Verbs change form to show the time that something takes place. These tense forms are called the principal parts of verbs. They are the present, the past, and the past participle. The present is used for things that happen now:

The <u>crowds</u> <u>gather</u>.

The past is used for things that happened before now:

The crowds <u>gathered</u>.

The past participle is also used for things that happened before now. But this form is always used with a helping word like *has*, *have*, or *had*.

The crowds <u>have gathered</u>.

The past participle is also used with the helping word *be*: *am, is, are, was, were, be*, or *been*.

The crowds <u>were gathered</u>.

Regular Verbs Regular verbs take the present-tense verb and add *d* or *ed* to the end to form the past and past participle. Some verbs that end in *y* change the *y* to *i* before adding *d* or *ed*. (See **51** for rules on this spelling.)

Present	*Past*	*Past Participle*
<u>verb</u>	<u>verb</u> + *ed*	<u>verb</u> + *ed*
gather	gathered	gathered
change	changed	changed
mow	mowed	mowed
study	studied	studied
pay	paid	paid

Irregular Verbs English has many verbs that change in some other way or ways to form the past and past-participle:

I <u>go</u> now. (Present)

I <u>went</u> before. (Past)

I <u>have</u> <u>gone</u> before. (Past Participle)

The past-participle form of the verb always uses a helping verb. (See **33** and **34**.) The helpers that can be used with the past participle are forms of *be*, *have*, *become*, and *get*.

be:
am, is, are (present time)
was, were (past time)
be, being, been (often uses still another helper — See 2.)

have:
have, has (present time)
had (past time)
having (always uses a form of *be* as still another helper)

become:
become (present time)
became (past time)
becoming (always uses a form of *be* as still another helper)

get:
get (present time)
got (past time)
getting (always uses a form of *be* as still another helper)

The only way to learn the forms of these irregular verbs is to memorize them. The following alphabetical list can serve as a checklist for you in choosing verbs.

Present	Past	Past Participle
am, is, are	was, were	(helper) been
arise	arose	(helper) arisen
awake	awoke/awaked	(helper) awoke/awaked, awoken
bear	bore	(helper) borne, born (with *be*, of infants)
become	became	(helper) become
begin	began	(helper) begun
bend	bent	(helper) bent
bet	bet	(helper) bet
bid	bid	(helper) bid
bind	bound	(helper) bound
bite	bit	(helper) bitten
bleed	bled	(helper) bled
blow	blew	(helper) blown
break	broke	(helper) broken
breed	bred	(helper) bred
bring	brought	(helper) brought
build	built	(helper) built
burst	burst	(helper) burst
buy	bought	(helper) bought
cast	cast	(helper) cast
catch	caught	(helper) caught
choose	chose	(helper) chosen
cling	clung	(helper) clung
come	came	(helper) come
cost	cost	(helper) cost
creep	crept	(helper) crept
cut	cut	(helper) cut
deal	dealt	(helper) dealt
dig	dug	(helper) dug
dive	dived (dove)	(helper) dived
does, do	did	(helper) done
draw	drew	(helper) drawn
drink	drank	(helper) drunk/drunken
drive	drove	(helper) driven
eat	ate	(helper) eaten
fall	fell	(helper) fallen
feed	fed	(helper) fed
feel	felt	(helper) felt
fight	fought	(helper) fought
find	found	(helper) found
fit	fitted/fit	(helper) fitted/fit

Present	Past	Past Participle
flee	fled	(helper) fled
fling	flung	(helper) flung
fly	flew	(helper) flown
forbid	forbad/forbade	(helper) forbidden
forget	forgot	(helper) forgotten/forgot
forgive	forgave	(helper) forgiven
forsake	forsook	(helper) forsaken
freeze	froze	(helper) frozen
get	got	(helper) got/gotten
give	gave	(helper) given
goes, go	went	(helper) gone
grind	ground	(helper) ground
grow	grew	(helper) grown
hang (not execute)	hung	(helper) hung
has, have	had	(helper) had
hear	heard	(helper) heard
hide	hid	(helper) hidden
hit	hit	(helper) hit
hold	held	(helper) held
hurt	hurt	(helper) hurt
keep	kept	(helper) kept
know	knew	(helper) known
lay	laid	(helper) laid
lead	led	(helper) led
leave	left	(helper) left
lend	lent	(helper) lent
let	let	(helper) let
lie	lay	(helper) lain
lose	lost	(helper) lost
make	made	(helper) made
mean	meant	(helper) meant
meet	met	(helper) met
mow	mowed	(helper) mowed/mown
pay	paid	(helper) paid
prove	proved	(helper) proved/proven
put	put	(helper) put
read	read (sound change)	(helper) read (sound is same as for past)
rent	rent	(helper) rent
ride	rode	(helper) ridden

Present	Past	Past Participle
ring	rang	(helper) rung
rise	rose	(helper) risen
run	ran	(helper) run
see	saw	(helper) seen
seek	sought	(helper) sought
sell	sold	(helper) sold
send	sent	(helper) sent
set	set	(helper) set
sew	sewed	(helper) sewed/sewn
shake	shook	(helper) shaken
shave	shaved	(helper) shaved/shaven
shed	shed	(helper) shed
shine	shone (shined, as polished)	(helper) shone (shined, as polished)
shoe	shod	(helper) shod
shoot	shot	(helper) shot
show	showed	(helper) showed/shown
shrink	shrank/shrunk	(helper) shrunk/shrunken
shut	shut	(helper) shut
sing	sang	(helper) sung
sink	sank	(helper) sunk/sunken
sit	sat	(helper) sat
slay	slew	(helper) slain
sleep	slept	(helper) slept
slide	slid	(helper) slid/slidden
slink	slunk	(helper) slunk
speak	spoke	(helper) spoken
speed	sped	(helper) sped
spend	spent	(helper) spent
spin	spun	(helper) spun
split	split	(helper) split
spread	spread	(helper) spread
spring	sprang	(helper) sprung
stand	stood	(helper) stood
steal	stole	(helper) stolen
stick	stuck	(helper) stuck
sting	stung	(helper) stung
stride	strode	(helper) stridden
strike	struck	(helper) struck
string	strung	(helper) strung
strive	strove/strived	(helper) striven/strived
swear	swore	(helper) sworn
sweep	swept	(helper) swept
swim	swam	(helper) swim
swing	swung	(helper) swung

Present	Past	Past Participle
take	took	(helper) taken
teach	taught	(helper) taught
tear	tore	(helper) torn
tell	told	(helper) told
think	thought	(helper) thought
throw	threw	(helper) thrown
wake	waked/woke	(helper) waked/woke, woken
wear	wore	(helper) worn
weave	wove	(helper) woven
weep	wept	(helper) wept
win	won	(helper) won
wind	wound	(helper) wound
wring	wrung	(helper) wrung
write	wrote	(helper written)

See lessons and exercises about verb tense forms in **33** and **34**.

9 Pronoun Agreement

A pronoun substitutes for a noun. A pronoun must agree with the noun in some ways so that the reader knows what noun it is substituting for. A pronoun must agree with the noun that it substitutes for in sex, number, and person.

Agreement in Sex The pronoun must agree in sex with its noun. If a noun names a woman, *she, her, hers,* or *herself* is the correct pronoun substitute. The pronouns *he, him, his,* and *himself* agree in sex with a noun naming a man. For something without sex, the pronouns *it, its,* and *itself* agree with the noun.

> The *mailman* lost *his* pocket watch.
> (masculine) (masculine pronoun)

Who/Which/That The pronoun *who* is used to refer to people. The pronoun *which* is used to refer to things. For animals, either *which* or *who* is used. The pronoun *that* is used to refer to people or to things. But it is used only to begin a clause that could not be left out of the sentence.

Agreement in Number If a noun means only one thing, its pronoun means one thing, too. If a noun means more than one, its pronoun substitute means more than one. This is agreement in number.

> The *baby whale* swam with *its* parents.
> (one)   (one)
>
> The *whales* swam through *their* home waters.
> (more than one)   (more than one)

Pronouns Meaning One	Pronouns Meaning More Than One
I, me, my, mine, myself	we, us, our, ours, ourselves
you, your, yours, yourself	you, your, yours, yourselves
he, him, his, himself, she, her, hers, herself, it, its, itself	they, them, their, theirs, themselves
this	these
that	those

Agreement in Person The person of a pronoun tells the relation of that pronoun to the writer or speaker. There are three kinds of person. *First person* names the person speaking. *Second person* means the person spoken to. *Third person* means the person or thing spoken about.

> *I* want to go *myself*. (first person)
> *You* will not leave *your* home. (second person)
> *They* have not been back since *he* fell over *her* shoe and knocked *her* down. (third person)

First Person	the person(s) speaking	I, me, my, mine, myself; we, us, our, ours, ourselves.
Second Person	the person(s) spoken to	you, your, yours, yourself, yourselves.
Third Person	the person(s) or thing(s) spoken about	he, him, his, himself, she, her, hers, herself, it, its, itself, they, them, their, theirs, themselves.

See lessons and exercises about pronoun agreement in **35**.

10 Pronoun Case

Although a pronoun substitutes for a noun, it does a job of its own in relation to other words in the sentence. This relation to other words in the sentence is called *case*. The case of a pronoun is always determined by its use in the sentence, not by the word it substitutes for. Different relations—different cases—use different forms of pronouns. Within a sentence, pronouns are related most closely to nouns or verbs or prepositions. See **2** about the use of nouns and pronouns in a sentence.

	Singular	Plural
Subjective Case	I	we
	you	you
	he, she, it	they
	who	who

	Singular	Plural
Objective Case	me you him, her, it whom	us you them whom
Possessive Case	my, mine your, yours his, her, hers, its whose	our, ours your, yours their, theirs whose

Subjective Case: subject The most important relation for a pronoun is the subject-verb relation. If a pronoun is the subject of a sentence, it is in the subjective case. This case uses the forms of the subject pronoun that are best known to us: *I, we, you, he, she, it, they, who.*

> *I* saw the cow.   *She* saw the cow.
> *We* saw the cow.   *It* saw the cow.
> *You* saw the cow.   *They* saw the cow.
> *He* saw the cow.   *Who* saw the cow?

subjective complements A pronoun that the verb says equals the subject is also in the subjective case. A linking verb says this about the pronoun. If the pronoun after a linking verb equals the subject, use the subjective case.

> The cow is *I*.   The cow is *she*.
> The cows are *we*.   The cow is *it*.
> The cow is *you*.   The cows are *they*.
> The cow is *he*.   The cow is *who*?

Objective Case The objective case forms of the pronouns are *me, us, you, him, her, it, them,* and *whom.* Notice that three of these forms—*him, them,* and *whom*—end in *m.* These forms are used whenever a pronoun is used as an object.

direct object A pronoun may receive the action of an action verb. It is then the direct object of the verb. Use the objective case for a pronoun receiving the direct action of a verb.

> The cow kicked *me*.   The cow kicked *her*.
> The cow kicked *us*.   The cow kicked *it*.
> The cow kicked *you*.   The cow kicked *them*.
> The cow kicked *him*.   The cow kicked *whom*?

indirect object The objective case is also used for a pronoun that indirectly receives the action of the verb. In other words, the pronoun names the person or thing to or for whom the action is done.

The cow kicked (to) me the bucket.

The cow kicked *me* the bucket.	The cow kicked *her* the bucket.
The cow kicked *us* the bucket.	The cow kicked *it* the bucket.
The cow kicked *you* the bucket.	The cow kicked *them* the bucket.
The cow kicked *him* the bucket.	The cow kicked *whom* the bucket?

object of
preposition
The objective case is also used for the object of a preposition, a word that a preposition relates to some other word in the sentence.

The cow stepped over *me*.	The cow stepped over *her*.
The cow stepped over *us*.	The cow stepped over *it*.
The cow stepped over *you*.	The cow stepped over *them*.
The cow stepped over *him*.	The cow stepped over *whom*?

Possessive
Case
A pronoun may show ownership or possession of a noun or another pronoun. The form used to show ownership is the possessive case. Because the form of the whole pronoun changes to show possession, no apostrophe is added to these pronouns to make them possessive. The possessive forms of the pronouns are *my, our, your, his, her, its, their,* and *whose*.

That was *my* cow.	That was *her* cow.
That was *our* cow.	That was *its* cow.
That was *your* cow.	That was *their* cow.
That was *his* cow.	That was *whose* cow?

Some pronouns have a second possessive form. This form is used when the noun owned is not named after the pronoun. Pronouns having this additional possessive form are *mine, ours, yours, hers,* and *theirs*.

The cow is *mine*.	The cow is *hers*.
The cow is *ours*.	The cow is *its*.
The cow is *yours*.	The cow is *theirs*.
The cow is *his*.	The cow is *whose*?

Reflexive
Pronouns
Pronouns with a *-self* or *-selves* ending are reflexive pronouns. They reflect the subject by repeating it in a different form.

Reflexives meaning one	Reflexives meaning more than one
myself	ourselves
yourself	yourselves
himself, herself, itself	themselves
oneself	

The reflexive form may be used as a direct object:

I (subject) hit *myself* (direct object).

I kicked *myself*.	She kicked *herself*.
We kicked *ourselves*.	It kicked *itself*.
You kicked *yourself*.	They kicked *themselves*.
You kicked *yourselves*.	
He kicked *himself*.	One kicked *oneself*.

The reflexive form may also be used for either of the other objective uses of pronouns. It may be used as an indirect object.

I (subject) gave *myself* (indirect object) a kick.

Or it may be used as the object of a preposition:

I (subject) was ashamed of *myself* (object of preposition).

The reflexive form may never be used as the subject because it is always repeating the subject. It is used instead of the subjective case if a predicate pronoun (subjective complement) completes and repeats the subject:

I (subject) am not myself (completer, equaling subject) today.

I am *myself*.	She is *herself*.
We are *ourselves*.	It is *itself*.
You are *yourself*.	They are *themselves*.
You are *yourselves*.	
He is *himself*.	One is *oneself*.

A final reason for using the reflexive form is to emphasize the pronoun subject:

I (subject) did it *myself* (repetition of subject for emphasis).

I *myself* am a cow.	She *herself* is a cow.
We *ourselves* are cows.	It *itself* is a cow.
You *yourself* are a cow.	They *themselves* are cows.
You *yourselves* are cows.	
He *himself* is a cow.	One *oneself* is a cow.

See lessons and exercises about pronoun case and reflexive pronouns in **36**.

Punctuation

Marks of punctuation separate, group, and qualify words and structures within the sentence for the convenience of the reader. They exist to make your writing more effective and are worth your careful study.

11 The Period

Location	Description
Sentences: • after the declarative sentence	Grammar is like medicine● (shows end of statement)
• after the imperative sentence	Go through that door● (shows end of command)
• after the indirect question	He asked if you will go● (shows statement is about a question)
• after the shortened sentence	Hello, Mary● (after a salutation) Alone● (after answer to a question)
Abbreviations • after permissible abbreviations	Dr●, Mr●, Ph●D● (titles) A● M●, P● M●, No●

12 The Question Mark

Location	Description
? after a direct question	Is this what you meant?

13 The Exclamation Mark

Location	Description
! to express strong emotion	Hey! Stop that! What a way to go!

14 The Semicolon

Location	Description
; between two independent clauses when a period or a coordinating conjunction does not separate them	*Independent clause* **;** *Independent clause.* (Use when the thoughts in the clauses are closely related and/or briefly expressed.)
; between two independent clauses with a conjunctive adverb like *however* between them	*Independent clause* **;** however, *Independent clause.* <div align="center">therefore, consequently, moreover, nonetheless, then, also</div> *She was not working* **;** therefore, *she budgeted carefully.*
; to set off groups within a series when the groups already contain commas	She visited the following places: Lexington, Kentucky **;** Baltimore, Maryland **;** and Galveston, Texas. The candidates are Howard Baker, senator from Tennessee **;** John Connally, former governor of Texas **;** and Eugene McCarthy, former senator from Minnesota.
; before words used to introduce an illustration or explanation that is a complete statement	She is never on time **;** for instance, she was late for her own wedding. <div align="center">for example, namely, that is.</div>

See lessons and exercises about semicolon use in **37**.

15 The Comma

Location	Description
, before the conjunction that joins independent clauses	*Independent clause* **,** and *Independent clause.* <div align="center">but or nor for so yet</div> I hired you **,** and I will fire you.
Introductory elements: **,** after introductory adverb clauses	Adverb clauses begin with adverbial conjunctions, also called subordinate conjunctions, such as *when, where, as, although, if.* See 2 for a list. *If you will allow me* **,** I'll pour a cup. *If* _____ **,** I'll pour a cup.

, after long introductory phrases or those likely to be misread	*In the course of each life,* long periods of boredom have to be endured _____ _____ **,** long periods of boredom have to be endured.
, after introductory infinitive phrases (*to* + verb)	An infinitive phrase always begins with *to* and is followed by a verb. See **3**. *To love,* one must first have been loved. *To*____ **,** one must first have been loved.
, after introductory participal phrase (-ing, -ed, -t, and -en endings)	A verb form usually ending with -*ing*, -*ed*, -*en*, or *t*. *Walking swiftly,* she turned a corner. See **3**. _____ **,** she turned a corner. *Disgusted with my excuse,* he hung up. _____ **,** he hung up.
, after introductory gerund phrases (-ing endings)	A verb form ending in -*ing*. See **3**. By *running in place,* you can build stamina. By _____ **,** you can build stamina.
Series **,** separating three or more words in a series	She eats apples, oranges, and pears. Independent clause _____ **,** _____ **,** and _____ .
, separating three or more phrases in a series	He searched *under the bed, in the closet,* and *on the bookshelf.* He searched _____ **,** _____ **,** and _____ .
, separating clauses in a series	We ate *before we sang, while we sang,* and *after we sang.* We ate _____ **,** _____ **,** and _____ .
Loose Modification Clauses **,** before (or before and after) an adjective clause that gives information not essential to the basic meaning of the sentence.	Begins with *who, whom, whose, which.* Nashville, *which is known as Music City,* is the capital of Tennessee. Nashville, _____ **,** is the capital of Tennessee.
Loose Modification Phrases **,** before (or before and after) a phrase giving information not essential to basic understanding of the word it modifies.	Mary, *wearing a red dress,* came down the stairs. Mary, _____ **,** came down the stairs.

Appositives
, on either side of a noun being closely modified by another noun

John Glenn, *the astronaut*, was the keynote speaker.

John Glenn, _____, was the keynote speaker.

Contrasted Elements
, before *not* (and after the *not* phrase)

Archie is the villain, not the hero.

Archie is the villain, _____.

Archie, *not Mike*, is the villain.

Archie, _____ , is the villain.

Place-Names in Addresses
, setting off place-names in addresses

Saundersville, Tennessee, is her home.

He lives at 621 West End, Tampa, Florida.

Dates
, setting off numbers in dates from each other

Friday 13, 1951, was a lucky day for me.

Parenthetical Expressions
, setting off particular sentence modifiers

Some parenthetical expressions are *therefore, consequently, besides, furthermore, accordingly, in the first place, I think, I hope.*

Nevertheless, I have decided.

_____ , I have decided.

They are not, *I think*, well pleased.

They are not, _____ , well pleased.

Direct Address
, setting off the name of person addressed

Albert, stop that.

We are, madam, yours truly.

Interjections
, setting off mild expressions of emotion

Oh, you startled me!

Well, have it your way.

Direct Quotations
, setting off actual words of speaker from speaker tag

"I want you to understand," said Captain Marvel.

She asked, "Where is he going?"

Yes and No
, setting off these words

Yes, we have no holiday.

No, I did not call you.

Such as, especially
, before these words

He derives special benefits, such as insurance.

	I like science fiction novels, especially those by Bradbury.
, between a statement and a question	A lie is hard to accept, isn't it?
, between double modifiers	Honest, loyal people do exist. (adjectives that modify the same noun)
Aids to Meaning **,** between words that confuse if not separated	After drinking, the cow continued grazing.
between repeated words	We have been told that what is, is right.
between numbers	In 1976, 4820 families were left homeless by floods.

See lessons and exercises about comma use in **38–47**.

16 Underlining

Location	Description
_____ Under titles of long works:	
Books	Mystery of the Bermuda Triangle
Magazines	Newsweek
Newspapers	The Tennessean or the Tennessean
Bulletins and Pamphlets	Prevention of Household Accidents
Musical Productions	Hair
Plays and Films	Romeo and Juliet; The Graduate
Long Poems	Paradise Lost
Ships, Trains, Aircraft	Queen Elizabeth; The Floridian; The Concorde
Painting, Sculpture	Duchamp's Nude Descending the Staircase; Brancusi's The Bird
Television Programs	Sixty Minutes; M*A*S*H
Letters, Words,	The p in pneumonia is silent.
Figures, and Symbols referred to as such	Your 2 looks like an 8.
	Do not use & for and.

17 Quotation Marks

Location	Description
Double Quotation Marks " around the *exact* words of the speaker	He answered, " Let me think about it." Speaker tag, " _____ ." "I am interested," she said, "but you will have to help me." " _____ ," she said, " _____ ." ___ . "You lead the way," she said. "I will follow." " _____ ," she said. " _____ ."
No Quotation Marks	Use quotation marks only when the words that the speaker actually used are quoted. Compare the following sentence with the examples above: She said that she was interested but that I would have to show her what to do.
" around the exact words of a writer	The poet is saying that happiness is like "a snowflake on the river, lasting but a moment." Lift the words you need, set them into your sentence, and punctuate and capitalize them as part of that sentence.
titles: short works or parts of a longer work " around chapter titles, magazine and journal articles, short essays, lectures, editorials, poems, songs, one-act plays	"The Old Manse" is the title of Chapter Three. "The Higher Literacy" can be read in *Harper's*. "The Pit and the Pendulum" is a short story by E. A. Poe. An essay by Thoreau is entitled " Civil Disobedience." "Chicago" is the title of a poem by Carl Sandburg. Keith Carradine sang "I'm Easy" in Nashville at the Exit/Inn.
Words " around a word definition written within a sentence	Adjacent means "near or beside."
" around words used in a special sense	The machine "justifies" margins. The note began, "Dear Friend." He is "real cool." He has a "complex" about it.

18 The Apostrophe

	Location	Description
'	between a singular noun owning something and the *s* added to show ownership	Both the *s* and the ' are needed to show possession when a singular noun is placed next to an object that it owns.

<table>
<tr><td>girl's
(singular
owner)</td><td>hair
(object
owned)</td></tr>
<tr><td>Robert Burns's*
(Singular owner)</td><td>poems
(objects owned)</td></tr>
</table>

*The second *s* is sometimes left off when a singular proper noun already ends in -*s*, but the apostrophe must be used.

Either   Robert Burns's poems

or

Robert Burns' poems.

	Location	Description
'	after a plural noun ending in *s* that owns something	girls' (plural owners) — hair (object owned)
'	between a plural noun not ending in *s* and the *s* added to show ownership	men's (plural owners) — hair (object owned) children's plural owners — hair object owned
'	Showing Omission where letter(s) or number(s) are left out	isn't (is *not*) class of '65 (1965) o'clock (*of the* clock) they're (they *are*)
'	between a letter or number and an *s* making it plural	Mind your *P*'s and *Q*'s. Add your 6's to the total. He lived in the 1700's.

See lessons and exercises about the apostrophe in **48**.

19 The Colon

	Location	Description
:	after an introductory statement preceding a list	I ordered the following: shock absorbers, hangers, and an expansion valve.

:	separating a statement from its restatement or clarification	Pole vaulting is for him more than exercise: it is his career. She thought of only one thing: revenge.
:	between title and subtitle	*Eliza Goodhue: Woman Who Led*
:	after the salutation in a business letter	Dear Sir:

20 The Hyphen

Location	Description
Words:	
- joining compound words	sister - in - law, delegate - at - large
- between two words used as an adjective before a noun	two - faced, black - eyed Susan.
- between numerals in compound numbers from twenty-one to ninety-nine	twenty - one, ninety - nine
- between parts of fractions	one - eighth, three - fourths
- after prefixes *ex, self, all,* and before the suffix *elect*	ex - senator, self - restraint, all - American, congresswoman - elect (*Semi* is hyphenated only in words beginning with *i*, or with a proper noun, like *semi - invalid* or *semi - European*.)

- at the end of a line in a word divided because of space	The excellent dinner made my father some - what drowsy.
	Words are divided *only* between syllables.
	  wrong: bookke - eper
	  right: book - keeper
	Words of one syllable cannot be correctly divided.
	  wrong: jump - ed
	  right: jumped
	Words cannot be correctly divided so that a single letter is set off from the rest.
	  wrong: hand - y e - nough
	  right: handy enough

Mechanics

21 Capitalization

A capital letter is used to call attention to something important, something that you want the reader to notice.

Capitals for Importance

Use a capital letter to begin the first word of every sentence. This is a signal that a sentence, an important unit of writing, is beginning.

The dog ran. It tumbled over the basket of wet clothes. It knocked over her flowers.

Use a capital letter to begin the first word of a quotation that is a complete sentence.

He said, "Flying is a kind of freedom."

Use capital letters at the beginning of the first word, the last word, and all important words in a title. This tells the reader that the title is important. It is the subject of what you will write next, or it is the particular name of something.

All in the Family.   *"White Christmas"*
(television program)   (a song)

My Greatest Adventure
(title of a student theme as it appears on a title page)

Use a capital *I* to refer to yourself. *I* is an important word because it names a person. But it is so short—only one letter long—that it needs to be capitalized so that it is not overlooked.

When I had measles, I was blistered all over.

Capitals for Names of Particular Persons, Places or Things

Names of particular persons, places, or things (proper nouns) are important, so their first letter should be capitalized. If you are referring to a general kind of person, place, or thing, do not capitalize the first letter.

McGavock High School (name of particular place—use capitals.)

my high school (reference to a general kind of place—no capitals.)

The general name of a school subject—algebra—is capitalized when a course number is placed after it—Algebra II. This number distinguishes it from Algebra I and other particular algebra courses.

> I take *P*sychology I. (a particular course)
> I study *p*sychology. (a general subject)

A name is always particular when it is the name of a nation. Any names that come from the particular name of a nation or its language begin with capital letters.

> The custom began in *S*pain.
> I study *S*panish.
> I am taking conversational *S*panish now.

Use a capital letter to begin the name of a direction or area only when the name is used *instead of* the particular names of states or countries.

> He moved to the *N*orth. (a particular group of states)
> He moved *n*orth. (a general direction)
> She is a citizen of the *T*hird *W*orld. (a particular group of countries)
> She is a citizen of the *w*orld. (a general place)

Use a capital letter to begin the names of the days of the week and months of the year.

> He left last *M*onday.
> She was born in *J*uly.

Use a capital letter to begin the name of a season only if you are writing about it as though it were a person.

> The *f*all was rainy.
> When *F*all marched in, he came in hip boots.

Use a capital letter to begin the title of a relative if that title is used instead of the person's particular name, or if it is used as part of the person's particular name.

> My *m*other helps me. (used as general relationship)
> I help *M*other. (used as name)
> I help *M*other *A*mes. (used as part of name)

Use a capital letter to begin the occupational title of a person only if the title is used instead of the person's name or as part of the name.

> Please help me, *D*octor. (used as name)

Dr. Austin came. (used as part of name)
The *doctor* came. (used as general occupation)

See lessons and exercises about capitalization in **49**.

22 Spelling

Learning to spell correctly in the English language is like playing Russian roulette in reverse. Keep at the roulette long enough and you're sure to lose. Keep at spelling long enough and you're sure to win. You can start learning how to help yourself become a better speller now. Start by consciously adopting the habits that aid the good speller.

**Spelling
Aids**

1. Look in a recent dictionary for the correct spelling of every doubtful word.
2. Record all your misspelled words in a form that you can study. A small notebook in which you can list words alphabetically will help. The notebook can be referred to easily when you are writing a composition.
3. Study the words on your list.
    Look—Notice their division into syllables.
    Hear—Say them to yourself.
    Write—Write them more than once to set up hand-to-brain patterns.
4. Study the Words section in the workbook (**50**) to clear up misuse of words that results in spelling problems.
5. Learn the spelling rules found in the workbook in the sections on Spelling, Plurals, and Numbers (**51–53**).

WORKBOOK
A Self-Instructional Review of Basic Problems in Writing

PART

INSTRUCTIONS FOR USE

This workbook provides review lessons on some problems in writing English. There are different lessons on different problems. You probably won't need all the lessons. On the next two pages you will find record sheets. Keep a record on these of the lessons that you work on.

Each teaching section has a pretest to show you whether or not you need to review that section. Take each pretest and check your answers. If you answer all the questions correctly, you do not need the instruction in that section. Record your perfect pretest score on the record sheet. Go on to the next pretest.

If you miss any questions in the first section, work on that section. Read the instructions for each step, do the practice exercises, and check your answers against the answer key. Finally, take the post-test. Show it to your instructor; or tear it out, write your name, course, and section number on it, and hand it to your instructor.

Continue with the next section.

Complete all of the sections, either by achieving a perfect score on the pretest or by completing the instructions, the practices, and the post-tests.

RECORD OF WORKBOOK ASSIGNMENTS COMPLETED

Name of Section	Comments
Sentence	
24. Fragments	
25 Fusion	
26. Comma Splices	
General Post-test	
Subject Verb Agreement	
27. General Agreement	
28. Agreement with Irregular Verbs	
29. Agreement with Compound Subjects	
30. Agreement of Separated Subject and Verb	
31. Agreement with Verb Before Subject	
32. Agreement with Pronoun Subjects	
General Post-test	
Verb Tense Forms	
33. Regular Verbs	
34. Irregular Verbs	
35. Pronoun Agreement	
36. Pronoun Case	
37. The Semicolon	
The Comma	
38. Commas Between Main Clauses	

Name of Section	Comments
39. Commas After Introductory Clauses	
40. Commas After Introductory Phrases	
41. Commas in a List	
42. Commas Between Adjectives	
43. Commas Setting Off Modifiers	
44. Commas Setting Off Conjunctive Adverbs	
45. Commas Before *Not*	
46. Commas with Speaker Tags	
47. Commas with Dates and Addresses	
48. The Apostrophe	
49. Capitalization	
Spelling	
50. Words	
51. Basic Rules	
52. Plurals	
53. Numbers	

Sentence Problems

SENTENCE PRETEST

Change the following sentences to make them correct while keeping the same meaning. You may put sentences together or separate them. You may add, take out, or change words or punctuation. Some sentences may not need changes.

24 1. I enjoy many things about being in school. Learning about myself and learning to express how I feel.

2. What I feel about Sundays. I like and dislike Sundays.

3. I have met all kinds of people. People from all walks of life.

4. These meetings helped Robin to understand the ways of others better. That their actions were justified although strange.

5. The shark bit him from the side. Then for some reason spat him out.

6. After dinner they always walked along the beach to relax with nothing to do but look at nature's wonders. To watch the gulls and some fish jumping once in a while.

7. My mother, grandmother, and aunt cook a big turkey dinner. While my father and uncle shoot pool.

25 1. March 4, 1789, was a good day this was when the Bill of Rights was written.

2. All at once he heard a scream a girl was drowning in the ocean.

3. But scouting does involve more than patriotism it also involves helping others.

4. Some people are fascinated by snakes, and others are frightened of them also there are those who seem indifferent.

5. People are like plants if they get a little affection, they grow bright.

26 1. Our nine-year-old daughter has just learned to swim, therefore she may decide to try waterskiing any day.

2. In 1967 a 3500 series Ford tractor sold for $3300, this year the same tractor sold for $10,000.

3. There is big money in pool nowadays, people gamble and try to hustle the other players.

4. The screen door slams, in comes Father yelling, "When will dinner be ready?"

5. Almost every campsite in the park has ample shade, this means campers don't have to hunt shade to eat in.

Ask your instructor to check your answers, or turn them in.

Key Block

If you missed any sentences above, check **23** Sentences below. If you missed any in **24**, check **24**; do the same for **25** and **26**. The groups that you have checked are the ones you need to study and practice. Skip any that you did not check.

23 Sentences _____	25. Fusion _____
24. Fragments _____	26. Comma Splice _____

23 Sentences

A sentence makes sense.

A sentence is a group of words that makes sense by itself. It names something and tells what that thing is or does, and it adds any other part needed to make a whole statement. It may be short or long. Each of the following is a sentence.

Plants grow.

"Fourscore and seven years ago, our forefathers brought forth upon this continent a new nation, conceived in liberty."

Each of these sentences names a thing (*plants, forefathers*) and tells what it is or does (*grow, brought forth*). The thing named is called the subject. What the subject does, or the word that means *is*, is called the predicate or verb. The relation between the <u>subject</u> and the <u>predicate</u> is the statement of the sentence. This statement must be complete to be a sentence. It may be long or short.

There may be other words in the sentence that tell about the subject or the verb. These are called modifiers. Or there may be words that answer the question *what* or *whom* after the predicate. These are called completers. Whether the sentence has modifiers and completers or not, the sentence must state something. It must be a complete statement.

Although you may not understand everything about the statement in a sentence from that sentence alone, the statement must be complete. See **3** for more information about the sentence core.

24 Fragments

A fragment is a group of words that does not make sense by itself. It is only a piece—a fragment—of an idea. It must be put together with other pieces to make a whole. Do not be misled by its length; a fragment can be long. But if it does not make sense by itself, do not punctuate it as a sentence. Either add it to a sentence that it is part of, or add to it enough to make it complete. There are many kinds of fragments and many causes of fragments.

Fragment Additions

PROBLEM

Often a writer ends a sentence and then thinks of something else that he or she wants to say. If the addition is part of the old statement, the writer may make a fragment by separating it from the sentence that it belongs with.

We decided that, on the hike, we would use lightweight dried food (a sentence). "Mountain food" (a fragment).

A hunter doesn't get a good open shot very often (a sentence). With his cramped position in a blind and the ducks flying up from almost anywhere (a fragment).

SOLUTION

Be sure that you are not making a fragment when you add to something that you have just said. If the addition is a complete statement, you must write it as a separate sentence. But if it is not complete, do not separate it from the sentence before it. Take out any semicolon or period between the sentence and the addition. Add a comma if it is needed. (See **38–47** about when commas are needed.)

We decided that on the hike we would use lightweight dried food, "mountain food" (a sentence).

A hunter doesn't get a good open shot very often with his cramped position in a blind and the ducks flying up from almost anywhere (a sentence).

HINT FOR FINDING FRAGMENT ADDITIONS

After you have written your paper, read it backwards. Read the last sentence first, then the next-to-the-last sentence, and so on. This will help you see when a group of words is not a complete statement. If you find a fragment, see if you can add it to the sentence before it.

In the following lessons, you will find several common kinds of fragment additions. Study each kind and watch for it to keep from writing fragment additions.

added lists and examples

PROBLEM

Many fragment additions help to explain something in the sentence before the fragment. Some of these fragment additions are lists.

Many kinds of dried foods are available. (a sentence)

For instance, carrots, peas, beans, corn, applesauce, noodles, rice, gravy, chicken, beef, coffee, hot chocolate, toast, and bread. (a fragment list)

Some paragraphs are mostly a list of one kind of thing, for instance, the specifications of a car. Any paragraph listing the details that describe something may contain fragment additions. Each item in the list must be part of a complete statement. Look at the following paragraph with fragment additions.

The Jeep has a paint job of deep, rich metallic blue (a sentence). A blue denim top with matching seats (a fragment addition). On the roll bar a thick, soft padding to protect tender bodies (a fragment addition). Also on the roll bar a set of blue denim saddle bags to carry odds and ends (a fragment addition).

Another kind of explanation added to a statement is an example. Using examples is part of good writing. But be sure that your example is either a complete statement by itself or part of a complete statement. Otherwise, it is a fragment addition.

I have many problems (a sentence). For example, finding time to do all that I want to (a fragment addition).

SOLUTION

Add a fragment addition to the sentence before it. If the addition is a list or example, put a comma before the list or before the word *for example, such as, for instance*, or before other words introducing the list or example. Usually, no comma is used before the word *like* if one short example follows it.

Many kinds of dried food are available, for instance, carrots, peas, beans, corn, applesauce, noodles, rice, gravy, chicken, beef, coffee, hot chocolate, toast, and bread (a sentence adding the list after a comma).

I have many problems, for example, finding time to do all that I want to (a sentence adding the example after a comma).

Sometimes a colon (:) is used instead of a comma before a list or example.

If the whole paragraph is a list, you probably will not want to join everything into one long sentence. You may need to add a subject or verb to some of the items in your list so that the fragments will be complete. Often *there is* or *there are* can be added to make one of these fragments complete. Also, the lesson Fragments Omitting Parts shows you ways to add subjects and verbs. If you make one sentence listing items, add the word *and* before the last item. Put commas between items and before *and* in a list of three or more items. Compare the following corrected paragraph with the fragment lists above.

(1)The Jeep has a paint job of deep, rich metallic blue. (2) Inside there are a blue denim top with matching seats, a roll bar with a thick, soft padding to protect tender bodies, and a set of blue denim saddle bags to carry odds and ends. (a correction made by combining the three fragments and by adding commas and the words *there are* and *and* to make the fragments complete)

Correct the fragment additions in the following sentences.

1. Customizing a van is a good hobby because it gives you pride in your own work. Like when you drive into a service station and everyone there wants to look inside.

2. The book's main concern is the way in which the plane is made to fly because of its parts. For instance, the shape of the wing.

3. He shows his great personality in many ways. For example, communicating with all the kids he meets and showing affection toward them.

4. Aunt Evie was so devout that she was always ready to do what she thought the Lord wanted her to. So humble that she was willing to do the tasks no one else would do. The most helpful, kind neighbor anyone ever had.

ANSWERS

1. Customizing a van is a good hobby because it give you pride in your own work, like when you drive into a service station and everyone there wants to look inside.
2. The book's main concern is the way in which the plane is made to fly because of its parts, for instance, the shape of the wing.
3. He shows his great personality in many ways, for example, communicating with all the kids he meets and showing affection toward them.
4. Aunt Evie was so devout that she was always ready to do what she thought the Lord wanted her to, so humble that she was willing to do the tasks no one else would do, and the most helpful, kind neighbor anyone had.

If you missed any, review the lesson and do the next exercise. Follow the direction for the last exercise.

1. Warm weather brings us good things to do that we can't do in winter. Like a baseball game or croquet match.

2. The older people were wonderful. Like the little old man who was sweeping the street with a broom made from twigs.

3. This country is as great as it is because of people's outstanding efforts and performance, such as Jan's dedication to helping the family find a new home, or the family's refusal to separate.

4. She has long, black, shiny hair. One of those hourglass figures men dream about. Dark-brown eyes that seem to sparkle and snap at the same time.

ANSWERS

1. Warm weather brings us good things to do that we can't do in winter, like a baseball game or croquet match.
2. The older people were wonderful, like the little old man who was sweeping the street with a broom made from twigs.

3. This country is as great as it is because of people's outstanding efforts and performances, such as Jan's dedication to helping the family find a new home, or the family's refusal to separate.
4. She has long, black, shiny hair, one of those hour-glass figures men dream about, and dark-brown eyes that seem to sparkle and snap at the same time.

added adjective clauses and appositives

PROBLEM

Another kind of fragment addition adds information about something in the sentence before it by describing it or renaming it Sometimes an adjective clause is used to describe it:

> Mr. Hughes is a superb teacher, whom I admire.
> (*Whom I admire* is an adjective clause describing *Mr. Hughes*. It gives more information about him.)

Adjective clauses begin with a word like *who, whose, whom, which, that, where*, or *when*. These words have other uses, too. But if they begin a description of something in the sentence before them, they are starting an adjective clause—only a part of the whole sentence. An adjective clause should not be separated from the sentence before it because it is not a complete thought. If it is added as a separate sentence, it is a fragment.

> The management sent to our department an older state agent (a sentence). Who was really a spy trying to find out if we were being paid correctly (an adjective clause fragment describing *agent* in the sentence before).

A writer may also give more information about something by renaming it. The new name used after the old name is called an appositive. An appositive repeats in a new way something that has just been said.

> This is my daughter, Mary. (*Mary* repeats *daughter* and gives information about it. *Mary* is an appositive for *daughter*.)
> There was only one problem on Sunday mornings, ten children and one bathroom. (*Ten children* and *one bathroom* explains *problem* by naming exactly what is meant by *problem*. The renaming words are an appositive.)

An appositive is not a complete statement. If is is separated from other sentences, it is a fragment.

> His son won the highest award that the school could give (a sentence). The James E. Dillehay Award (a fragment appositive telling about *award*).

SOLUTION

Join adjective clauses and appositives to the sentences that come before them. Remember that they are part of that sentence because they are not complete statements themselves. Replace the period before the fragment with a comma unless the adjective clause or appositive is necessary to identify the word it refers to. If it does identify the word, do not use a comma. See **43** about such commas.

All the students there wear a uniform (a sentence).

A white shirt with dark-blue pants (an appositive fragment telling about *uniform*).

All the students there wear a uniform, a white shirt with dark-blue pants. (a sentence with an appositive)

The boss replaced it with a new machine (a sentence).

Which was always breaking down (an adjective clause fragment telling about *machine*).

The boss replaced it with a new machine, which was always breaking down. (a sentence with an adjective clause added)

Correct any fragments in the following sentences by joining them to the sentence before them. Put a comma between the sentence and the fragment if the fragment is not necessary to identify the word to which it refers.

1. My whole family enjoys many outdoor sports. That require warm weather.

2. My best gift was my parents' last birthday gift to me. A 1968 Honda 175 motorcycle.

3. During his four years in the Navy he spent almost half of the time overseas. Which he thought was great.

4. It is the story of a group of fighter pilots. Who are all troublemakers in the eyes of the outfit on the next island.

5. Michael is preparing to attend a Bible school. Zion Bible Institute in Providence, Rhode Island. An interdemoninational school.

6. Jane's happiest memories were of her girlhood. Memories of doing things with her brother, her dog, or her grandparents.

7. Blake has an unusual lifestyle. His dislike of city life and money and his escape from it all in a little yellow plane.

ANSWERS

1. My whole family enjoys many outdoor sports that require warm weather.
2. My best gift was my parents' last birthday gift to me, a 1968 Honda 175 motorcycle.
3. During his four years in the Navy he spent almost half of the time overseas, which he thought was great.
4. It is the story of a group of fighter pilots, who are all troublemakers in the eyes of the outfit on the next island.
5. Michael is preparing to attend Bible school, Zion Bible Institute in Providence, Rhode Island, an interdenominational school.
6. Jane's happiest memories were of her girlhood, memories of doing things with her brother, her dog, or her grandparents.
7. Blake has an unusual lifestyle, his dislike of city life and money and his escape from it all in a little yellow plane.

If you missed any of these, review the lesson above and then do the next exercise. Follow the directions for the last exercise.

1. On his right hand are two diamond rings. One larger than two carats.

2. I can't get my sounds together. Which causes me to get my letters in the wrong places.

3. When I first became an N.C.O., he taught me the principle of leadership. The principle of looking out for the welfare of my men.

4. I enjoy the other characters in the show. Richie, Ralph, and Potsie, three high-school friends that get into all kinds of mischief.

5. Eleven years later she moved to Greenbrier. Where she went to John Doss High School.

6. Walt's brother has bought forty houses. About half of which are duplexes that need drastic repair.

7. I have two fine children. A daughter born January 15, 1969, and a son born June 17, 1971.

ANSWERS

1. On his right hand are two diamond rings, one larger than two carats.
2. I can't get my sounds together, which causes me to get my letters in the wrong place.
3. When I first became an N.C.O., he taught me the principle of leadership, the principle of looking out for the welfare of my men.
4. I enjoy the other characters in the show, Richie, Ralph, and Potsie, three high-school friends that get into all kinds of mischief.
5. Eleven years later she moved to Greenbrier, where she went to John Doss High School.
6. Walt's brother has bought forty houses, about half of which are duplexes that need drastic repair.
7. I have two fine children, a daughter born January 15, 1969, and a son born June 17, 1971.

See **5** about adjective clauses and **3** about appositives.

added exceptions, contrasts, and emphasized parts

PROBLEM

Some very common fragment additions change what has just been said in some way. Three such additions are *exceptions*, *contrasts*, and *emphasized parts*.

An exception changes a statement by saying that the statement does *not* apply to something. Often it begins with *except*. If the exception is not a complete statement itself but is separated from the statement before it, the exception is a fragment addition.

> The courses that he is taking do not relate directly to what he wants to be (a sentence). Except for Introduction to Aviation (a fragment adding an exception).

A contrast shows how the thing just said is different from something else. Often it begins with *not* or *rather than* or *instead of*. If it is not a complete statement, it is sometimes written as a fragment.

People must sometimes think of others (a sentence). Rather than only of themselves (a fragment adding a contrast).

They were crooks (a sentence). Not just greedy but vicious people (a fragment adding a contrast).

An emphasized part calls attention to one part of a group that is being talked about. Usually an emphasized part begins with the word *especially*. It is often written as a fragment.

She enjoys doing things for people (a sentence). Especially the ones that cannot help themselves (a fragment emphasizing one part of *people* in the sentence before).

SOLUTION

Either make a complete sentence out of a contrast, an exception, or an emphasized part, or attach it to the sentence before it. A comma usually replaces the period before *except*, *not*, and *especially*. With other words, often no punctuation is used between the complete statement and the fragment.

The courses that he is taking do not relate directly to what he wants to be, except for Introduction to Aviation (a sentence).

People must sometimes think of others rather than only of themselves (a sentence).

They were crooks, not just greedy but vicious men (a sentence).

She enjoys doing things for people, especially the ones that cannot help themselves (a sentence).

Correct the fragment additions in the following sentences.

1. Mammals are warm-blooded and usually have fur or hair on their bodies. With the exception of whales, which are the largest living mammals known to humans.

2. It is better to go swimming with someone. Rather than to go swimming alone.

3. Rick enjoys reading fiction. Especially historical novels and science fiction.

ANSWERS

1. Mammals are warm-blooded and usually have fur or hair on their bodies, <u>with</u> the exception of whales, which are the largest living mammals known to humans.
2. It is better to go swimming with <u>someone rather</u> than to go swimming alone.
3. Rick enjoys reading fiction, <u>especially</u> historical novels and science fiction.

If you missed any, review the lesson and do the next exercise. Follow the directions for the last exercise.

1. What I like about motorcycling is cross-country racing. Not big-time, 288-miles-an-hour racing.

2. She works hard in her courses. Especially if they are related to her major.

3. No one had ever before listened to him say what he wanted to do. Except his grandmother, who had lived with his family until he was seven.

ANSWERS

1. What I like about motorcycling is cross-country racing, <u>not</u> big-time, 288-miles-an-hour racing.
2. She works hard in her courses, <u>especially</u> if they are related to her major.
3. No one had ever before listened to him say what he wanted to do, except his grandmother, <u>who</u> had lived with his family until he was seven.

added compounds   ### PROBLEM

Another kind of fragment addition is a second part that is like a part already included in the sentence. Two parts doing the same thing in a sentence are called compounds if they can be joined by *and, or, nor,* or *but.*

Often a sentence has two or more compound predicates (verbs) for the same subject. The last predicate (verb) is sometimes written as though it were a new sentence although it is part of the old sentence. This predicate cannot be complete since its subject is in the old sentence. Because it is not complete, it is a fragment.

He had a motorcycle wreck, broke his ankle, and chipped a bone in his foot (a sentence). And stayed in a cast for four months (a compound verb fragment).

Complements (completers) after a verb may be compound, too. There may be two or more complements answering the questions *what* or *whom* after the verb. They are part of the old sentence rather than new sentences, so, if they are written as new sentences, they are fragments.

What I like about the place I live is the friendliness of the neighbors (a sentence). The location close to a shopping center (a fragment). And the trees and lot around my house (a fragment).

SOLUTION

Remember that a sentence may be long. Do not divide a sentence into two parts unless both parts are complete, even though it may seem long to you. Completeness is more important than length.

If you have two or more verbs for the same subject, be sure not to separate the last verb(s) from the subject by a period. The last verb should be joined by the word *and* to the sentence that it is part of.

He had a motorcycle wreck, broke his ankle, chipped a bone in his foot, and stayed in a cast for four months (a sentence with compound verbs).

Also, be sure that the last complement (completer) in a group of compound complements is part of the sentence that it is completing. Add the compound complement to the sentence that it is completing. Put *and* before the last complement. If there are three or more compounds, put commas between them, too. If there are only two, do not use a comma between them; the word *and* is enough.

> What I like about the place I live is the friendliness of the neighbors, the location close to a shopping center, and the trees and lot around my house (a sentence).

Correct the fragment additions in the following by connecting them to the sentences that they are part of.

1. She has a son who is eighteen and will graduate this spring. And a daughter who is a sophomore in college.

2. I enjoy going to church. Being involved in Sunday School class and helping the youth. Thinking about the sermon and my own life.

3. The wrestler who gets the take-down gets two points. And is winning the match.

4. The car smells of tobacco smoke. But is a nice car to ride in.

ANSWERS

1. She has a son who is eighteen and will graduate this <u>spring and</u> a daughter who is a sophomore in college.
2. I enjoy going to church, <u>being</u> involved in Sunday School class and helping youth, <u>and</u> thinking about the sermon and my own life.
3. The wrestler who gets the take-down gets two <u>points and</u> is winning the match.
4. The car smells of tobacco <u>smoke but</u> is a nice car to ride in.

If you missed any, review the lesson and do the next exercise. Follow the directions for the last exercise.

1. The best part of fishing is the excitement of trying to catch the biggest fish in the whole lake. And trying to get it out of the water without losing it.

2. Other things you will learn are how to get along in the community in which you work. The types of people you will come in contact with.

3. He stopped his friend from bleeding and called for a medi-vac chopper. And then sat beside his friend to wait.

4. My son is twelve years of age. And goes to Union Elementary School. Plays the trumpet in the school band.

ANSWERS

1. The best part of fishing is the excitement of trying to catch the biggest fish in the whole <u>lake and</u> trying to get it out of the water without losing it.
2. Other things you will learn are how to get along in the community in which you <u>work and</u> the types of people you will come in contact with.

3. He stopped his friend from bleeding and called for a medi-vac <u>chopper and</u> then sat beside his friend to wait.

4. My son is twelve years of age, <u>goes</u> to Union Elementary School, <u>and</u> plays the trumpet in the school band.

Fragments with Omitted Parts A fragment may be incomplete simply because one or more parts have been left out. Usually, the missing parts must be added to correct these fragments.

omitted subjects making fragments The subject *you* in a command is the only subject that can be left out and be understood. So, although we often leave out other subjects in speaking, we may not leave them out in writing.

Go clean up your car. (subject *you* understood)
You go clean up your car. (subject *you* expressed)

PROBLEM

The subject *I* is often left out, making a fragment, especially if it has been used before in the same paragraph.

I am thirty-seven years old, the mother of six children (a sentence). Am now working at Twilight Hours Nursing Home as a Licensed Practical Nurse (a fragment omitting the subject *I*).

SOLUTION

Use the subject *I* whenever it is meant. Do not expect your reader to supply it.

I am thirty-seven years old, the mother of six children. I am now working at Twilight Hours Nursing Home as a Licensed Practical Nurse. (two complete sentences)

PROBLEM

Sometimes other subjects are omitted after the first time they are used. A sentence without a subject is a fragment.

The puppy that she found has become a very good pet (a sentence). Does not chase cars any more (a fragment omitting the subject).

SOLUTION

Repeat a subject or use a pronoun for the subject to correct a fragment with an omitted subject.

The puppy that she found has become a very good pet. *The puppy* does not chase cars any more. (two sentences repeating the subject)

or

The puppy that she found has become a very good pet. *He* does not chase cars anymore. (two sentences, the second using a pronoun subject)

PROBLEM

Occasionally a writer will omit a subject that has not been used just before the fragment. This is an especially confusing fragment to the reader.

James is handsome, dresses well, and has a good personality (a sentence). Been good friends for years (a fragment omitting the subject).

SOLUTION

Be sure that every sentence has its subject expressed unless the subject is *you* and the sentence is a command.

James is handsome, dresses well, and has a good personality. He and I have been friends for years. (two sentences, the second with a subject added)

Correct the following fragments by adding subjects where they are needed.

1. He would come in and fix up her apartment. Even keep her dog when it was lonesome.

2. I work at the <u>Times</u>. Have worked there for twelve years, first as a secretary and now as an editor.

3. We come to school together, taking turns driving. Have double-dated before.

ANSWERS

The second sentences in each pair should read:

1. <u>He</u> would even keep her dog when it was lonesome.
2. <u>I</u> have worked there for twelve years. . .
3. <u>We</u> have double-dated before.

If you missed any of these, review **1** and **3**. Then review the lesson above and do the next exercise. Follow the directions for the last exercise.

1. They have taken several trips together. Went to Bryce Canyon and the Tetons last summer.

2. I drank the milk left over from lunch. Was beginning to spoil.

3. Thanksgiving is a time for us to gather and share our blessings. Makes us aware of how much we should be grateful for each other.

ANSWERS

The second sentence in each group should read:

1. <u>They</u> went to Bryce Canyon and the Tetons last summer.

2. <u>It</u> was beginning to spoil.

3. <u>It</u> makes us aware of how much we should be grateful for each other.

omitted In many ways, the verb is the most necessary part of a sentence. In writing, it may *never*
verbs be left out, for without it, a sentence cannot be complete.

making
fragments   **PROBLEM**

The linking verbs *am, is, are, was,* and *were* are sometimes left out of a sentence.
They are like equal marks. They say that a subject is equal to something that comes
after it (a predicate noun or predicate adjective). They link subjects to these complements.
If they are left out, the relation between the subject and the complement may not be
clear.

> He very friendly with children.
> (a fragment omitting a linking verb)

SOLUTION

Check your sentences to be sure that each has a verb. If a linking verb has been left
out, put it in.

> He <u>is</u> very friendly with children.
> (a sentence)

These are the most common forms of the linking verb that can be used as the predicate
of a sentence.

am, is, are	(present time)
was, were	(past time)
shall be, will be	(future time)

Usually, it is one of these that has been left out. There is a complete list of the forms
of *be* in **2**.

Add the linking verb between the things it links to correct the following fragments.

1. The two players wanted stiff competition, so that the way they played.

2. *Blazing Saddles* the funniest picture I have watched.

3. I don't depend on anyone because it up to me to get my learning.

4. He bought a Burmese; it also a very expensive cat.

ANSWERS

1. The two players wanted stiff competition, so that <u>was</u> the way they played.
2. *Blazing Saddles* <u>is</u> the funniest picture I have watched.
3. I don't depend on anyone because it <u>is</u> up to me to get my learning.
4. He bought a Burmese; it also <u>is</u> a very expensive cat.

If you missed any, study **2** and **3** and review the lesson above; then do the next exercise. Follow the directions for the last exercise.

1. The dog also very protective of their home when they not there.

2. We expected to win the game, and that what we did.

3. Compared to Corbin, Louisville a very big city.

4. I have been educated about what wrong or right even if I don't always follow these rules.

ANSWERS

1. The dog is also very protective of their home when they are not there.
2. We expected to win the game, and this is what we did.
3. Compared to Corbin, Louisville is a very big city.
4. I have been educated about what is wrong.

omitted thoughts making fragments

PROBLEM

Sometimes a writer leaves out so much of his or her idea that the reader really has trouble figuring out what is meant. For instance, the following leaves out both the subject and the verb.

> Then as always, time to go to church. (a fragment)

Or the writer may assume that readers will know what he means although he does not say it.

> It was the most enjoyable trip I can remember. The camping out in the van and the beauty of the lake. (a fragment)

SOLUTION

Be sure to check your groups of words between periods or semicolons to see that each has a subject and a verb and makes a complete statement by itself. If it does not, it is a fragment. Add the rest of your thought to make it a sentence.

> Then as always, it is time to go to church. (a sentence)

> It was the most enjoyable trip I can remember because of the camping out in the van and the beauty of the lake. (a sentence)

Add whatever is necessary to make the following complete thoughts.

1. I went to school in Clarksville all my life. First and second grade at Smith Elementary School.

2. The rider doesn't know if the horse is going to stand perfectly still or arch his back and go straight up trying to throw the rider to the ground. The excitement of man and horse trying each to control and command the other.

3. Furthermore, humans must stay in control. That they should make the computer a slave, not themselves.

ANSWERS

The second sentences may read:
1. I attended first and second grade at Smith Elementary School.
2. That is the excitement of man and horse trying each to control and command the other.
3. Humans must see that they should make the computer a slave, not themselves.

You may have correctly added something different to some of these incomplete thoughts. If your answers are different from these, show your instructor. If you missed any, review 2 and 3 and the lesson above; then do the next exercise. Follow the directions for the last exercise.

1. My car will not start as soon as the temperature hits five degrees below zero. The disgust of waking up to a cold house and a car that will not start.

2. She was a very special dog to me. The way she scratched the door when she wanted to play or eat.

3. The love of the wild, adventure, and the excitement of the unknown make me want to go on the trip. A sort of thrill of victory.

ANSWERS

The second sentences may read:
1. I am disgusted by waking up to a cold house and a car that will not start.
2. I remember the way she scratched the door when she wanted to play or eat.
3. The trip may give me a thrill of victory.

If your answers are different from these, they still may be correct. Show them to your instructor.

Fragments with Incomplete Forms of Verbs A fragment may have what seems to be a predicate (verb) but is really a form of the verb that cannot be the predicate of a sentence by itself. Sometimes such incomplete predicates (verbs) also lack subjects. They are often a special type of fragment addition to the preceding sentence but not always.

fragments using only *be* as verb PROBLEM

The word *be* is a verb, but it is not a verb form that can be the predicate (verb) of a sentence by itself.

Children *be* thinking that Santa Claus *be* coming to bring toys and goodies. (a fragment without a predicate)

SOLUTION

Sometimes you can change *be* to a form of the verb *be* that can be used as the predicate (verb) of a sentence. These are the forms of *be* that can act as predicates (verbs) by themselves.

am, is, are (present time)
was, were (past time)

If the sentence above is about something in the present time, it can be corrected this way:

Children <u>are</u> thinking that Santa Claus <u>is</u> coming to bring toys and goodies. (a sentence with <u>are</u> and <u>is</u> as predicates)

Often a helping word can be added to *be* to make it the predicate (verb). The most common helping words are forms of *be* itself; *has, have, had; shall, will; can, may;* and *do, did*. (Some other helpers are listed in **2**, where there is also a list of forms of *be* with and without helping words.) The *be* fragment above could be corrected by adding helpers, for instance:

Children <u>will</u> <u>be</u> thinking that Santa Claus <u>will</u> <u>be</u> coming to bring toys and goodies. (a sentence with the helping verb <u>will</u> added to <u>be</u> to make a predicate)

Correct the fragments in the following sentences by changing *be* to another form that can be a predicate or by adding a helping verb to make *be* part of a predicate.

1. Every day I be tired at 6:00.

2. A bully always be somebody tougher then everybody else be.

3. They be doing that every day.

ANSWERS

1. Every day I <u>am</u> tired at 6:00.
2. A bully always <u>is</u> somebody tougher than everybody else <u>is</u>.
3. They <u>are</u> doing that every day.

If you missed any of these, review the lesson on *be* fragments and do the next exercise. Follow the directions for the last exercise.

1. She always be too slow for me.

2. Mr. Cook be my coach last year.

3. We be too busy to go.

ANSWERS

1. She always <u>is</u> too slow for me.
2. Mr. Cook <u>was</u> my coach last year.
3. We <u>are</u> too busy to go.

infinitive fragments

PROBLEM

Another form of the verb that cannot be used as the predicate for a complete thought is the infinitive. An infinitive is the form of the verb used with *to*: for example, *to go*, to *sing*, *to think*, *to be*, *to have*. This verb form is always used as a noun, an adjective, or an adverb. If it is used as a verb, it makes a fragment.

That is another reason I am going to college (a sentence). To expand my knowledge in different areas to find one that I like (a fragment with an infinitive instead of a verb).

SOLUTION

Usually, these infinitive fragments are used as nouns closely related to the preceding sentence, so they can be added to the sentence. If they are the second of two compounds (see compound complements), they are added after the word *and*. If they explain a word in the preceding sentence (like *reason* in the example above), they are added after a comma. (See added appositive.)

That is another reason I am going to college, to expand my knowledge in different areas to find one that I like. (a sentence)

If a sentence begins with an infinitive (*to* plus a verb), be sure that it makes a complete statement by itself and is not just an addition to the preceding sentence. If it is a fragment, add it to the preceding sentence or add the parts (including a verb) needed to make it complete.

Add the following infinitive fragments to the sentence that they are a part of.

1. I like to be alone. To sit and think things out in their entirety.

2. Studying wildlife conservation has taught me a new attitude. To take care of the trees and plants, the ponds and campsites. To respect every living thing that I see.

ANSWERS

1. I like to be <u>alone and to sit</u> and think things out in their entirety.
2. Studying wildlife conservation has taught me a new <u>attitude, to</u> take care of the trees and plants, the ponds and <u>campsites, and to</u> respect every living thing that I see.

If you missed any of these, review the lesson above and do the next exercise. Follow the directions for the last exercise.

1. Traveling offers many opportunities. To see how other people live. To understand their views.

2. The job requires me to be at work on time every day. To help whenever emergencies come up.

ANSWERS

1. Traveling offers many opportunities to see how other people live <u>and to</u> understand their views.
2. The job requires me to be at work on time every day <u>and to</u> help whenever emergencies come up.

**fragments
using *ing*
forms as verbs**

PROBLEM

The *ing* form of a verb is often used as the predicate of a sentence, but this form by itself cannot be a predicate. Either it must have a helping verb with it or it must be related to a verb that is a predicate of the same sentence.

> I like the competition involved in tennis (a sentence). Playing with different people. (an *ing* fragment)

SOLUTION

To find an *ing* fragment, look for an *ing* verb that does not have a helping verb with it and is not related to a verb that is a predicate of the same sentence. There are several kinds of *ing* fragments and several ways to correct them. Choose the one that fits your meaning best.

If the *ing* fragment is an addition to the preceding sentence, add it to that sentence. If it is another item like one you have just named (a compound), put *and* or *or* between the two similar items. See compounds for more about this.

> I like the competition involved in tennis and playing with different people. (a sentence naming two things I like).

Some *ing* fragment additions describe a word in the preceding sentence.

> From being a small, bony kid, he has developed into a rock (a sentence). Standing 5 feet, 11 inches tall and weighing 170 pounds of muscle (a fragment describing what the sentence before means by *rock*).

This kind of fragment can be added to the sentence before with a comma between.

> From being a small, bony kid, he has developed into a rock, standing 5 feet, 11 inches tall and weighing 170 pounds of muscle (a sentence).

For other *ing* fragment additions, add connecting words that show the relation of the complete sentence to the fragment addition.

> Leaders controlled the townspeople (a sentence). Taking a few and training them to use the rest (a fragment).

Correct such fragment additions by using a connecting word (usually a preposition) between the sentence and the *ing* fragment addition.

> Leaders controlled the townspeople *by* taking a few and training them to use the rest (a sentence adding the fragment with the connecting word *by*).

Correct the *ing* fragment additions by adding them to the preceding sentence.

1. I get a sensational feeling from letting the boat pull me up out of the water. Feeling the power of the boat and water as I skim along.

2. With heavy heart we packed to come home. Knowing that someday we would come back to the beautiful island of Jamaica.

3. I have often used the camera. Taking pictures around the house, on trips, and on special occasions and holidays.

ANSWERS

1. I get a sensational feeling from letting the boat pull me up out of the <u>water and feeling</u> the power of the boat and water as I skim along.
2. With heavy heart we packed to come home, <u>knowing</u> that someday we would come back to the beautiful island of Jamaica.
3. I have often used the <u>camera for taking</u> pictures around the house, on trips, and on special occasions and holidays.

If you missed any of these, review the lesson above and do the next exercise. Follow the directions for the last exercise.

1. At Thanksgiving I give thanks for whatever I am thankful for. Having the turkey dinner.

2. People become closer because of traveling together. Getting to be with one another in many different situations.

3. I decided to go to a school I could commute to. Thus saving myself and my family the expense of dormitory bills.

ANSWERS

1. At Thanksgiving I give thanks for whatever I am thankful <u>for, like</u> having the turkey dinner.
2. People become closer because of traveling <u>together and getting</u> to be with one another in many different situations.
3. I decided to go to a school I could commute <u>to, thus</u> saving myself and my family the expense of dormitory bills.

PROBLEM

If the *ing* fragment is not a part of the sentence that precedes it, the fragment itself must be changed to make it complete.

SOLUTION

Again, different changes correct different kinds of *ing* fragments.

Some *ing* fragments have subjects. For these, a predicate is needed. Sometimes adding a helping verb to the *ing* verbal makes it a predicate. The helping verb *be* makes a predicate out of an *ing* verb form. These are the forms of *be* that can be used with an *ing* verb form:

am, is, are	(present time)
was, were	(past time)
shall be, will be	(future time)
has been, have been	(present perfect time)
had been	(past perfect time)

The perfect-time helpers are not often used. This is how a helping verb can correct an *ing* fragment with a subject.

All pilots fear in-flight fire in the battery box because of toxic fumes (sentence). Pilots also checking very closely for loose connections or bad wiring (a fragment with an -*ing* verb form instead of a predicate).

CORRECTION

Pilots <u>are</u> always <u>checking</u> very closely for loose connections or bad wiring. (a sentence with <u>are checking</u> as its predicate)

Another way to correct an *ing* fragment with a subject is simply to change the *ing* form of the verb to a form that can be a predicate.

CORRECTION

Pilots always <u>check</u> very closely for loose connections or bad wiring. (a sentence with <u>check</u> as its predicate)

See 1 if you are not sure what subjects and predicates are.
See 2 for information about verb forms and helping verbs.
See 8 about verb tenses (time) if you need to.

PROBLEM

Sometimes, neither the subject nor the predicate is given for an *ing* fragment, and the fragment does not make sense if added to the sentence before it.

My first choice of all sports I know would be water sports (a sentence). Getting out in the hot sun on a summer day (a fragment).

SOLUTION

Add to the fragment so that it has a subject and a verb. You may add both a subject and a verb:

I *enjoy* getting out in the hot sun on a summer day. (a sentence)

Or you can change the *ing* verb form to a predicate form and add only a subject.

I *get* out in the hot sun on a summer day. (a sentence)

Sometimes you can use the *ing* words themselves as the subject of the sentence. See **2**, gerund, and **5** about using a group of words as a subject.

Getting out in the hot sun on a summer day is fun. (a sentence using the *ing* phrase as a subject and adding a predicate and complement)

Correct the *ing* fragments in the following sentences by adding needed parts or by changing the *ing* to a predicate.

1. I work in a rest home and get great satisfaction from it. Dialing a phone for someone who cannot see the numbers.

2. The future of wildlife depending on our decision now.

3. Other people trying to break someone's marriage up.

ANSWERS

Your corrections may read like this:
1. I work in a rest home and get great satisfaction from it. I *enjoy* dialing a phone for someone who cannot see the numbers.
2. The future of wildlife *depends* (or *is depending*) on our decisions now.
3. Other people *are trying* (or *try*) to break someone's marriage up.

If your answers are not like these, ask your instructor to check them. They may still be correct. If you missed any of these, review the lesson above and do the next exercise.

1. The bandit having the policeman's car hood torn off.

2. The cops chasing the bandit, who wrecked the motorcycle.

3. The most noticeable season of the year is fall. The changing of the forest or just the trees in the yard.

ANSWERS

Your corrections may read:
1. The bandit *had* (or *was having*) the policeman's car hood torn off.
2. The cops *were chasing* (or *chased*) the bandit, who wrecked the motorcycle.
3. The most noticeable season of the year is fall. I *notice* the changing of the forest or just the trees in the yard.

If your answers are not like these, ask your instructor to look at them. They may still be correct.

PROBLEM

The verb form *being* cannot be the predicate of a sentence but is often used as a predicate. This makes a fragment.

> There are two schools of thought on this subject (a sentence). The first being that of hunters who favor the bolt-action rifle (a fragment with *being* for the predicate).

SOLUTION

Being fragments are additions to the sentence before them. So they can be corrected by adding them to that sentence. Use a comma instead of the period between the sentence and the fragment, and begin the fragment with a lowercase letter, not a capital. Then it will be part of a complete thought.

> There are two schools of thought on this subject, the first being that of hunters who favor the bolt-action rifle. (a sentence adding a fragment to the complete statement)

Or, if you want two separate sentences, change *being* to a form of the verb *be* which can be used as a predicate. These forms are:

am, is, are	(present time)
was, were	(past time)
shall be, will be	(future time)

There are two schools of thought on this subject. The first is that of hunters who favor the bolt-action rifle. (a sentence using *is* for its predicate)

Correct the *being* fragments below by adding them to the sentence before or by changing *being* to a predicate verb.

1. My chief interests are art and automobiles. Automobiles being my more profitable interest.

2. He wants to move into the country. His reason being that his neighbors do not control their children.

3. I like humorous, exciting movies. My favorite being *Smoky and the Bandit*.

ANSWERS

1. My chief interests are art and automobiles, automobiles being my more profitable interest. (*or* Automobiles are my more profitable interest.)
2. He wants to move into the country, his reason being that his neighbors do not control their children. (*or* His reason is that his neighbors do not control their children.)
3. I like humorous, exciting movies, my favorite being *Smoky and the Bandit*. (*or* My favorite is *Smoky and the Bandit*.)

If you missed any of these, review the lesson above and do the next exercise. Follow the directions for the last exercise.

1. We had to start crawling on our stomachs. The tunnels being too small for us to crawl on our hands and knees.

2. He has several friends. The closest being his cousin Mark.

3. The kind of music I prefer is hard rock, the kind people can get down to. My favorite song being "Burnin' Sky."

ANSWERS

1. We had to start crawling on our stomachs, <u>the</u> tunnels being too small for us to crawl on our hands and knees. (*or* The tunnels <u>were</u> too small for us to crawl on our hands and knees.)
2. He has several friends, <u>the</u> closest being his cousin Mark. (*or* The closest <u>is</u> his cousin Mark.)
3. The kind of music I prefer is hard rock, the kind people can get down to, <u>my</u> favorite song being "Burnin' Sky." (*or* My favorite song <u>is</u> "Burnin' Sky.")

Adverb-Clause Fragments

PROBLEM

An adverb clause is always a part of a sentence, never a complete statement. It is a group of words with a subject and a predicate (a clause). But it begins with a word that says that it is only part of a more important idea that is a complete statement. Without this word (an adverbial conjunction or subordinating conjunction), the adverb clause itself would be a complete statement.

> Ann does not wear much make-up. (a complete statement)
> She has very smooth skin. (a complete statement)

> | Complete statement—main clause. |

> | Complete statement—main clause. |

But, when a subordinating conjunction is added to one of these complete statements, the statement is no longer complete. The conjunction says that it is part of another, more important idea.

> Ann does not wear much make-up (complete)
> because she has very smooth skin. (incomplete)

> | Complete statement (main clause) |
> (Conjunction) | Incomplete statement (adverb clause). |

The incomplete statement—the adverb clause—may come after the complete statement as in the example above. Or it may come before the complete statement.

> Because she has very smooth skin, Ann does not wear much make-up.

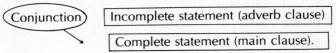

Notice that a comma separates the clauses when the adverb clause comes first. The conjunction separates the clauses when the adverb clause follows the main clause, so no comma is needed to separate them.

Ann does not wear much make-up (because) she has very smooth skin.

Because the subordinating conjunction makes the adverb clause part of a more important idea, an adverb clause cannot be a sentence by itself. If it is separated from its main clause, it is a fragment.

Ann does not wear much make-up (a sentence).
Because she has very smooth skin (an adverb-clause fragment).

SOLUTION

Learn the subordinating conjunctions that begin adverb clauses. The most common are *because, if, when, before, until, till, after, since, while, as, the day that, unless,* and *although (though)*. A longer list is found in 2. Look for these words before a clause. If an adverb clause is not connected to a main idea, it is a fragment.

CORRECTION 1

To correct adverb-clause fragments, add them to the sentence that contains the main idea that they are related to. This sentence may be before the adverb clause or after it.

Ann does not wear much make-up because she has very smooth skin. (a sentence)

If it is after the adverb clause, separate the clauses with a comma.

Because Ann has very smooth skin, she does not wear much make-up. (a sentence)

Correct the adverb-clause fragments in the following groups by adding them to the main ideas they are related to.

1. I enjoy the milder weather that comes with Spring. After winter has passed, taking with it its snow, ice, and sleet.

2. Some people call this harmless, and as far as I'm concerned, it is. As long as it does not go any further than this.

3. She particularly likes plants that bloom. Although a few of the ones she likes do not bloom.

4. Some parents believe that the values instilled in them in their childhood are outdated. While others believe that permissive parents are causing our children to decay morally.

5. Humans need the computer for their future. Because, in the future, new problems will require new and better services.

ANSWERS

1. I enjoy the mild weather that comes with <u>spring after</u> winter has passed, taking with it its snow, ice, and sleet.
2. Some people call this harmless, and as far as I'm concerned, <u>it is</u> as long as it does not go any further than this.
3. She particularly likes plants that <u>bloom although</u> a few of the ones she likes do not bloom.
4. Some parents believe that the values instilled in them in their childhood are <u>outdated while</u> others believe that permissive parents are causing our children to decay morally.
5. Humans need the computer for their <u>future because,</u> in the future, new problems will require new and better services.

If you missed any of these, review the lesson above, **2** on adverbs, and **5** on dependent clauses. Then do the next exercise. Follow the directions for the last exercise.

1. My hobbies are skating, swimming, tennis, horseback riding, and painting. Although I take my painting more seriously than most people take a hobby.

2. He used to work at Memorial Hospital as an orderly. Till he got another job.

3. If I can get the dress cut out today. Then maybe I can finish it this week.

4. She wrote her term paper on Lindbergh and enjoyed it. Even though it was difficult to find information about him.

5. I would like to live in Los Angeles or New York. Because someday I hope that I will be a baseball player on a team for one of those cities.

ANSWERS

1. My hobbies are skating, swimming, tennis, horseback riding, and <u>painting although</u> I take my painting more seriously than most people take a hobby.
2. He used to work at Memorial Hospital as an <u>orderly till</u> he got another job.
3. If I can get the dress cut out <u>today, then</u> maybe I can finish it this week.
4. She wrote her term paper on Lindbergh and enjoyed <u>it even</u> though it was difficult to find information about him.
5. I would like to live in Los Angeles or <u>New York because</u> someday I hope that I will be a baseball player on a team for one of those cities.

CORRECTION 2

If there is no main idea for the adverb clause to relate to, take out the subordinating conjunction that says the idea should be related to something.

Because Ann has very smooth skin. (an adverb-clause fragment)

Ann has very smooth skin. (a sentence)

Correct the adverb-clause fragments in the following groups by taking out the subordinating conjunction. Remember to capitalize the first letter of the new sentence.

1. After a horrible game I go home in a bad mood, never wanting to play again. Then when I sit down to think about what I did wrong and how I am going to correct it.

2. Under this type of economy people can freely control their economic affairs. Since the profits earned belong to the person who earned them.

3. Fred's rebellion makes him retreat underground. While the Harlequin, on the other hand, rebels openly and tries to change the people around him.

4. Each student is steered toward making the best grades. While sports and extracurricular activities are of little importance.

5. I can remember the first time I tried to smoke. One day while the grownups were outside carrying on a big conversation about how life had changed and was changing.

ANSWERS

The second sentences can be corrected to read:
1. Then I sit down to think about what I did wrong and how I am going to correct it.
2. The profits earned belong to the person who earned them.
3. The Harlequin, on the other hand, rebels openly and tries to change the people around him.
4. Sports and extracurricular activities are of little importance.
5. One day the grownups were outside carrying on a big conversation about how life had changed and was changing.

If you missed any of these, review the lesson above, **2** on adverbs, and **5** on dependent clauses. Then do the next exercise. Follow the directions for the last exercise.

1. He was stationed at Bin Hoe, South Viet-Nam, which was not a bad place to be. Simply because nothing ever happened around there.

2. I do not plan to get married for a while. Though I do have a boyfriend I have dated for three years.

3. With both the hard and soft contact lenses one can see no matter which way the eyeball is turned. Whereas with glasses one can see clearly only when looking straight ahead.

4. The boat shows that the family likes to spend time around the water. While the skis show that it is sports-minded.

5. Thanksgiving is a satisfying holiday for me. Because I come home from an exciting ball game and sit down and start digging into my mother's cooking.

ANSWERS

The second sentences can be corrected to read:
1. Nothing ever happened around there.
2. I do have a boyfriend I have dated for three years.
3. With glasses one can see clearly only when looking straight ahead.
4. The skis show that it is sports-minded.
5. I come home from an exciting ball game and sit down and start digging into my mother's cooking.

Paragraph Topics as Fragments

PROBLEM

A new paragraph begins a new part of a paper. So the writer needs to let the reader know what new part of the subject the new paragraph is about. Sometimes the writer writes a title (a fragment) for the paragraph instead of writing a sentence. But a title is correctly used only for a whole paper, not for a paragraph. A paragraph is only a part of a paper. The paragraph's beginning must be a whole statement, a sentence.

What Sundays are like after our evening meal. (fragment)

SOLUTION

When beginning a new paragraph, be sure that the new part of the paper—the topic of the paragraph—is named in a sentence, not a fragment. Remember that a sentence not only names a thing (Sundays); it also makes a complete statement about the thing that it names.

Sundays are quiet after our evening meal. (sentence)

Label each of the following either a sentence (S) or a title (T).

_____ 1. How I feel about marijuana.

_____ 2. The first thing to look for is any change in facial features.

_____ 3. When my husband and I went to Florida.

_____ 4. Finally, the man is narrow-minded.

_____ 5. The day I graduated from high school.

ANSWERS

1. T   2. S   3. T   4. S   5. T

If you missed any of these, review sentence completeness in **3** and **23** and then do the next exercise. Follow the directions for the last one.

_____ 1. What it takes to get a quality education.

_____ 2. To conclude my thoughts on the ambulance service.

_____ 3. What I like most about spring.

_____ 4. Another sport that I really enjoy is hunting.

_____ 5. The way to make an indoor plant garden.

ANSWERS

1. T   2. T   3. T   4. S   5. T

The handbook discusses the sentence core in **3** and phrases and clauses in **4** and **5**. Now do Post-test A.

NAME

24. FRAGMENTS

Post-Test A

Correct any fragments in the following. Some groups of words are already complete sentences.

1. A man gets to be hard to get along with. When he spends his time with people whose personalities are as good as dogs'.
2. He helped in the planning and layout of the warehouse part. Which is for receiving, storage, and shipping.
3. Why I am in college. I am going to college to learn to be a pharmacist.
4. My life began on a small farm in Green County. A family of six, two brothers, one sister, Mother, and Dad.
5. Two friends and I decided that we wanted to go on a trip. Not just an ordinary trip of a couple of weeks, but a trip that lasted for two months.
6. I hope all my memories be good ones.
7. When my father was young, he was impressed by many things. Things that made him what he is today, like the way he combs his hair and even his political views.
8. Sunday afternoons I go out, feed my pigs again, then talk to them a while. Walk around the yard and see what has to be done the next week.
9. The next time I want to see a movie, the best bet I have to leave that crazy friend at home.
10. I could do whatever I wanted while I was on the trip. The only exception being that I had to call home at least twice.

Ask your instructor to check your answers, or turn them in.

The instructor may want the student to review parts of the lesson and then take Post-test **B** or the general post-test over all sentence errors after **26**. See **36–47** about commas and **54–56** for writing assignments.

NAME _____

24. FRAGMENTS

Post-Test B

Correct any fragments in the following. Some groups of words are already complete sentences.

1. As I watched her hands, I can tell that she is nervous. The tense, twitching fingers.
2. Thirty years ago, people depended upon their neighbors. Who always helped them in time of need.
3. Every day when I be walking through the woods, I would always stop and eat my lunch.
4. What I feel about my work. I both like and dislike my work.
5. There are many reasons for belonging to a softball team. For exercise, competition, friendship, and sportsmanship.
6. It was hard for others to join our little group of friends. Not because we didn't like them but because they didn't share our interests.
7. Another weakness is the police force. If that is what you want to call it.
8. Watching a mother who has elected to stay awake while giving birth is very exciting. Seeing the look on her face when she sees her baby for the first time.
9. The author tells how the computer will benefit humans. How it already has destroyed the barriers between theoretical and practical knowledge.
10. She wears attractive clothing. Especially the dresses and coats.

Ask your instructor to check your answers, or turn them in.

25 Fused Sentences

A fusion puts two things together to make one. Metal is fused when it is welded or soldered together. Two layers of cloth may be fused together. Sentences are fused when they are put together with nothing between them.

> complete statement complete statement

My neighbor called and asked me to fix the storm door on her basement when I got home she said she had tried but could not. (a fusion of two complete statements)

Complete statements must be separated from each other. Fused sentences confuse readers because they cannot tell where the first statement ends and the second begins. In the sentence above, we don't know when it was that the neighbor said that she tried to fix the door herself. The usual way to separate complete statements is with a period and capital letter.

Complete statement. Complete statement.

My neighbor called and asked me to fix the storm door on her basement when I got home. She said she had tried but could not. (two sentences)

A semicolon (;) or a co-ordinating conjunction after a comma may also separate complete statements. (A comma alone is not enough to separate complete statements.) These are the co-ordinating conjunctions that sometimes separate sentences.

, and	, nor	, so
, but	, for	, yet
, or		

Put a comma before one of these conjunctions when it separates sentences.

Fusion in Closely Related Statements
Fusions often occur because a writer does not separate two very closely related ideas. Because they relate to each other, the writer puts them together. But they may be confusing if not separated. They must be separated by punctuation to show that they are different complete statements.

sequence, question and answer, statement and comment, added details

PROBLEM

Below are several kinds of close relations that lead to fusions. Be aware of the kinds of sentences that lead to fusions so that you can check them and separate complete statements if necessary.

One close relation leading to fusion is sequence, that is, one event coming just after another.

She tried to pet a cow it got scared and chased her down toward the creek. (a fusion of two events happening close to each other)

Another very close relation leading to fusions is the relation between a question and its answer.

The scoutmaster asked if anyone had decided not to go everyone said no. (a fused question and answer)

Sometimes a writer makes a statement and then comments on how he or she feels about this statement. The close relation between the statement and the comment may lead to fusion.

I asked her out again don't ask me why. (a fusion of a statement and a comment about the statement)

Often a second statement will give more details about the first. This close relation may lead to a fusion.

We traveled by bus it took fourteen hours to get there. (a fusion with the second statement giving more details about the first)

SOLUTION

Separate complete statements, even if they are very closely related to each other. Some close relations to watch out for are sequence (telling about one thing happening right after another), a question and its answer, a statement and a comment about the statement, and a statement plus another statement giving details about the first. Separate complete statements like this with a period and capital letter.

CORRECT SEPARATIONS

She tried to pet a cow. It got scared and chased her down toward the creek. (sequence)

The scoutmaster asked if anyone had decided not to go. Everyone said no. (question and answer)

I asked her out again. Don't ask me why. (statement and comment)

We traveled by bus. It took fourteen hours to get there. (added details)

Each of the correct separations ends the first statement with a period and begins the second with a capital letter.

Correct all the following fusions by separating complete statements from each other.

1. He was caught in the snow his skis were broken all to pieces.
2. I visited the Great Smoky Mountains it was in the fall of the year the trees had turned gold.
3. You won't believe this he thought his wife wouldn't find out.
4. She asked if he would at least refund her money he said no.

ANSWERS

These answers show a period and capital letter as the only separation. You may correctly separate with a semicolon or a coordinating conjunction after a comma instead.

1. He was caught in the <u>snow. His</u> skis were broken all to pieces.
2. I visited the Great Smoky <u>Mountains. It</u> was the fall of the <u>year. The</u> trees had turned gold.
3. You won't believe <u>this. He</u> thought his wife wouldn't find out.
4. She asked if he would at least refund her <u>money. He</u> said no.

If you missed any of these, review the lesson above and do the next exercise. Follow the directions for the last exercise.

1. I hope that I shall be a good actor that is all I can say.
2. It really works farm families to get ready for the winter they have to cut and gather wood and put up food.
3. Carrie arrives home her mother is waiting for her.
4. He wanted to know if I was still angry I said that I was.

ANSWERS

These answers show a period and capital letter as the only separation. You may correctly separate with a semicolon or a coordinating conjunction after a comma instead.

1. I hope that I shall be a good <u>actor. That</u> is all I can say.
2. It really works farm families to get ready for the <u>winter. They</u> have to cut and gather wood and put up food.
3. Carrie arrives <u>home. Her</u> mother is waiting for her.
4. He wanted to know <u>if I</u> was still <u>angry. I</u> said that I was.

explanation
and contrast

PROBLEM

The most common kinds of close relations leading to fusions are explanation and contrast. Often a writer wants to explain more about what he or she has just said, so the writer uses another way of saying it or gives a specific example to explain the general statement. If both the explanation and the thing being explained are complete statements, they may be fused.

Some of my goals in life are quite simple I would like to have a wife, some children, and a good home. (a statement about simple goals fused with an explanation of what simple goals are)

The other most common close relation, contrast, is really a kind of explanation, too. Often one statement says something negatively, and another says the same thing positively. Often one statement uses the word *not*.

I will do what I want no one will stop me. (a positive statement fused to a negative statement of the same idea)

Or two statements tell about different things that are being compared to each other.

I was doing sixty-five the speed limit was forty-five. (a fusion of two things being contrasted)

SOLUTION

Be sure to separate complete statements, even if one is explaining the other or one is contrasted with the other. End the first statement with a period and begin the second with a capital letter.

CORRECT SEPARATIONS

Some of my goals in life are quite simple. I would like to have a wife, some children, and a good home. (two sentences)

I will do what I want. No one will stop me.
(two sentences)

I was doing sixty-five. The speed limit was forty-five. (two sentences)

Correct fusions in the following by separating complete statements.

1. I like to read Asimov he is a very imaginative writer.
2. Time flew by before we knew it, our hour was up.
3. I enjoyed the skating party very much I was worn out, though.
4. Don't give up your goals keep on working for what you really want.

ANSWERS

These answers show a period and capital letter as the only separation. You may also correctly separate with a semicolon or a coordinating conjunction after a comma.
   1. I like to read Asimov. He is a very imaginative writer.
   2. Time flew by. Before we knew it, our hour was up.
   3. I enjoyed the skating party very much. I was worn out, though.
   4. Don't give up your goals. Keep on working for what you really want.

If you missed any of these, review the lesson above and do the next exercise. Follow the directions for the last exercise.

1. In the morning when the campfire was cooking breakfast, the smell made us taste the eggs and bacon even the woodchucks and ground squirrels came out.
2. My father showed us how to make snow cream it is like ice-cream or a snow cone.
3. They did not want to hurt her they just wanted to make her understand.
4. I love mountains they are so beautiful.

ANSWERS

These answers show a period and capital letter as the only separation. You may correctly separate with a semicolon or a coordinating conjunction after a comma instead.
   1. In the morning when the campfire was cooking breakfast, the smell made us taste the eggs and bacon. Even the woodchucks and ground squirrels came out.

2. My father showed us how to make snow cream. <u>It</u> is like ice cream or a snow cone.
3. They did not want to hurt her. <u>They</u> just wanted to make her understand.
4. I love mountains. <u>They</u> are so beautiful.

Fusions Caused by Pronouns

PROBLEM

Two complete statements are often fused if the writer thinks one statement is not complete because it contains a pronoun referring to the other statement.

Other schools have these classes to help students that is why I think credit for them should transfer. (a fusion with the pronoun *that* in the second statement substituting for the idea of the first statement)

SOLUTION

Remember that you do not have to be able to understand everything about a statement for the statement to be complete. Most sentences depend on the sentences around them for full understanding. But, if a statement names a thing and completes an assertion about it, the statement is complete. It is a sentence.

The book pleased her.

In this sentence, we do not know what book or who she is. But the sentence is a complete statement. So a pronoun does not have to be in the same sentence as the word or idea that it is substituting for.

Think of it this way. If a football coach sends a substitute in for his starting halfback, the team using the substitute is still complete. If a writer uses any pronoun (except a relative pronoun) to substitute for a word or idea in another sentence, the statement using the pronoun substitute is as complete as it would be with whatever the pronoun substitutes for. When a complete statement containing one of these pronoun substitutes is not separated from the complete statement that the pronoun refers to, the statements are incorrectly fused. The pronouns most common in fusions are:

he	this	many
she	that	some
it	these	both
they	those	others

Be sure to separate complete statements containing these pronouns from complete statements containing the words or ideas that they substitute for.

Other schools have these classes to help students. That is why I think credit for them should transfer. (two sentences separated with a period and a capital letter)

Correct any fusions in the following sentences.

1. I get angry when people hammer nails into trees this kills them.
2. The celebration has a name it is the Feast of Tabernacles.

3. I took my little girl she enjoyed the trip as much as I did.

4. Birthdays to my family are very special they have been observed the same way as long as I can remember.

ANSWERS

These answers show a period and capital letter as the only separation. You may correctly separate with a semicolon or a coordinating conjunction after a comma instead.

1. I get angry when people hammer nails into trees. <u>This</u> kills them.
2. The celebration has a name. <u>It</u> is the Feast of Tabernacles.
3. I took my little girl. <u>She</u> enjoyed the trip as much as I did.
4. Birthdays to my family are very special. <u>They</u> have been observed the same way as long as I can remember.

If you missed any, review the lesson and do the next exercise. Follow the directions for the last exercise.

1. From my notes I have drawn these conclusions he is a middle-aged gentleman who is a bricklayer and a ladies' man.
2. I like only spaniels, pointers, and dachshunds these are my favorite dogs.
3. I never did like poetry it was because of all the memory work.
4. I spent my first twenty-one years in Wisconsin that is why I love the change of seasons so much.

ANSWERS

These answers show a period and capital letter as the only separation. You may correctly separate with a semicolon or a coordinating conjunction after a comma instead.

1. From my notes I have drawn these conclusions. He is a middle-aged gentleman who is a bricklayer and a ladies' man.
2. I like only spaniels, pointers, and dachshunds. <u>These</u> are my favorite dogs.
3. I never did like poetry. <u>It</u> was because of all the memory work.
4. I spent my first twenty-one years in Wisconsin. <u>That</u> is why I love the change of seasons so much.

Fusions Caused by Conjunctive Adverbs

PROBLEM

Because it is correct to separate complete statements with coordinating conjunctions, a word that seems to be a conjunction but is not sometimes causes fusions.

We have our youth meeting then we adjourn so that we can go somewhere. (a fusion of two complete statements with *then* between them)

SOLUTION 1

Learn the coordinating conjunctions.

and	nor	so
but	for	yet
or		

Remember that any other words between complete statements cannot separate. Add a separation (period and capital, semicolon, or coordinating conjunction after a comma).

We have our youth meeting. Then we adjourn so that we can go somewhere. (two sentences)

SOLUTION 2

The words that cause fusions because they look like conjunctions are called conjunctive adverbs. Learn the most common of these.

NOT CORRECT SEPARATIONS

then	also	however
next	plus	therefore
soon	at least	thus
finally	for example	consequently
moreover		

If one of these is the only separation between complete statements, separate the statements with a period or semicolon.

I passed the ball then the receiver was tackled.
(a fusion)

I passed the ball. Then the receiver was tackled.
(two sentences)

Correct the following fusions caused by conjunctive adverbs.

1. Her new job offers her a great chance of a good promotion also she is getting over the disappointment about her last job.
2. After the filler has been applied, let it set approximately ten minutes then remove it with a putty knife or steel wool.
3. Everyone was ready to go swimming until we felt the water then we decided we would wait until tomorrow.
4. I have had about three jobs so far I have not found one that I like.

ANSWERS

These answers show a period and capital letter as the only separation. You may correctly separate with a semicolon instead.
1. Her new job offers her a great chance of a good promotion. Also she is getting over the disappointment about her last job.
2. After the filler has been applied, let it set approximately ten minutes. Then remove it with a putty knife or steel wool.
3. Everyone was ready to go swimming until we felt the water. Then we decided we would wait until tomorrow.
4. I have had about three jobs. So far I have not found one that I like.

If you missed any of these, review the lesson above. Then do the next exercise, following the directions for the last exercise.

1. I played basketball in junior high school then in high school I played basketball and ran track.
2. Businesses compete by trying to outdo each other thus the people always have improved products to choose among.
3. I drag myself out of bed and try to think about what I will wear then I put on my socks and my shoes and a pair of jeans.
4. The meadowlarks are easy to recognize if you can see their breasts however, they hop around with just their backs and heads showing most of the time.

ANSWERS

These answers show a period and capital letter as the only separation. You may correctly separate with a semicolon instead.

1. I played basketball in junior high school. Then in high school I played basketball and ran track.
2. Businesses compete by trying to outdo each other. Thus the people always have improved products to choose among.
3. I drag myself out of bed and try to think about what I will wear. Then I put on my socks and my shoes and a pair of jeans.
4. The meadowlarks are easy to recognize if you can see their breasts. However, they hop around with just their backs and heads showing most of the time.

See lessons on sentence completeness in **3**. Now do Post-test A.

NAME _____

25. FUSED SENTENCES
Post-Test A

Correct all the following fusions by separating complete statements from each other.

1. I should not complain about my work it could be worse.
2. Rhonda has a little boy now he is two years old his name is Joshua.
3. I don't know let's try to make it to Wichita before we stop.
4. Most people think that a dent in the can does not mean much, but it does the food could be spoiled or old, and you should not buy it.
5. The dogs are well fed they are not skinny.
6. My heat-system went out on me I got it fixed.
7. I enjoy "playing the stick" that is slang for baseball.
8. The tune is sweet and sad also the words tell about an unhappy love affair.
9. I asked if they were tired they said no.
10. I had trouble getting it to turn over then I flooded it.

Ask your instructor to check your answers, or turn them in.

The instructor may want the student to review parts of the lesson and then take Post-test B. See the general post-test on sentence errors after 26. See the writing assignments in 54–56.

25. FUSED SENTENCES

Post-Test B

Correct all the following fusions by separating complete statements from each other.

1. You don't have to have many to enjoy life you just have to know how to enjoy it without spending money.
2. I saw some blue lights flashing I knew they were after me.
3. She is friendly by this I mean that she is interested in other people.
4. He drove to New York City it was his first trip without his parents.
5. Beat the whites till they are stiff next fold in the flour mixture.
6. Don't get me wrong I want to earn a good salary, too.
7. That area is beautiful there are hills and mountains.
8. The actors seemed to be living their parts there was fighting during an argument that was spontaneous.
9. He wanted to know how to take it apart no one knew.
10. We decided to take her car that meant I had to transfer the CB radio to it.

Ask your instructor to check your answers, or turn them in.

26 Comma Splices

A comma splice is an error that occurs when only a comma is used to separate two complete statements. A comma is used to separate many smaller parts of a sentence, so it is not enough to stop a reader at the end of what could be a whole sentence.

I am a veteran   ,   I was in the Navy four years. (comma splice)

| Complete statement | , | complete statement. |

The usual way to separate complete statements is to end the first with a period and to begin the second with a capital letter.

I am a veteran. I was in the Navy four years.

| Complete statement | • | Complete statement. |

Sometimes a question mark or exclamation point is needed instead of a period to end the first statement. A semicolon (;) or a coordinating conjunction after a comma (see 2, Conjunctions) are two other ways to separate complete statements.

| A comma alone is not acceptable between complete statements. |

Comma Splices in Closely Related Sentences
Many comma splices are written because the two complete statements are closely related to each other in their ideas. They are so closely related that the writer does not think they should be separated. But if they are not separated, the reader may be confused. So even closely related statements must be separated from each other.

sequence, question and answer, statement and comment, added details

PROBLEM

There are several kinds of statements in which one statement very closely follows another. The writer needs to be aware of these kinds to prevent making comma splices when he or she writes them.

One kind is sequence. The first statement tells about one thing that happened and another statements tells about what happened right after the first. Because the events are closely related in time, the writer sometimes does not separate them enough; he or she makes a comma splice. This is especially likely if the events are exciting and interesting.

I looked at my receivers, two of them were open (a comma splice). I pulled up to pass, the halfback read *pass* very quickly, I had plenty of time to throw (two more comma splices).

A question is usually followed by an answer, and this close relation sometimes causes comma splices.

I asked if she would go out with me, she said yes.
(a comma splice)

Another close relation appears when a writer makes a statement and also comments on the statement. That is, the writer says something and also gives his or her own attitude toward what has been said. If both the statement and the comment are complete statements, they must be separated with more than a comma.

Don't misunderstand me, I really do like my job.
(a comma splice joining a comment that is a complete statement to the complete statement about which it comments)

Statements are also closely related when one gives details about something in the other. If the statements are not properly separated, they make a comma splice.

When I was three years old, we moved to South Dakota, there we lived in three different towns.
(a comma splice joining details about living in South Dakota to the general statement that I lived there)

SOLUTION

If a second statement is closely related to the first in one of these ways, check to see if both statements are complete. If they are, be sure that they are separated by more than a comma.

CORRECT SEPARATIONS

I looked at my receivers. Two of them were open. I pulled up to pass. The halfback read *pass* very quickly. I had plenty of time to throw. (sequence)

I asked if she would go out with me. She said yes. (question and answer)

Don't misunderstand me. I really like my job. (comment and statement)

When I was three years old, we moved to South Dakota. There we lived in three different towns. (statement and details)

These corrections all separate by ending the first statement with a period and beginning the second with a capital letter. A semicolon or a conjunction after a comma may also be correctly used to separate complete statements.

Correct comma splices in the following sentences by separating all complete statements from each other with more than just a comma.

1. The principal announced that I was the valedictorian, for a few moments I was on cloud nine.
2. He was average in looks, he was about 6 feet tall and weighed about 165 pounds.
3. The last two weeks came, I believe they were the hardest.
4. He asked if they should stop at a service station along the way, she said she thought they could make it to town.

ANSWERS

These answers show a period and capital letter as the only separation. You may correctly separate with a semicolon or a coordinating conjunction after a comma instead.

1. The principal announced that I was the <u>valedictorian. For</u> a few moments I was on cloud nine.
2. He was average in <u>looks. He was</u> about 6 feet tall and weighed about 165 pounds.
3. The last two weeks <u>came. I believe</u> they were the hardest.
4. He asked if they should stop at a service station along the <u>way. She said</u> she thought they could make it to town.

If you missed any of these, review the lesson above and do the next exercise. Follow the directions for the last exercise.

1. Compacts cost less than components, usually compacts sell from fifty to five hundred dollars.
2. As I cut my first rafter on my own, I was really nervous, the boss put the rafter in place and grinned broadly.
3. We wondered if they would have room for us in the Citroën, they said we could ride in the sling.
4. The pain in his leg must have been terrible, I don't know how he stood it.

ANSWERS

These answers show a period and capital letter as the only separation. You may also correctly separate with a semicolon or a coordinating conjunction after a comma.

1. Compacts cost less than components. <u>Usually</u> compacts sell from fifty to five hundred dollars.
2. As I cut my first rafter on my own, I was really <u>nervous. The</u> boss put the rafter in place and grinned broadly.
3. We wondered if they would have room for us in the Citroën. <u>They</u> said we could ride in the sling.
4. The pain in his leg must have been terrible. <u>I</u> don't know how he stood it.

explanation
and
contrast

PROBLEM

The close relations of ideas that most often cause comma splices are explanation and contrast. A complete statement often explains something about the statement before or after it. Because of this close relation, the two are sometimes incorrectly written as a comma splice.

These two girls have always helped me when I needed them, they have become like sisters to me. (a comma splice in which the first complete statement explains the second)

A similar close relation between statements is contrast. This means that one statement may say what is and the other what is not, or the two statements may show a difference in some other way. It is like explanation because one statement explains what the other is not, or it explains what the other is different from. Often, one of the statements uses the word *not*. Two contrasting statements like this are sometimes incorrectly written as a comma splice, also.

> People don't think of the good points of motorcycling, they think only of its danger. (a comma splice containing two contrasting statements)

SOLUTION

Remember that two complete statements must be separated from each other even if they are closely related. A comma is not enough to separate complete statements. End the first one with a period, and begin the second with a capital letter.

CORRECT SEPARATIONS

> These two girls have always helped me when I needed them. They have become like sisters to me.

> People don't think of the good points of motorcycling. They think only of the danger.

Correct the comma splices in the following by separating complete statements.

1. The shore line is clean, the park officials clear it every day.
2. His face has many wrinkles, his eyes do not look old.
3. She was fortunate to have me as her friend, she went through many changes, but I stuck by her.
4. Lee does not walk, he stalks as if he were Genghis Khan about to topple the whole Chinese dynasty.

ANSWERS

These answers show a period and capital letter as the only separation. You may correctly separate with a semicolon or a coordinating conjunction after a comma instead.
   1. The shore line is <u>clean. The park</u> officials clear it every day.
   2. His face has many <u>wrinkles. His</u> eyes do not look old.
   3. She was fortunate to have me as her <u>friend. She went</u> through many changes, but I stuck by her.
   4. Lee does not <u>walk. He</u> stalks as if he were Genghis Khan about to topple the whole Chinese dynasty.

If you missed any of these, review the lesson above and then do the next exercise. Follow the directions for the last exercise.

1. I will be glad to see this storm come up, maybe it will cool things off.
2. I never have trouble putting my ideas on paper, the problem is spelling them so they can be read.
3. He was not upset by his lack of material possessions, he seemed content to sleep on the ground when he had no better bed.
4. New Year's Eve is a real time for celebration, we have made it though another year after all.

ANSWERS

These answers show a period and capital letter as the only separation. You may correctly separate with a semicolon or a coordinating conjunction after a comma instead.

1. I will be glad to see this storm come <u>up. Maybe</u> it will cool things off.
2. I never have trouble putting my ideas on <u>paper. The</u> problem is spelling them so they can be read.
3. He was not upset by his lack of material <u>possessions. He</u> seemed content to sleep on the ground when he had no better bed.
4. New Year's Eve is a real time for <u>celebration. We</u> have made it through another year after all.

Comma Splices with Pronouns

PROBLEM

Another major cause of comma splices is that a writer often does not think a complete statement is complete. The cause for this is usually a pronoun. A pronoun substitutes for a noun or an idea that comes before it. If a statement begins with a pronoun, the writer sometimes thinks that the pronoun statement cannot be separated from the statement containing the noun or the idea. So he or she separates the pronoun statement from the noun statement only with a comma, which is not enough.

One reason for the popularity of the film was the music, it set the mood for many scenes. (a comma splice)

The last statement in the example can seem incomplete because the word *it* is not completely understood by itself; *it* substitutes for *music* in the first statement. So the statement has not been separated from the statement before it as it should be.

SOLUTION

There is a difference between complete understanding of a statement and a complete statement. The reader does not necessarily understand everything about a complete statement. Few sentences could be taken out of a paper and be completely understood on their own. But every sentence is a complete statement; that is, it names something, says what that thing is or does, and adds any complements (completers) needed. So a statement can be complete although the reader does not understand everything about that statement.

Also, the use of a pronoun does not keep a statement from being complete. A pronoun is a substitute. If a coach takes a starting player out of a game and sends in a substitute instead, the team is still complete. When a writer uses a pronoun to substitute for a thing named earlier, the pronoun substitute does not keep the statement from being complete.

Watch out for the following pronouns, for they are the ones most often causing a comma splice.

he	this	both
she	that	many
it	these	some
they	those	others

Always separate complete statements with more than a comma, even if one statement substitutes one of these pronouns for a noun or idea in the other statement.

One reason for the popularity of the film was the music (a complete statement). It set the mood for many scenes (a complete statement).

Correct the comma splices in the following sentences by replacing the comma with one of the three separations above.

1. The first part of the song is slow, this increases her nervousness.
2. Only one person responded to the call, it was Jessie.
3. Then the land was sold for development as a shopping center, that explained why he had bought it.
4. My youngest brother is Bobby, he has just gotten married.

ANSWERS

These answers show a period and capital letter as the only separation. You may correctly separate with a semicolon or a coordinating conjunction after a comma instead.
1. The first part of the song is slow. This increases her nervousness.
2. Only one person responded to the call. It was Jessie.
3. Then the land was sold for development as a shopping center. That explained why he had bought it.
4. My youngest brother is Bobby. He has just gotten married.

If you missed any answers, review **23** and the lesson above. Then do the next exercise. Follow the directions for the last exercise.

1. Tennis is a healthful sport, it exercises the heart and lungs as well as increasing strength.
2. Her best friend is James Carver, he is an insurance underwriter.
3. The trail was easier at the beginning, it would get much harder as they climbed higher.
4. He wanted to buy a new airplane, that was why he was saving.

ANSWERS

These answers show a period and capital letter as the only separation. You may also correctly separate with a semicolon or a coordinating conjunction after a comma.
1. Tennis is a healthful sport. It exercises the heart and lungs as well as increasing strength.
2. Her best friend is James Carver. He is an insurance underwriter.
3. The trail was easier at the beginning. It would get much harder as they climbed higher.
4. He wanted to buy a new airplane. That was why he was saving.

Comma Splices with Conjunctive Adverbs

PROBLEM

A writer may make a comma splice because he or she thinks that a conjunction after a comma is separating statements when really there is not a conjunction but only a conjunctive adverb. A conjunctive adverb cannot separate complete statements. But it does look like a conjunction.

We unwrapped the package, then we gasped in amazement. (a comma splice)

The word *then* looks like a conjunction but cannot correctly be used to separate complete statements. So the sentence above is not correctly separated.

SOLUTION

There are two ways to avoid this kind of comma splice. The first way is to memorize all the conjunctions that can correctly separate complete statements.

CORRECT SEPARATIONS

and	nor	so
but	for	yet
or		

There are no other coordinating conjunctions that can correctly separate complete statements. So use more than a comma unless one of these is the word you are checking.

The second way to avoid this kind of comma splice is to learn the most common conjunctive adverbs. The following are by far the ones most often found in comma splices.

NOT ACCEPTABLE SEPARATIONS

then	finally	at least	therefore
next	also	for example	consequently
soon	plus	however	moreover

If one of these begins a complete statement, you still need to add some separation before it.

We unwrapped the package. Then we gasped in amazement. (two sentences correctly separated)

Correct the following comma splices by replacing the comma with one of the separations.

1. The school gave him a chance to be on a state championship baseball team, therefore, he is grateful to it.
2. The wedding was over and everything had gone well, now the parents' nerves were calm again.
3. I get very angry when someone does not believe me, for example, a sales clerk would not accept my word about the price of an unmarked item, and so I would not buy it.
4. First the court was announced, then the queen was crowned and seated on her throne.

ANSWERS

These answers show a period and capital letter as the only separation. You may correctly separate with a semicolon instead.

1. The school give him a chance to be on a state championship baseball team. Therefore, he is grateful to it.
2. The wedding was over and everything had gone well. Now the parents' nerves were calm again.
3. I get very angry when someone does not believe me. For example, a sales clerk would not accept my word about the price of an unmarked item, and so I would not buy it.
4. First the court was announced. Then the queen was crowned and seated on her throne.

If you missed any of these, review the lesson above and then do the next exercise. Follow the instructions for the last exercise.

1. My parents took pictures of us in our prom clothes, then we went to his home, and his sister took pictures.
2. He does not care much for money, however, he does take pride in his clothes.
3. Many units are used for distant contact (DX) work, therefore, the units must be able to receive and reproduce faint signals.
4. He has skill in handling problems, also he gets along well with people.

ANSWERS

These answers show a period and capital letter as the only separation. You may also correctly separate with a semicolon.

1. My parents took pictures of us in our prom clothes. Then we went to his home, and his sister took pictures.
2. He does not care much for money. However, he does take pride in his clothes.
3. Many units are used for distant contact (DX) work. Therefore, the units must be able to receive and reproduce faint signals.
4. He has skill in handling problems. Also he gets along well with people.

See the sentence core in **3**.
Now do Post-test A.

26. COMMA SPLICES
Post-Test A

Correct all the comma splices in the following sentences.

1. Tom offered to help by operating on her foot, she refused.
2. Money is not the important part of nursing, it is caring about people and giving of yourself to a total stranger.
3. We had a good water battle, everyone got wet.
4. Our foster child's name was Amy, she was six years old.
5. We stood there for a few minutes and stared at each other, then we said goodbye and left.
6. We had already bought a place to live, it was a mobile home.
7. He was shy, for example, he didn't like to eat his lunch in front of the other children.
8. Then I finally got unpacked, I lay down on the bed and slept for about three hours.
9. Heroin and marijuana accumulate in the body in different ways, they also differ in the physical and mental effects.
10. I couldn't believe it, it was the new bike I had wanted.

Ask your instructor to check your answers, or turn them in. Your instructor may want you to review parts of the lesson and then take Post-test B. See the general post-test after Post-test B. See writing assignments in **54–56**.

<u>NAME</u>

26. COMMA SPLICES

Post-Test B

Correct all the comma splices in the following sentences.

1. I reminded them that they still had time to back out if they wanted to, the answer was no.
2. My friends stayed for an hour, then they left us alone together.
3. The trees are of countless variety and size, no two are the same.
4. So I told him, soon everyone else woke up.
5. We dated the night after graduation, that was the last time I saw him until after we had both married someone else.
6. The representative from Saudi Arabia makes a speech suggesting peace with Israel, the Arab underground arranges to assassinate him.
7. I thought it was useless, I went with them, anyway.
8. The town is for old people, there is no place to take a date.
9. Compacts cost less than components, usually compacts sell for anything from fifty to five hundred dollars.
10. The truck missed me by inches, that gave me a scare.

Ask your instructor to check your answers, or turn them in.

<u>NAME</u>

SENTENCE PROBLEMS : *Fragments, Fused (Run-On) Sentences, Comma Splices*

~~General~~ Post-Test

Correct any errors in the following groups of words. Some may be correct sentences as written. You may add, take out, or change words or punctuation.

1. The neighbors and I sometimes have a cookout and sit around and just talk, I enjoy that.
2. I have two brothers their names are Edward and James.
3. What I enjoy doing. I like to play tennis.
4. There seemed to be little need for others in his life, for example, he took lightly any romantic feelings that girls had for him.
5. Sociology was my worst subject in high school. Simply because at the time I would not give oral reports.
6. She finds it easy to get to know people. To learn to understand and love them.
7. He plans for what he wants most first, and that nothing but being smart.
8. People enjoy holidays for different reasons some are widely held, and others are personal.
9. Lisa made a face at me then I popped the question, "Did you put that writing on the auditorium?"
10. There were many exciting moments during our trip to Hawaii. The best being my first experience surfing.
11. The best restaurant is Kuennings Suburban, it has a terrific salad and good steaks.
12. I don't know why he helped he is not kin.
13. The Marines train their people to attack on the ground, then they can move back to the water.
14. Janet was a help to me. While Beverly just sat around looking decorative.
15. Her complexion is light brown, therefore she seldom wears make-up.

Ask your instructor to check your answers, or turn them in. See reviews of sentence parts in **1–6**. See writing assignments in **54–56**.

Relationships Within a Sentence

SUBJECT-VERB AGREEMENT

Pretest

Underline the correct verb for each of the following sentences.

27   1. No school (teaches, teach) us to be ideal parents.
     2. I shall stay with him until he (hurts, hurt) me in some way.
     3. Dressmaking (interests, interest) him because he (wants, want) to become a fashion designer.
     4. Physical fitness (seems, seem) more important than money.
     5. Some people (says, say) that he was innocent.
     6. The Bill of Rights (gives, give) us many basic liberties.

29   7. We (was, were) digging one another.
     8. My main interests (be, am, is, are) farming and sport hunting.
     9. It (be, am, is, are) a male dog, and it (doesn't, don't) like strangers at all.
     10. When it rains, the students (has, have) to run across the campus, and most of them (be, am, is, are) soaked.

29 11. The spring and a low area combined (creates, create) a streak of swampy land.
     12. The hen or her chickens (be, am, is, are) scratching up my flowers.
     13. Not only the boys but also Ellen (wants, want) a pony.
     14. Neither the singer nor the musicians (was, were) trained.
     15. My mother and sister (does, do) the dishes.

30 16. Mornings usually (starts, start) out quietly.
     17. My dog always (pays, pay) my neighbor a visit every day.
     18. The people working on this service (be, am, is, are) crazy.
     19. Bright high beams from oncoming traffic (makes, make) it difficult to see what is on the shoulder of the road, also.
     20. A friend that is honest and can be trusted (be, am, is, are) worth a little trouble now and then.

21. We arrived late and (was, were) not permitted to tour inside.

31 22. There (be, am, is, are) not as many major crimes here as in the cities.

23. If there (was, were) dormitories, more students would come to school here.

24. (Does, Do) this problem change with the child's age?

25. Next (was, were) the husband's suicide.

32 26. I played baseball for a Babe Ruth team when I (was, were) in junior high school.

27. New Year's Eve I always (be, am, is, are) with my family listening to music.

28. I (has, have) had all kinds of trouble out of the car, but I still (likes, like) it.

29. On Fifties Day everybody (dresses, dress) up like the fifties and (has, have) a dance with fifties songs and dances.

30. My boys are different also in the hobbies each of them (likes, like).

31. My mother is always around when either (needs, need) help in any way.

32. Both (does, do) the same kind of work.

33. Most of my friends (has, have) moved away.

34. Most of the money (be, am, is, are) gone.

35. I like the two racing stripes that (runs, run) along the sides.

36. He is a person who (likes, like) to move.

ANSWERS

Mark below the ones that you missed.

27.   1. teaches   2. hurts   3. interests, wants   4. seems   5. say   6. gives.
28. 7. were   8. are   9. is, doesn't   10. have, are.
29. 11. create   12. are   13. wants   14. were   15. do.
30. 16. start   17. pays   18. are   19. make   20. is   21. were.
31. 22. are   23. were   24. Does   25. was
32. 26. was   27. am   28. have, like   29. dresses, has   30. likes   31. needs   32. do
       33. have   34. is   35. run   36. likes.

Now mark the number of each section in which you missed a verb.

27. _____   29. _____   31. _____
28. _____   30. _____   32. _____

The sections you marked are the ones you need to study in the following pages. Skip each section you did not mark.

27   General Subject-Verb Agreement

PROBLEM

A subject and its verb (predicate) must agree with each other. That means that the form of the verb changes to show how many things the subject means. Only present-

time verbs (those talking about things that are happening now) and one verb used for past time (*was-were*) change forms to agree with the number of things that are the subject.
    Subjects that mean only one agree with verbs with *s* added:

He (one) likes (s) lizards.

Subjects that mean more than one agree with verbs that do not have an added *s*:

They (more) like (no s) spiders.

SOLUTION

Ask yourself how many the subject means. Then choose the correct verb form to agree with that number.

In each sentence underline the subject. Write how many the subject represents, one or more than one; then underline the correct verb for that number.

    Example: Irene (works, work) hard.

1. He (likes, like) to wear jeans.
2. They (likes, like) horses.
3. Those men (likes, like) sky-diving.
4. My mother (gets, get) the whole show on the road.

ANSWERS

    1. He—one—likes.
    2. They—more—like.
    3. men—more—like.
    4. mother—one—gets.

If you missed any, review the lesson. Then do the next exercise. Follow the instructions for the last exercise.

1. Mrs. Johnson (tells, tell) everyone about her grandchildren.
2. The honor that the tournament (brings, bring) is worth the long hours of practice and training.
3. She (knows, know) that her parents would do anything for her.
4. The different seasons (makes, make) it possible to have winter crops and summer crops here.

ANSWERS

    1. Mrs. Johnson—one—tells.
    2. tournament—one—brings.
    3. She—one—knows.
    4. seasons—more—make.

PROBLEM

If a verb always ends in s or an s sound (like *ch* in *catch*), it changes by adding *es* to agree with a subject meaning only one:

<u>Snakes</u> (more) <u>hiss</u> (no added s), but a <u>snake</u> (one) <u>hisses</u> (es).

SOLUTION

If your subject means only one, add *es* to a verb that ends in s or an s sound. Underline each subject. Write how many the subject means. Then underline the verb that agrees with it.

1. The boat (whizzes, whiz) by.
2. The hen (hatches, hatch) geese eggs.
3. She (misses, miss) him.

ANSWERS

1. <u>boat</u>—one—<u>whizzes</u>.
2. <u>Hen</u>—one—<u>hatches</u>.
3. <u>She</u>—one—<u>misses</u>.

If you missed any, review the lesson and do the next exercise. Follow the directions for the last exercise.

1. The troopers (searches, search) all night for the lost hikers.
2. Polio (reaches, reach) epidemic proportions where vaccine is not given.
3. Grandfather (outfoxes, outfox) me every time we play checkers.

ANSWERS

1. <u>troopers</u>—more—<u>search</u>.
2. <u>Polio</u>—one—<u>reaches</u>.
3. <u>Grandfather</u>—one—<u>outfoxes</u>.

PROBLEM

We almost never hear the *s* added to verbs that already end in an *s* sound plus a consonant like *k* or *t*. But these verbs, too, need *s* added to agree with a subject meaning one:

<u>They</u> <u>ask</u> for frogs, but <u>he</u> <u>asks</u> for frogs.

SOLUTION

Be sure that words like *ask* and *suggest* have an added *s* when the subject means only one.

Underline each subject. Write how many the subject means. Then underline the verb that agrees with it.

1. An egg (costs, cost) more than a nickel.
2. We (suggests, suggest) that you go.
3. He (asks, ask) for bread.

ANSWERS

1. egg—one—costs.
2. We—more—suggest.
3. He—one—asks.

If you missed any, review the lesson and do the next exercise. Follow the directions for the last.

1. The subject (interests, interest) me.
2. It (costs, cost) about thirty dollars more.
3. We (trusts, trust) his judgment.

ANSWERS

1. subject—one—interests.
2. It—one—costs.
3. We—more—trust.

PROBLEM

Some words that mean only one look or sound as though they mean more because they end with an *s* or an *s* sound. The word *this* is an example. So are the names of some school subjects, like *physics* and *mathematics*. Many words also end in *-ience* or *-ness* but mean only one. If a subject is a word that means only one but ends in an *s* or an *s* sound, it may cause a subject-verb disagreement.

Physics (require, requires) much study. (*Requires* is correct because *physics* is only one thing, one school subject.)

SOLUTION

Ask whether the subject that ends in *s* or an *s* sound really means more than one. Make the verb agree with however many the subject really means.

Underline each subject. Write how many the subject means. Then underline the verb that agrees with the subject.

1. Mathematics (helps, help) with accounting.
2. Prettiness (fades, fade) with time.
3. This (provides, provide) me with something to do.

ANSWERS

1. Mathematics—one—helps.
2. Prettiness—one—fades.
3. This—one—provides.

If you missed any, review the lesson and do the next exercise. Follow the directions for the last exercise.

1. Confidence (shows, show) in his manner.
2. This (gives, give) me a laugh every time.
3. Aeronautics (takes, take) quick thinking.

ANSWERS

1. <u>Confidence</u>—one—<u>shows</u>.
2. <u>This</u>—one—<u>gives</u>.
3. <u>Aeronautics</u>—one—<u>takes</u>.

PROBLEM

Sometimes a subject does not look as though it means more than one, but it does. Many plurals in English do not end in *s*. But if they mean more than one, the verb that agrees with them must not have an *s*.

People (likes, like) their independence. (*People* means more than one, so *like* agrees with it.)

SOLUTION

If the subject means more than one, leave the *s* off the verb even if there is no *s* on the subject.

Underline each subject. Write how many the subject means. Then underline the verb that agrees with the subject.

1. The men (goes, go) through the woods shooting at whatever moves.
2. People (spends, spend) too much on toys that tear up.
3. The mice (gnaws, gnaw) through the box to get at the seed.

ANSWERS

1. <u>men</u>—more—<u>go</u>
2. <u>People</u>—more—<u>spend</u>.
3. <u>mice</u>—more—<u>gnaw</u>.

If you missed any, review the lesson and do the next exercise. Follow the directions for the last.

1. My children (likes, like) the wrappings as well as the presents.
2. The goose (eats, eat) anything it sees.
3. The people (wants, want) to be friendly.

ANSWERS

1. <u>children</u>—more—<u>like</u>.
2. <u>goose</u>—one—<u>eats</u>.
3. <u>people</u>—more—<u>want</u>.

PROBLEM

The words in a title of something created (like a song, book, or painting) may themselves mean more than one. But the title itself means only one, that one created thing.

"The Bells" <u>was</u> <u>written</u> by Poe.

SOLUTION

Use the verb that agrees with one in writing about one creation, even though its title may mean more than one.

Write how many the subject means. Then underline the verb form that agrees with the subject.

1. *Days of Our Lives* (tells, tell) about unlikely happenings.
2. *The Muppets* (pleases, please) my children.
3. *Blazing Saddles* (keeps, keep) me laughing.

ANSWERS

1. one—<u>tells</u>.
2. one—<u>pleases</u>.
3. one—<u>keeps</u>.

If you missed any, review the lesson and do the next exercise. Follow the directions for the last exercise.

1. *Roots* (tells, tell) of the struggle to keep human dignity.
2. "Blue Suede Shoes" (shows, show) Presley's typical style.
3. "That's When the Music Takes Me" (gives, give) an opportunity for a big production number.

ANSWERS

1. one—<u>tells</u>.
2. one—<u>shows</u>.
3. one—<u>gives</u>.

Now take the Post-test.

NAME _____

27. GENERAL SUBJECT-VERB AGREEMENT
Post-Test

Underline the correct verb in each of the following sentences.

1. A child (likes, like) privacy at times.
2. My parents (relaxes, relax); the children are quiet.
3. In baseball you can lead off from the base and steal when the ball (crosses, cross) the plate.
4. DuPont High School (contrasts, contrast) favorably with McGavock in providing an ideal setting in which to learn.
5. My patience (wears, wear) thin.
6. Older people (forgets, forget) what it is like to be young.
7. Dan Rather's *Sixty Minutes* (interviews, interview) all kinds of people.
8. Our training (consists, consist) of ninety hours of class time and ten hours in a hospital.
9. Sometimes my husband (makes, make) a good, sound decision when I am not at home.
10. The drinks (makes, make) them feel better.

Ask your instructor to check your answers, or turn them in.

See more about agreement in **7**, a general post-test after **32**, or writing assignments in **54–56**.

28 Agreement with Irregular Verbs

PROBLEM

Four very common verbs do not just add *s* to their root when they agree with subjects meaning only one. They change their pronunciation and form more than the other verbs do. These four are

Agreeing with Subject Meaning One	Agreeing with Subject Meaning More
is	are
was	were
does	do
has	have

SOLUTION

Remember that these four verbs are like the rest in that their forms with an *s* (*is*, *was*, *does*, *has*) agree with subjects meaning one, and their forms without an *s* (*are*, *were*, *do*, *have*) agree with subjects meaning more.

Study each of these verbs closely, for they cause many problems of subject-verb agreement.

VERB 1: *is—are*

The verb *be* is the most irregular in English, and it is the most often used. Its name, *be*, can never be used without a helping verb as the predicate (verb) of a sentence, so there is no problem of agreement with this form. Another present-time form, *am*, agrees only with the subject *I*. So *is* and *are* are the only present-time forms that cause trouble in agreement. Remember that *is* can agree only with a subject meaning only one; it has an *s*.

He *is* tall.

With a subject meaning more than one, *are*, the form without an *s*, must be used.

They *are* tall.

Underline the correct verb in each of the following sentences.

1. All of us (be, am, is, are) in the den now.
2. The Corvette (be, am, is, are) really expensive if it has split-back windows.
3. These items are what a woman's wardrobe (be, am, is, are) built around.
4. Elton (be, am, is, are) my first cousin.

ANSWERS

1. are
2. is
3. is
4. is

If you missed any of these, review the lesson and do the exercise below.

1. The weather (be, am, is, are) rainy there.
2. He (be, am, is, are) too young to support himself.
3. The classes (be, am, is, are) pretty boring sometimes.
4. They (be, am, is, are) my favorite foods.

ANSWERS

1. is
2. is
3. are
4. are

VERB 2: *was—were*

The past-tense form of the verb *be* is *was—were*. It, too, has an *s* in the form agreeing with one, *was*.

He *was* going with us.

There is no *s* in the form that agrees with more than one.

They *were* going with us.

Underline the correct verb in each sentence.

1. My senior year (was, were) the best.
2. You (was, were) not bored for a minute throughout the movie.
3. They (was, were) trained for that work.
4. He (was, were) always late.

ANSWERS

1. was
2. were
3. were
4. was

If you missed any, review the lesson and do the next exercise.

Underline the correct verb in each sentence.

1. She always interrupted them before they (was, were) finished.

2. After the basketball season (was, were) over, I started getting letters from colleges.

3. Some boys (was, were) sitting in the lobby doing nothing.

4. Christmas (was, were) approaching fast.

ANSWERS

1. were
2. was
3. were
4. was

VERB 3: *does—do*

The verb *do* is often misused. But, like all other present-time verbs, it uses an *s* to agree with a subject meaning only one.

He *does* plumbing.

The form that agrees with a subject meaning more than one has no *s*.

They *do* plumbing.

Underline the correct verb in each sentence.

1. She (does, do) not have to know about things to figure them out.

2. We (does, do) not have much time.

3. The older students (does, do) not get involved enough

4. His mother (does, do) not work.

ANSWERS

1. does
2. do
3. do
4. does

If you missed any, review the lesson and do the next exercise.

Underline the correct verb in each sentence.

1. She (does, do) laundry to help support the family.

2. The baseball players (does, do) better when they are on the road, for some reason.

3. The horse (does, do) whatever he is told.

4. People (does, do) all kinds of things to get out of trouble.

ANSWERS

1. does
2. do
3. does
4. do

VERB 4: *has—have*

The verb *has—have* is the last of the four that are irregular in their forms for agreement with a subject. But, like the other three and like all regular verbs, it has an *s* in the form that agrees with a subject meaning only one.

He *has* measles.

It has no *s* in the form that agrees with a subject meaning more than one.

They *have* measles.

Underline the correct verb in each sentence.

1. My mother (has, have) never told me anything wrong.
2. The farmer is successful when he (has, have) the proper tools and good weather.
3. With a family like mine, things (has, have) to be organized.
4. Football (has, have) more body contact than basketball.

ANSWERS

1. has
2. has
3. have
4. has

If you missed any, review the lesson and do the next exercise.

Underline the correct verb in each sentence.

1. The restaurants (has, have) good food at reasonable prices.
2. We (has, have) to finish the puzzle before we can start anything else.
3. The teachers (has, have) the best places to park.
4. He (has, have) to learn how to lose well.

ANSWERS

1. have
2. have
3. have
4. has

Now take the post-test.

NAME _____

28. IRREGULAR VERBS IN AGREEMENT
Post-Test

Underline the correct verb in each sentence.

1. The people (was, were) laughing there also.
2. But, as you know, it (doesn't, don't).
3. They go home whenever they get ready and (does, do) as they please.
4. The teachers (was, were) so old that they fell asleep during class.
5. When we (have, has) a disagreement, we talk about it.
6. Basketball (have, has) another kind of set-up.
7. Three days (be, am, is, are) not terrifying.
8. To me Sundays (be, am, is, are) very relaxing.
9. When friends need to borrow money, if she (has, have) it, they can get it.
10. Those people (does, do) not understand.

Ask your instructor to check your answers, or turn them in.

See more about agreement in **7**, the general post-test after **32**, or writing assignments in **54–56**.

29 Agreement with Compound Subjects

Two or more words may be used as a compound subject. The sentence is equally about both words in the compound subject. They are joined by a conjunction, and they share a verb.

PROBLEM

If the compound subjects are joined by *and*, they mean more than one and the verb must agree with more than one:

The <u>hogs</u> <u>eat</u>. (The one-word subject means more than one.)

The <u>sow</u> and <u>boar</u> <u>eat</u>. (The two words make a compound subject that means more than one.)

One *and* one are more than one.

SOLUTION

Remember that one subject *and* one subject *are* more, so the verb for a compound subject paired by *and* must agree with more than one.

Write how many the first subject means, one or more. Then circle the conjunction joining the subjects. Next, write how many the second subject means. Then underline the correct verb to agree.

Example: Mary *one* (and) Gary *one* (bites, <u>bite</u>) hard.

1. The crickets and the owl (sings, sing) at night.
2. The Joneses and the Browns (likes, like) water-skiing.
3. The cat and the dog (fights, fight).
4. My teammates and coach (means, mean) so much to me.

ANSWERS:

1. many (and) one—sing.
2. many (and) many—like.
3. one (and) one—fight.
4. more (and) one—mean.

If you missed any, review the lesson and do the next exercise. Follow the directions for the last.

1. Her happy attitude, her serious side, and her loving nature (makes, make) Kathy my best friend.
2. My parents' standards and example (was, were) great character-building for me.
3. Wreckless driving and drunk driving (is, are) two things to think about.
4. My parents and my husband's mother (has, have) dinner with us on Easter.

ANSWER

1. one (and) one   and one—make.
2. more (and) one—were.
3. one (and) one—are.
4. more (and) one—have.

PROBLEM

Compound subjects joined by *or, nor,* or *but* do not both agree with the verb. Only the subject closer to the verb is considered in choosing the verb:

The sows or the <u>boar</u> <u>eats</u>.

The boar or the <u>sows</u> <u>eat</u>.

SOLUTION

Look at the conjunction joining compound subjects. If it is *or, nor,* or *but,* cover up the subjects separated from the verb by the conjunction. Make the verb agree with the subject still showing:

~~The sows~~ (or) the <u>boar</u> <u>eats</u>.

~~The boar~~ (or) the <u>sows</u> <u>eat</u>.

Cover up or mark out the subjects separated from the verb by *or, nor,* or *but.* Then choose the verb that agrees with the subject closer to the verb.

1. My head or my shoulders (is, are) coming loose.
2. Not only Tom but also Edward (was, were) stoned.
3. Neither frogs nor a spider (seems, seem) good to pet.
4. Not only the flowers but the trees (starts, start) bursting into bloom.

ANSWERS

1. are
2. was
3. seems
4. start

If you missed any, review the lesson and do the next exercise. Follow the directions for the last exercise.

1. Either Dupont or TVA (has, have) emitted industrial waste into the lake.
2. Not only my parents but also my grandmother (has, have) influenced me.
3. Neither the blue nor the brown (looks, look) good on him.
4. Ellen or the boys (manages, manage) to find something to argue about.

ANSWERS

1. has
2. have
3. looks
4. manage

Now take the post-test.

NAME

29. AGREEMENT WITH COMPOUND SUBJECTS
Post-Test

Underline the correct verb for each sentence.

1. My cousins and family (comes, come) home on holidays.
2. Either Keith or his friends (has, have) gotten the idea that they should start a band.
3. The goat and the horse (gets, get) along well together.
4. Either English or math (takes, take) up every weekend.
5. The transmission and engine (is, are) dropped in to check the weight variance.
6. In this song, not only the words but also the music (projects, project) a good picture of what is happening.
7. Basketball and baseball (is, are) both good exercise.
8. The setting and the style (is, are) beautiful.
9. Neither the calls nor the letter (makes, make) me feel better.
10. Not only circumstances but also a choice (limits, limit) us.

Ask your instructor to check your answers, or turn them in.

See more about agreement in 7, the general post-test after 32, or writing assignments in 54–56.

30 Agreement of Separated Subjects and Verbs

A word or words coming between the subject and the verb may seem to be the subject. Then the verb may agree with the word between instead of with the real subject.

Do not think about any word or words between the subject and verb when you choose the verb form. Think of the real subject and how many it means.

PROBLEM

A single word coming between a subject and verb may seem like the subject and make you choose the wrong verb form. Two words especially to watch out for are *always* and *sometimes*.

He always goes. (goes must agree with He, not with any word between)

SOLUTION

Pay no attention to such words, but make the verb agree with the real subject.

Put parentheses ( ) around the separating words in the following sentences. Then underline the verb that agrees with the real subject.

1. The best actor always (plays, play) the role.
2. Margaret sometimes (brings, bring) cheese.
3. We always (takes, take) the bus.
4. He also (likes, like) to give his friend advice.

ANSWERS

1. Actor (always) plays.
2. Margaret (sometimes) brings.
3. We (always) take.
4. He (also) likes.

If you missed any of these, review the lesson and do the next exercise. Follow the directions for the last exercise.

1. Henry always (tries, try) to look at both sides of the situation before making a decision.
2. It also (gives, give) people the courage of getting used to the water.
3. She always (takes, take) pride in herself.
4. We seldom (buys, buy) anything there.

ANSWERS

1. Henry (always) tries.
2. It (also) gives.
3. She (always) takes.
4. We (seldom) buy.

PROBLEM

A group of words—a phrase—coming after the subject may seem like the subject or part of the subject and make you choose the wrong verb form.

One (of the vases) was empty.

Arthur (along with Howard) was best.

The boy (holding his ears) was hit.

The box (to go to the Ellises) was green.

SOLUTION

When the sentence gives many words before the verb, be sure to ask who or what the sentence is really about, that is, who or what the real subject is. Pay no attention to other words that separate the subject and the verb.

Put parentheses ( ) around the separating phrases in the following sentences. Then underline the correct verb forms to agree with the real subjects.

1. Minnesota, the Land of Ten Thousand Lakes, (is, are) my parents' home.
2. Two of my friends (is, are) Jim and Tom.
3. Dale along with Frank (tries, try) to sing.
4. The dog covered with red spots (has, have) some Irish Setter blood.
5. The show to watch on Tuesdays (is, are) M*A*S*H.

ANSWERS

1. Minnesota (the Land of Ten Thousand Lakes,) is
2. Two (of my friends) are
3. Dale (along with Frank) tries
4. dog (covered with red spots) has
5. show (to watch on Tuesdays) is

If you missed any, review the lesson and study **4** about phrases, **2** about prepositions, and **3** about verbals. Then do the next exercise. Follow the directions for the last exercise.

1. Summers around the farm (is, are) fun.
2. My feelings toward pollution (is, are) that it is easier to prevent than to cure.
3. In a small college, the size of the classes (is, are) small enough that the student gets to know his teachers.
4. Fishing trips at my house (begins, begin) about daybreak.
5. The trash dumped in area creeks (causes, cause) much pollution.

ANSWERS

1. Summers (around the farm) are
2. Feelings (toward pollution) are

3. <u>size</u> (of the classes) <u>is</u>
4. <u>trips</u> (at my house) <u>begin</u>
5. <u>trash</u> (dumped in area creeks) <u>causes</u>

PROBLEM

A dependent clause may come after the independent-clause subject and before the verb. Because the dependent clause may contain many words and phrases, you may confuse some part of the dependent clause with the real subject.

The <u>girl</u> (that likes candy and other sweets) <u>spends</u> too much money on them.

SOLUTION

Most of these clauses begin with *that, who,* or *which.* They include a subject and a verb and, perhaps, complements. When you find one of these clauses between the subject and the verb, decide what words complete the idea of that clause. Then take these words out of the sentence and decide what verb form agrees with the real subject of the independent clause. In other words, the separating clause is like a word or phrase separating subject and verb, though it may be longer. Treat it like a separating word or phrase.

Put parentheses (   ) around any dependent clause separating the subject and verb of the independent clause. Then underline the verb form that agrees with the real subject.

1. People who live in the past (dreams, dream) too much.
2. The place that I grew up (is, are) Portland.
3. The three things I like best about Noland (is, are) his honesty, his loyalty, and his sense of humor.
4. When my best friends, whom I have not seen for a long time, (comes, come) home, I want to have a party.
5. The only instructions he gave Steele (was, were) to leave the ball alone.

ANSWERS

1. <u>People</u> (who live in the past) <u>dream</u>
2. <u>place</u> (that I grew up) <u>is</u>
3. <u>things</u> (I like best about Noland) <u>are</u>
4. <u>friends</u> (whom I have not seen for a long time) <u>come</u>
5. <u>instructions</u> (he gave Steele) <u>were</u>

If you missed any, review the lesson and study **5** about clauses. Then do the next exercise, following the directions for the last exercise.

1. The tales that my uncle told (was, were) very exciting.
2. Some of the reasons that it is different (is, are) that it appeals to a different kind of player.
3. The main reason I like these holidays (is, are) that they come in different seasons.

4. The subjects I like most (is, are) math, accounting, and physical education.
5. One way by which I was able to tell that he was middle-aged (was, were) the wrinkles on his face and hands.

ANSWERS

1. <u>tales</u> (that my uncle told) <u>were</u>
2. <u>some</u> (of the reasons) (that it is different) <u>are</u>
3. <u>reason</u> (I like these holidays) <u>is</u>
4. <u>subjects</u> (I like most) <u>are</u>
5. <u>way</u> (by which I was able to tell that he was middle-aged) <u>was</u>

PROBLEM

There may be two or more verbs for the same subject. So the first verb or verbs and their completing words separate the subject from the later verb. But the later verbs must agree with the real subject, not with some of the separating words.

The <u>trees</u> (<u>shade</u> the house in summer and) <u>provide</u> a wind-break in winter.

Put a circle around the subject in the following sentences. Then underline each verb that goes with it. If any verbs do not agree, change them.

1. This aircraft is able to travel at 170 miles per hour, has a range of 650 miles, and average 14 miles to a gallon of fuel.
2. She never gets angry at anyone and start using foul language.
3. They make me laugh and leaves me feeling lighthearted
4. My other sister stays back in her room and listen to the radio.
5. The mind filters out information and bring a picture for us to see.

ANSWERS

The changes in verbs are encircled.
1. aircraft <u>is</u> able . . . <u>has</u> a range . . . and <u>average</u>(s) 14 . . . .
2. She never <u>gets</u> angry at anyone and <u>start</u>(s) using foul language.
3. They <u>make</u> me laugh and <u>leave</u>( ) me . . . .
4. sister <u>stays</u> back in her room and <u>listen</u>(s) to the radio.
5. The mind <u>filters</u> out information and <u>bring</u>(s) a picture for us to see.

If you missed any, review the lesson and do the next exercise. Follow the directions for the last exercise.

1. She cooks three meals a day and wash dishes without any help.
2. Sara ignores a rude person and even turn her back on him.
3. We all go into the den, gets around the fireplace, and starts talking about the good old days.
4. He is always honorable and stand for loyalty and honesty.
5. It does not run up big fuel bills and cost little to maintain.

ANSWERS

The changes in verbs are encircled.

1. She <u>cooks</u> three meals a day and <u>wash</u>(es) dishes . . .
2. Sara <u>ignores</u> a rude person and even <u>turn</u>(s) her back on him.
3. We all <u>go</u> into the den, get( ) around the fireplace, and <u>start</u>( ) . . .
4. He <u>is</u> always honorable and <u>stand</u>(s) for . . .
5. It <u>does</u> not run up big fuel bills and <u>cost</u>(s) little to maintain.

Now do the post-test.

NAME _____

30. AGREEMENT OF SEPARATED SUBJECTS AND VERBS
Post-Test

Underline the correct verb in each sentence.

1. A Thunderbird always (keeps, keep) its value.
2. The comedy shows help to relieve tensions of the day and (lifts, lift) my spirit.
3. The three best gifts that I have received (is, are) a charm bracelet, a stereo tape deck, and a picture.
4. The scouts in Japan (is, are) about the same as the American scouts.
5. He is about five feet, eight inches tall and (weighs, weigh) about one hundred fifty pounds.
6. The hours I work (depends, depend) upon the hours I take classes.
7. The people of Wilson County (has, have) a good firefighter service.
8. Annie just (loves, love) going around singing the Wind Song commercial.
9. Parts of the letter (is, are) indented
10. The eggs hidden in the lawn (is, are) hardest to find.

Ask your instructor to check your answers, or turn then in.

See more about agreement in **7**, the general post-test after **32**, or writing assignments in **54–56**.

31 Agreement When the Verb Comes Before the Subject

Usually, English sentences begin with the subject, and the verb follows. But questions and sentences beginning with the expletive *there* put the verb before the subject. Sometimes other sentences do this. For these, you must look past the verb to find the real subject before you choose the form of the verb you need.

PROBLEM

Most of the time, we write the verb after the subject. But questions often put the verb or a part of the verb before the subject. So, in many questions, the verb comes before the subject that it must agree with.

Does   Lewis   like   oranges?
(verb) (subject) (verb)

How   do   we   get there?
   (verb) (subject)

SOLUTION

Think beyond the verb to find the real subject. Then make the verb form agree with the real subject. Turn the question into its answer if this helps you to find the subject.

Lewis <u>does</u> <u>like</u> oranges.

<u>We</u> <u>do</u> <u>get</u> there how.

Then choose the verb that agrees with the subject. *Lewis* means only one, so *does* is the correct verb. *We* means more than one, so *do* agrees with it.

Underline the real subject in each of the following questions. Then underline the verb form that agrees.

1. (Was, Were) they going?
2. (Doesn't, Don't) she need to do that?
3. (Is, Are) he ready?
4. (Hasn't, Haven't) they finished yet?

ANSWERS

1. they—Were.
2. she—Doesn't.
3. he—Is.
4. they—Haven't.

If you missed any, review the lesson and do the next exercise. Follow the directions for the last exercise.

1. (Isn't, Aren't) you bored?
2. (Doesn't, Don't) he make enough money?

3. Why (isn't, aren't) she ready yet?

4. When (does, do) they plan on finishing?

ANSWERS

1. you—Aren't.
2. he—Doesn't.
3. she—isn't.
4. they—do.

PROBLEM

A word telling time, place, order, or frequency may begin a sentence: *There* are fine bargains. *Next* came Lucy. These words are not subjects. They tell something about the subject, but the subject comes later in the sentence, after the verb.

There   are   fine bargains.
(place) (verb)   (subject)

Next   came   Lucy.
(order) (verb) (subject)

These sentences follow this order:

Word	Verb	Subject

The word *there* is also used as an expletive, that is, a filler to begin a sentence until the subject is given. It means that the subject exists, that it is. *There* is not the subject, and the verb cannot agree with it. The verb must agree with the subject, which comes after the verb.

There   were   four men in the car.
(expletive) (verb) (subject)

There	verb	subject

SOLUTION

Do not think that the expletive *there* or these words of time, place, order, or frequency (*there, here, next, then, seldom, second,* and others) are subjects when they begin a sentence. They tell something about a subject, which will come after a verb. Look beyond the verb to find the real subject and choose the verb form to agree with it.

Draw a line under the real subject in each sentence below. Then underline the verb form that agrees with it.

1. In Amsterdam, there (was, were) twelve of us that went to the red light district.

2. Never (does, do) he go.

3. Usually, there (is, are) seventy-five people that go on this picnic.
4. Then (comes, come) the fun.
5. There (is, are) not many important things to tell about me.

ANSWERS

1. twelve—were.
2. he—does.
3. people—are.
4. fun—comes.
5. things—are.

If you missed any of these, review the lesson and do the next exercise. Follow the directions for the last exercise.

1. Following this there (was, were) various skits put on by the student body.
2. First (is, are) five strings.
3. There (has, have) been many good times at that old bridge.
4. Here (is, are) two hundred acres to walk around in.
5. There (was, were) about fifty statues in the house.

ANSWERS

1. skits—were.
2. strings—are
3. times—have.
4. acres—are.
5. statues—were.

Now take the post-test.

31. AGREEMENT WHEN THE VERB COMES BEFORE THE SUBJECT
Post-Test

Underline the correct verb for each number.

1. Why (does, do) she always act like that?
2. There (is, are) five people at my house.
3. There (is, are) seventeen vocational courses available for adults.
4. Then (comes, come) the presentation of gifts.
5. There (is, are) enough groups organized in the city.
6. (Wasn't, Weren't) they all going together?
7. (Doesn't, Don't) complaints like that worry you?
8. There (was, were) the three loons, swimming in front of the campsite.
9. Here (is, are) my point.
10. (Wasn't, Weren't) he in the wrong?

Ask your instructor to check this, or turn it in.

See more about agreement **7**, questions and expletives in **3**, the general post-test after **32**, or writing assignments in **54–56**.

32   Agreement with Pronoun Subjects

Pronouns substitute for nouns. Usually, the number of a pronoun is the same as the number of the noun for which it substitutes. But sometimes this noun is hard to find. And sometimes the pronoun does not substitute for any *definite* noun. And agreement with the pronoun *I* does not follow usual rules. So all of these pronouns need extra attention when they are subjects.

PROBLEM

Agreement with the pronoun *I* does not follow the usual pattern. *I* means only one, but no present-tense verb used with it ends in an added *s*. The verb *was* is the only verb that follows the normal pattern with *I*.

SOLUTION

Learn the following three special rules for agreement with *I*.

> 1.   Remember to use *am* (not *be, is,* or *are*) with the subject *I* when writing about the present time.

I *am* hopeful.

> 2.   Use *was* (not *were*) when writing about the past.

I *was* shy.

> 3.   For all other verbs, choose the form without the *s* to agree with the subject *I*.

I *have* measles. (not *has*)
I *do* exercises. (not *does*)
I *buy* clothes. (not *buys*)

Remember that *was* is the only verb form adding *s* that agrees with *I*. Use the form without added *s* for all other verbs to agree with *I*.

Underline the correct verb for each number.

1. I (likes, like) to cook for people.
2. I (goes, go) home on the weekends.
3. I (be, am, is, are) not happy about the situation.
4. I (was, were) tired of it.

ANSWERS

1. like
2. go
3. am
4. was

If you missed any, review the lesson and do the next exercise. Follow the directions for the last exercise.

1. I (goes, go) to the movies often.
2. The reason I (likes, like) scouting is that it keeps me outdoors.
3. I (was, were) the youngest one on the trip.
4. I (be, am, is, are) ready to start out on my own now.

ANSWERS

1. go
2. like
3. was
4. am

PROBLEM

Indefinite pronouns do not substitute for a definite noun. So most of the indefinite pronouns have a number that is always the same. But the number for a particular pronoun may not seem logical to you.

Several are through.
(more than one)

Everyone is going.
    (one)

SOLUTION

Learn each of the indefinite pronouns with a fixed number according to its group. The following pronouns always mean more than one and take a verb form with no *s* added:

both	few
several	fewer
many	fewest

Underline the correct verb to agree with the indefinite pronoun subjects below:

1. Both (was, were) lost.
2. Few (finds, find) trouble.
3. Many (wants, want) more.

ANSWERS

1. were
2. find
3. want

If you missed any, review the lesson and do the next exercise. Follow the directions for the last exercise.

1. Several (wants, want) to leave.
2. Fewer (was, were) at the second service.
3. The fewest (has, have) come to work.

ANSWERS

1. want
2. were
3. have

The following pronouns always mean only one:

another	anything	everyone
anyone	each	everybody
anybody	either	everything
no one	none	someone
nobody	neither	somebody
nothing	one	something

To test some of these to see why they mean only one, take them apart into the words they put together: *everybody* means *every body* (one; not *bodies*—which is more than one). These pronouns as subjects agree with the verbs that *do* end in *s*.

Underline the verb form which agrees with each of the indefinite pronoun subjects in the following sentences.

1. Each (was, were) glad.
2. Everyone (likes, like) him.
3. Something (has, have) been taken.
4. Everybody there (was, were) friends.

ANSWERS

1. was
2. likes
3. has
4. was

If you missed any, review the lesson and do the next exercise. Follow the directions for the last exercise.

1. One (is, are) educated in what is right and wrong.
2. Everyone (seems, seem) to be talking at once.

3. No one (has, have) bought anything all morning.
4. At my wife's mother's home, everybody (was, were) waiting to see us.

ANSWERS

1. is
2. seems
3. has
4. was

PROBLEM

A few indefinite pronouns mean one when they refer to things thought of as one mass, one total amount.

Some of the flour is whole wheat.

These pronouns mean more than one when they refer to things that are counted as separate things.

Some of the houses are brick.

The indefinite pronouns of this sort are:

any	some
more	a lot
most	lots

SOLUTION

If these pronouns talk about some one thing that is thought of as a whole, they mean *one* and use a verb with an *s*. If they talk about things that are counted, they mean more than one and use a verb without an *s*.

Underline the verb form that agrees with the indefinite pronoun subjects in the following sentences.

1. Any of the papers (is, are) all right.
2. Most of the ice cream (is, are) gone.
3. A lot of candy (was, were) taken.

ANSWERS

1. are
2. is
3. was

If you missed any, review the lesson and do the next exercise. Follow the directions for the last exercise.

1. Some of the people (was, were) downright mean.

2. The next day, more of the silver (was, were) gone.

3. Lots of snow (drifts, drift) across their drive during each storm.

ANSWERS

1. were
2. was
3. drifts

PROBLEM

A relative pronoun (*who, which, that*) always substitutes for a word in another part of the sentence. The number of the relative pronoun (one or more than one) is always the same as the number of the word for which it substitutes.

The ball that has gone over the fence was mine.

That substitutes for *ball*, which means one. Therefore, *that* means one. The verb must agree with one.

The balls that have gone over the fence were mine.

That substitutes for *balls*, which means more than one. Therefore, *that* means more than one. The verb must agree with more than one.

SOLUTION

Find the word for which a relative-pronoun subject substitutes. Decide how many that word means. Then make the verb form agree with that number.

Underline the relative-pronoun subjects in the following sentences. Then encircle the word for which each pronoun is substituting. Write above the word how many it is, one or more than one. Then underline the correct verb form to agree with that number. The first one is done for you.

1. The (star) that (shines, shine) brightest is Arcturus.
2. Aunt Gail, who (gives, give) good presents, is coming for my birthday party.
3. The new boys, who (plays, play) hard, are Herman and Claude.
4. Examples of these are things that (has, have) recently happened.
5. I misplaced some of the parts that (was, were) needed.

ANSWERS

1. given
2. (Aunt Gail) who gives
3. (boys) who play
4. (things) that have
5. (parts) that were

If you missed any, review the lesson and do the next exercise. Follow the directions for the last exercise.

1. He is the type of person that (believes, believe) in treating others right.
2. First is our bathroom, which (stays, stay) crowded all the time.
3. I have three friends that (lives, live) on the same street that I do.
4. This is one of two types of communication receivers that (is, are) available for general use.
5. He is part secretary, part bookkeeper, and he performs the other office jobs that (is, are) necessary

ANSWERS

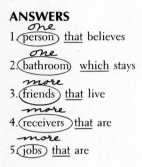

1. *one* (person) that believes
2. *one* (bathroom) which stays
3. *more* (friends) that live
4. *more* (receivers) that are
5. *more* (jobs) that are

Now do the post-test.

NAME _____

32. AGREEMENT WITH PRONOUN SUBJECTS
Post-Test

Underline the correct verb for each choice.

1. After I (gets, get) through practicing, I (goes, go) home to study.
2. Everyone (is, are) very close to him.
3. I (has, have) lived in Tucson all my life.
4. Some (says, say) that we live in the country.
5. During football season my sophomore year, I (was, were) getting many write-ups.
6. He is not the kind of person that (does, do) not want to learn.
7. Both (is, are) going to live with their father.
8. If everyone who (drinks, drink) would not drive, there would be fewer wrecks.
9. To know why someone (acts, act) a certain way, we must know something about him.
10. The dog that (lives, live) at my house is a nuisance.

Ask your instructor to check your answers, or turn them in.

See more about agreement in 7, the general post-test after this page, or writing assignments in **54–56**.

SUBJECT-VERB AGREEMENT
General Post-Test

Underline the correct verb in each of the following sentences.

27 1. As the song (says, say), "I get by with a little help from my friends."
2. He does everything that the jobs (requires, require) to be done.
3. The school (teaches, teach) carpentry, electricity, upholstery, and masonry.
4. A typical weekend (consists, consist) of cleaning, laundry, and resting.
5. When this (happens, happen), the dog barks.
6. Many people (lets, let) their children act impolitely in stores.
7. *The New York Times* (prints, print) all the news that is fit to print, it says.

28 8. You (be, am, is, are) always trying to put points up because you (be, am is, are) playing against the machine.
9. But they (was, were) not the real reasons he left.
10. Whatever they (does, do), they seem to get in trouble.
11. The outdoorsmen (has, have) an easy time finding lakes that they like in that area.
12. Other minor characters (be, am, is, are) the head nurse and the young doctor.
13. She (does, do) the best she can to bring her children up right.
14. We (was, were) on a gravel road, so it (was, were) not too hard to shake them up.
15. Los Angeles (has, have) more loyal fans than Detroit.

29 16. His sense of humor, loyalty, and honesty (shows, show) his fine features.
17. A broken play or a long pass (pulls, pull) the crowd right out of their seats.
18. Not only her interest in other people but also her unselfish acts (makes, make) me admire her.
19. Either his habits or his goal (has, have) to change.
20. In Troy the air, water, and soil (provides, provide) pollution that we can see.
21. The door and the fender (was, were) bent.

30 22. He always (goes, go) to Martha's Vineyard on vacation.
23. The men working that shift (has, have) a good foreman.
24. The best holidays for me (is, are) Thanksgiving Day and Christmas.
25. They bring their trash out to our road and (dumps, dump) it.
26. The three qualities that stand out most (is, are) her sense of humor, her faith, and her kindness.

31   27. There (is, are) enough lakes and streams for everybody.

28. First (is, are) my parents and my two brothers.

29. Even rarer (is, are) a quiet moment.

30. (Doesn't, don't) he know any better?

32   31. Dresses made with material that (clings, cling) to the body are popular.

32. I (was, were) and still (be, am, is, are) proud of it.

33. It is a pleasure to have an old car that (has, have) been restored and (looks, look) as new as the day it was made.

34. A lot of people (drives, drive) like race-car drivers.

35. More of the students (does, do) not join any groups.

36. I (likes, like) to go with them.

37. Everyone (leaves, leave) all the work for her to do.

38. Several (has, have) affected my life.

Ask your instructor to check your answers, or turn them in.

See subjects and verbs in 1–3, subject-verb agreement in 7, or writing assignments in 54–56.

VERB TENSE FORMS

Pretest

Underline the accepted verb form for the following sentences.

1. My car had (break, broke, broken) down.
2. He (do, did, done) what he could.
3. The pants were (wear, wore, worn) out.
4. They (lie, lay, lain, laid) down yesterday.
5. Herman (know, knew, known, knowed) Jim in high school.
6. Mother had (take, took, taken) her medicine.
7. They had (eat, ate, eaten) all the pie.
8. We (see, saw, seen, seed) the show.
9. I have (write, wrote, written) seven pages.
10. The dog (begin, began, begun) to bark.
11. The fever (become, became) worse.
12. He (was, been) sick.
13. The bubble (busted, burst).
14. He (use, used) to go.
15. We are (suppose, supposed) to stay.
16. We (spend, spent) the night there and enjoyed ourselves.
17. I have (return, returned) to school for several reasons.
18. If he has a flat tire, he has to make sure it gets (fix, fixed) himself.
19. He hunts bear with a very (high-power, high-powered) rifle.
20. He (knock, knocked) a woman's purse from her shoulder.

ANSWERS

1. broken
2. did
3. worn
4. lay
5. knew
6. taken
7. eaten
8. saw
9. written
10. began
11. became
12. was
13. burst
14. used

15. supposed
16. spent
17. returned
18. fixed
19. high-powered
20. knocked

If you missed any, study the following lessons.

33 Regular Verbs

PROBLEM

When we speak, we often leave the endings off words. So you may not be used to hearing the *ed* or *d* at the end of the past and past participle forms of regular verbs. If you have not heard the *d* or *ed* ending of these verb forms, you probably will not say or write it.

SOLUTION

Add *d* or *ed* to the end of regular verbs when you use the past tense or past participle.

Present	Past	Past Participle
(used about things happening now)	(used about things happening before)	(never used as a verb without a helping word; the time of the helping word shows when things happen)
I kick.	I kicked.	I am kicked.
		I had kicked.
verb kick	verb + *ed* kicked	helper + verb + *ed* am kicked had kicked

If you do not know whether a verb is regular, look in the dictionary. For regular verbs, the dictionary either lists *ed* after the word or it lists nothing. If the verb is irregular (that means that it does not just add *d* or *ed*), the dictionary will always list its past and past-participle forms.

The helping word used with the past participle is usually a form of *have* or *is*. But some other linking verbs (for instance, *become* or *get*) may also be helping verbs with the past participle. See **2** for lists of these and forms of the verb *be*.

The following are the most common forms of helping verbs used with the past participle.

Present:	am kicked	
	is kicked	
	are kicked	
Past:	was kicked	
	were kicked	
Future:	shall be kicked	
	will be kicked	
Present Perfect:	has been kicked	has kicked
	have been kicked	have kicked
Past Perfect:	had been kicked	had kicked

Future Perfect:	shall have been kicked	shall have kicked
	will have been kicked	will have kicked

Be especially careful with the words ⟨used⟩ , ⟨supposed⟩ , and ⟨asked⟩ . They often come before the word ⟨to⟩ , and the ⟨t⟩ sound that begins ⟨to⟩ absorbs the ⟨d⟩ sound at the end of ⟨used⟩ : ⟨used to⟩ . So it is likely that the ⟨d⟩ or ⟨ed⟩ on these words will be left off. Add ⟨d⟩ or ⟨ed⟩ to these regular verbs when you write about the past or when you use a helping word with the past participle.

She was used to noise.

They were supposed to go.

Put *ed* or *d* after the past-time or past-participle verbs in the following sentences.

1. The first bad driving habit that I have witness is driving under the influence of alcohol.
2. My friend was kill in the wreck.
3. We were waken about three o'clock in the morning and made to clean up the barrack.
4. Tim, who had been pacing across the room, lean over and answer the phone.
5. I had been doing pretty well until the store owner call my father.
6. The first person that sees an officer is suppose to call for attention.

ANSWER

Ed or *d* should be added only to the following:
1. witnessed
2. killed
3. wakened
4. leaned, answered
5. called
6. supposed

If you missed any, review the lesson and do the next exercise. Follow the directions for the last exercise.

1. We went in and ask the manager if we could still be served.
2. I use to think that I wanted to join the Navy.
3. This has broaden our mental and physical limits.
4. My sister drove her camper to the party, and we all stay in it.
5. The look of hurt in my father's eyes when he found out bother me most.
6. I gave them their food when I check their packs and gear.

ANSWER

Only the following verbs should have *ed* or *d* added:
1. asked
2. used

3. broadened
4. stayed
5. bothered
6. checked

**ed on
participles
as adjectives**

PROBLEM

Past participles may also be used as adjectives to modify (tell more about) a noun.

He killed a six-point, white-tail<u>ed</u> buck.

(White-<u>tailed</u> tells about the buck.)

The *d* or *ed* making a past participle is often left off when the participle is used as an adjective.

He killed a six-point, white-tail__ buck.

SOLUTION

Add *d* or *ed* to the verb form used as an adjective telling about a noun. Study **2** if you do not know what an adjective is. Study **3** on participles.

Add *d* or *ed* to verb forms used as adjectives.

1. We came to a barb wire fence.
2. He bought a use car.
3. I have seen players play with broken noses, jam fingers, or pulled ham strings.
4. The cat was decease.

ANSWERS

1. barbed
2. used
3. jammed
4. deceased

If you missed any, review the lesson and do the next exercise. Follow the directions for the last exercise.

1. He was an interest party to the divorce.
2. The car is jack up in the back.
3. He sent me long-stem roses.
4. She has been a change person since she married.

ANSWERS

1. interested
2. jacked
3. long-stemmed
4. changed

drown   **PROBLEM**

Common speech adds a *d* sound twice to the end of *drown* to make *drownded*. This is not an accepted form.

SOLUTION

Remember that *drown* is regular and needs only one added *ed*: *drowned*.

Present	Past	Past Participle
verb	verb + ed	helper + verb + ed
drown	drowned	had drowned

Add *ed* where it is needed.

1. The kitten was drown in a sack.
2. Sally almost drown when she was caught by a current.
3. After they broke up, he drown his sorrows in a fifth of gin.

   ANSWERS

   1. drowned
   2. drowned
   3. drowned

34 Irregular Verbs

PROBLEM

We hear the wrong forms of irregular verbs every day, so we learn the verbs incorrectly.

SOLUTION

Learn the forms—the principal parts—of the following common irregular verbs. The principal parts of irregular verbs are the same as those of regular verbs. Each part is used in the same way for regular and for irregular verbs.

Present (used about things happening now)	Past (used about things happening before)	Past Participle (never used as a verb without a helping word; the time of the helping word shows when things happen)
I go.	I went.	I will be gone.
		I have gone.

The helping verbs used with the past participle are usually forms of *have* or *be*. Sometimes some other linking verb is used. See **2**, forms of *be* and other linking verbs. See **33** for the most common helpers used with the past participle.

principal parts according to sounds

Study the principal parts of these irregular verbs. They are grouped together when they sound alike. Say the forms to yourself so that you are used to their sound.

Present	Past	Past Participle
burst	burst	(helper) burst
bring	brought	(helper) brought
catch	caught	(helper) caught
teach	taught	(helper) taught
send	sent	(helper) sent
spend	spent	(helper) spent
shoot	shot	(helper) shot
get	got	(helper) got
feel	felt	(helper) felt
keep	kept	(helper) kept
meet	met	(helper) met
deal	dealt	(helper) dealt
lose	lost	(helper) lost
find	found	(helper) found
hear	heard	(helper) heard
lead	led	(helper) led
strike	struck	(helper) struck
sit	sat	(helper) sat

This verb means "to rest." The verb meaning "to put something down" is:

Present	Past	Past Participle
set	set	(helper) set
break	broke	(helper) broken
speak	spoke	(helper) spoken
choose	chose	(helper) chosen
freeze	froze	(helper) frozen
swear	swore	(helper) sworn
tear	tore	(helper) torn
wear	wore	(helper) worn
lie	lay	(helper) lain

This verb means "to rest." The verb often confused with it, meaning "to place," is:

Present	Past	Past Participle
lay	laid	(helper) laid
blow	blew	(helper) blown
fly	flew	(helper) flown
grow	grew	(helper) grown
know	knew	(helper) known
throw	threw	(helper) thrown

Present	Past	Past Participle
burst	burst	(helper) burst
take	took	(helper) taken
shake	shook	(helper) shaken
draw	drew	(helper) drawn
eat	ate	(helper) eaten
fall	fell	(helper) fallen
give	gave	(helper) given
see	saw	(helper) seen
drive	drove	(helper) driven
ride	rode	(helper) ridden
rise	rose	(helper) risen
write	wrote	(helper) written
does, do	did	(helper) done
goes, go	went	(helper) gone
drink	drank	(helper) drunk
shrink	shrank	(helper) shrunk
sink	sank	(helper) sunk
ring	rang	(helper) rung
sing	sang	(helper) sung
spring	sprang	(helper) sprung
begin	began	(helper) begun
swim	swam	(helper) swum
come	came	(helper) come
become	became	(helper) become
run	ran	(helper) run
The verb *to be*: am, is, are	was, were	(helper) been
The verb *to have*: has, have	had	(helper) had
may	might	

These are the irregular verbs most often misused. There is a longer list of irregular verbs in the handbook in 8.

> To practice learning these irregular verbs, cover up the last two columns. Look at the present and write the other forms of the verbs. Then uncover the past and past-participle forms and check your answers. Repeat this until you know the forms.

ed on irregular verbs

PROBLEM

Most of our verbs add *d* or *ed* to show that something happened in the past. But some of our verbs are not regular. They change in some other way. Often writers and speakers treat one of these irregular verbs as though it were regular. They add *d* or *ed* when the verb does not change its form in that way.

WRONG: He <u>knowed</u> them.   The balloon <u>busted</u>.

ACCEPTED: He <u>knew</u> them.   The balloon <u>burst</u>.

SOLUTION

The way to avoid adding *d* or *ed* to an irregular verb is to know the accepted forms of the irregular verb and use them. Study the lists and examples below. They will help you learn the use of these regular verbs. Remember that the irregular verbs should not have *ed* added. Say the first three forms and the examples to yourself to get to know them.

burst	burst	(helper) burst	NOT busted

I <u>burst</u> bubbles now. (present)

I <u>burst</u> bubbles yesterday. (past)

I <u>have</u> <u>burst</u> bubbles before. (past participle)

Bubbles <u>were</u> <u>burst</u>. (past participle)

catch	caught	(helper) caught	NOT catched

I <u>catch</u> balls now. (present)

I <u>caught</u> balls yesterday. (past)

I <u>have</u> <u>caught</u> balls before. (past participle)

Balls <u>were</u> <u>caught</u>. (past participle)

teach	taught	(helper) taught	NOT teached

I <u>teach</u> art now. (present)

I <u>taught</u> art yesterday. (past)

I <u>have</u> <u>taught</u> art before. (past participle)

Art <u>was</u> <u>taught</u>. (past participle)

hear	heard	(helper) heard	NOT heared

I <u>hear</u> music now. (present)

I <u>heard</u> music yesterday. (past)

I <u>have</u> <u>heard</u> music before. (past participle)

Music <u>was</u> <u>heard</u>. (past participle)

lie	lay	(helper) lain	NOT laid

I <u>lie</u> down now. (present)

I lay down yesterday. (past)

I have lain down before. (past participle)

blow	blew	(helper) blown	NOT blowed

I blow bubbles now. (present)

I blew bubbles yesterday. (past)

I have blown bubbles before. (past participle)

Bubbles were blown. (past participle)

grow	grew	(helper) grown	NOT growed

I grow now. (present)

I grew yesterday. (past)

I have grown before. (past participle)

I was grown. (past participle)

know	knew	(helper) known	NOT knowed

I know now. (present)

I knew yesterday. (past)

I have known before. (past participle)

I was known. (past participle)

throw	threw	(helper) thrown	NOT throwed

I throw tantrums now. (present)

I threw tantrums yesterday. (past)

I have thrown tantrums before. (past participle)

Tantrums were thrown. (past participle)

draw	drew	(helper) drawn	NOT drawed

I draw water now. (present)

I drew water yesterday. (past)

I have drawn water before. (past participle)

Water was drawn. (past participle)

see	saw	(helper) seen	NOT seed

I see daffodils now. (present)

I saw daffodils yesterday. (past)

I have seen daffodils before. (past participle)

Daffodils <u>were</u> <u>seen</u>. (past participle)

run	ran	(helper) run	NOT runned

I <u>run</u> now. (present)
I <u>ran</u> yesterday. (past)
I <u>have</u> <u>run</u> before. (past participle)
Races <u>were</u> <u>run</u>. (past participle)

Write the accepted form of the verb at the beginning of the sentence in the blank.

1. (lie) Yesterday he _____ down on the bed.
2. (know) As soon as he spoke, I _____ who he was.
3. (burst) When they fell, the soap bubbles _____ .
4. (see) After he had gone, she _____ his hat on the chair.
5. (teach) I have _____ a church class of twelve-year-olds.

ANSWERS

1. lay
2. knew
3. burst
4. saw
5. taught

If you missed any, review the lesson and do the next exercise. Follow the directions for the last exercise.

1. (throw) He had _____ another curve ball.
2. (catch) At the picnic last week I _____ cold.
3. (hear) After I _____ about their date, we did break up.
4. (blow) The sounds of all those people _____ my mind that day.
5. (run) The car was something, for it _____ the way it looked.

ANSWERS

1. thrown
2. caught
3. heard
4. blew
5. ran

past and past participle confused

PROBLEM

Speakers and writers confuse the past form with the past-participle form of some verbs.

SOLUTION

Remember that the second part (the past) is never used WITH a helping word. The third part (the past participle) is never used as the verb WITHOUT a helping word. It is always used with <u>be</u>, <u>am</u>, <u>is</u>, <u>are</u>, <u>was</u>, <u>were</u>, <u>been</u>, <u>has</u>, <u>have</u>, <u>had</u>, or a combination of two of these, or one of the other linking verbs like <u>become</u> or <u>get</u>.

I <u>am</u> <u>sent</u> home (*am* is a helper).

I <u>have</u> <u>sent</u> it (*have* is a helper).

I <u>will</u> <u>have</u> <u>been</u> <u>sent</u> home (*will have been* are helpers).

Subject	past

or

Subject	Helper + past participle

Study the following principal parts and examples. Say them to yourself so that you get used to their sounds.

break	broke	(helper) broken

I <u>broke</u> the vase yesterday. (past)

I <u>have</u> <u>broken</u> vases before. (past participle)

Vases <u>are</u> <u>broken</u>. (past participle)

speak	spoke	(helper) spoken

I <u>spoke</u> yesterday. (past)

I <u>have</u> <u>spoken</u> before. (past participle)

Wisdom <u>was</u> <u>spoken</u> seldom. (past participle)

steal	stole	(helper) stolen

I <u>stole</u> yesterday. (past)

I <u>have</u> <u>stolen</u> before. (past participle)

Hearts <u>will</u> <u>be</u> <u>stolen</u>. (past participle)

Underline each correct verb form.

1. He has (break, broke, broken) his promise.
2. They had (steal, stole, stolen) his car.
3. Long promises were (speak, spoke, spoken).

ANSWERS

1. broken
2. stolen
3. spoken

If you missed any, review the lesson and do the next exercise. Underline each correct verb form.

1. The chair is (break, broke, broken).
2. The jewelry was (steal, stole, stolen).
3. She had (speak, spoke, spoken) her piece.

ANSWERS

1. broken
2. stolen
3. spoken

choose	chose	(helper) chosen

I <u>chose</u> him yesterday. (past)

I <u>had</u> <u>chosen</u> him before. (past participle)

He <u>would</u> <u>have</u> <u>been</u> <u>chosen</u>. (past participle)

freeze	froze	(helper) frozen

I <u>froze</u> a rose yesterday. (past)
I <u>have</u> <u>frozen</u> a rose before. (past participle)
Roses <u>are</u> <u>frozen</u>. (past participle)

Underline each correct verb form.

1. I have (freeze, froze, frozen) ten pints.
2. She was (choose, chose, chosen) to go.

ANSWERS

1. frozen
2. chosen -

If you missed any, review the lesson and do the next exercise.

1. I have (choose, chose, chosen) two approaches to try.
2. When the car starts, I am (freeze, frozen, frozen).

ANSWERS

1. chosen
2. frozen

swear	swore	(helper) sworn

I <u>swore</u> yesterday. (past)
He <u>was</u> <u>sworn</u> before. (past participle)
Oaths <u>have</u> <u>been</u> <u>sworn</u>. (past participle)

tear	tore	(helper) torn

I tore paper yesterday. (past)
I had torn paper before. (past participle)
Paper is torn. (past participle)

wear	wore	(helper) worn

She wore a yellow ribbon yesterday. (past)
She has worn it before. (past participle)
Ribbons will be worn. (past participle)

Underline each correct verb form.

1. The dress is (tear, tore, torn) from top to bottom.
2. He (swear, swore, sworn) to me then.
3. They have (wear, wore, worn) her out.

ANSWERS

1. torn
2. swore
3. worn

If you missed any, review the lesson and do the next exercise.

Underline each correct verb form.

1. The players are (wear, wore, worn) out.
2. His clothes were (tear, tore, torn) by thorns.
3. They had (swear, swore, sworn) a blue streak.

ANSWERS

1. worn
2. torn
3. sworn

blow	blew	(helper) blown

We blew the test yesterday. (past)
We had blown tests before. (past participle)
The test was blown. (past participle)

grow	grew	(helper) grown

They grew weeds yesterday. (past)
They have grown weeds before. (past participle)
Weeds are grown everywhere. (past participle)

know	knew	(helper) known

He <u>knew</u> his lesson yesterday. (past)
He <u>has</u> <u>known</u> his lesson before. (past participle)
The lesson <u>will</u> <u>be</u> <u>known</u>. (past participle)

throw	threw	(helper) thrown

She <u>threw</u> it away yesterday. (past)
She <u>has</u> <u>thrown</u> it away before. (past participle)
It <u>was</u> <u>thrown</u> away. (past participle)

Underline each correct verb form.

1. She had (know, knew, known) him a long time.
2. They had (grow, grew, grown) apart.
3. He had (blow, blew, blown) his chance.
4. Time is (throw, threw, thrown) away.

ANSWERS

1. known
2. grown
3. blown
4. thrown

If you missed any, review the lesson and do the next exercise.

Underline each correct verb form.

1. I got (throw, threw, thrown) by the horse.
2. They have (know, knew, known) each other for years.
3. The storm has now (blow, blew, blown) over.
4. The corn has (grow, grew, grown) taller than he is.

ANSWERS

1. thrown
2. known
3. blown
4. grown

take	took	(helper) taken

I <u>took</u> it yesterday. (past)
I <u>had</u> <u>taken</u> it before. (past participle)
I <u>was</u> <u>taken</u> in by his story. (past participle)

shake	shook	(helper) shaken

We <u>shook</u> hands yesterday. (past)
We <u>have</u> <u>shaken</u> hands before. (past participle)
Hands <u>were</u> <u>shaken</u>. (past participle)

draw	drew	(helper) drawn

I <u>drew</u> water yesterday. (past)
I <u>have</u> <u>drawn</u> water before. (past participle)
Water <u>has</u> <u>been</u> <u>drawn</u>. (past participle)

Underline each correct verb form.

1. Mary had (draw, drew, drawn) his portrait.
2. His faith is (shake, shook, shaken).
3. She has (take, took, taken) his part.

ANSWERS

1. drawn
2. shaken
3. taken

If you missed any, review the lesson and do the next exercise.

Underline each correct verb form.

1. I have (take, took, taken) the challenge.
2. The mixture is (shake, shook, shaken) well.
3. He had (draw, drew, drawn) two aces.

ANSWERS

1. taken
2. shaken
3. drawn

eat	ate	(helper) eaten

He <u>ate</u> dinner yesterday. (past)
He <u>had</u> <u>eaten</u> dinner before. (past participle)
Dinner <u>was</u> <u>eaten</u>. (past participle)

fall	fell	(helper) fallen

She <u>fell</u> yesterday. (past)
She <u>has</u> <u>fallen</u> before. (past participle)
Leaves <u>were</u> <u>fallen</u>. (past participle)

give	gave	(helper) given

I <u>gave</u> apples yesterday. (past)
I <u>have</u> <u>given</u> apples before. (past participle)
Apples <u>are</u> <u>given</u>. (past participle)

see	saw	(helper) seen

You <u>saw</u> me yesterday. (past)
You <u>have</u> <u>seen</u> me before. (past participle)
I <u>am</u> <u>seen</u>. (past participle)

Underline each correct verb form.

1. Last night he (eat, ate, eaten) pretty well.
2. Has he (fall, fell, fallen) down again?
3. Her tears have (give, gave, given) her away.
4. Shirley had (see, saw, seen) her sister.

ANSWERS

1. ate
2. fallen
3. given
4. seen

If you missed any, review the lesson and do the next exercise.

Underline each correct verb form.

1. That was the best seafood I have ever (eat, ate, eaten).
2. Many people have carelessly (fall, fell, fallen) overboard.
3. He never (see, saw, seen) a fox in that area.
4. The pup was (give, gave, given) to me.

ANSWERS

1. eaten
2. fallen
3. saw
4. given

drive	drove	(helper) driven

He <u>drove</u> a truck yesterday. (past)
He <u>had</u> <u>driven</u> a truck before. (past participle)
Trucks <u>were</u> <u>driven</u> up. (past participle)

ride	rode	(helper) ridden

She <u>rode</u> yesterday. (past)
She <u>has ridden</u> before. (past participle)
Horses <u>are ridden</u>. (past participle)

| rise | rose | (helper) risen |

I <u>rose</u> yesterday. (past)
I <u>have risen</u> before. (past participle)

| write | wrote | (helper) written |

He <u>wrote</u> letters yesterday. (past)
He <u>had written</u> letters before. (past participle)
Letters <u>are written</u>. (past participle)

Underline each correct verb form.

1. The horse was (ride, rode, ridden) to death.
2. He had (rise, rose, risen) early.
3. The stories were (write, wrote, written) before she was twenty.
4. He has (drive, drove, driven) the animal unmercifully.

ANSWERS

1. ridden
2. risen
3. written
4. driven

If you missed any, review the lesson and do the next exercise.

Underline each correct verb form.

1. I have (ride, rode, ridden) bulls.
2. He had (write, wrote, written) the recipe down.
3. The dough had (rise, rose, risen).
4. Alice had not drive, drove, driven) for years.

ANSWERS

1. ridden
2. written
3. risen
4. driven

| does, do | did | (helper) done |

She <u>did</u> it yesterday. (past)

She <u>has</u> <u>done</u> it before. (past participle)
It <u>was</u> <u>done</u>. (past participle)

goes, go	went	(helper) gone

They <u>went</u> yesterday. (past)
They <u>have</u> <u>gone</u> before. (past participle)
They <u>were</u> <u>gone</u>. (past participle)

Underline each correct verb form.

1. He had (do, did, done) what I told him to do.
2. They (go, went, gone) when she left.
3. After that we (do, did, done) all the work.
4. It has (go, went, gone) away.

ANSWERS

1. done
2. went
3. did
4. gone

If you missed any, review the lesson and do the next exercise.

Underline each correct verb form.

1. While we were here, we (do, did, done) a lot of exploring.
2. Everyone had (go, went, gone) home except this guy and me.
3. That year I (do, did, done) pretty well.
4. Five days had (go, went, gone) by.

ANSWERS

1. did
2. gone
3. did
4. gone

drink	drank	(helper) drunk

I <u>drank</u> yesterday. (past)
I <u>had</u> <u>drunk</u> before. (past participle)
I <u>was</u> <u>drunk</u>. (past participle)

shrink	shrank	(helper) shrunk

His clothes <u>shrank</u> yesterday. (past)

His clothes <u>have shrunk</u> before. (past participle)
His clothes <u>are shrunk</u>. (past participle)

sink	sank	(helper) sunk

The ship <u>sank</u> yesterday. (past)
The ship <u>had sunk</u> before. (past participle
the ship <u>was sunk</u>. (past participle)

Underline each correct verb form.

1. When it rained, her spirits (sink, sank, sunk).
2. When it rained, the new suit (shrink, shrank, shrunk).
3. When it rained, the cattle (drink, drank, drunk).

ANSWERS

1. sank
2. shrank
3. drank

If you missed any, review the lesson and do the next exercise.

Underline each correct verb form.

1. We had (drink, drank, drunk) all the coffee we could take.
2. His appetite had (shrink, shrank, shrunk).
3. The boat (sink, sank, sunk).

ANSWERS

1. drunk
2. shrunk
3. sank

ring	rang	(helper) rung

The bell <u>rang</u> yesterday. (past)
The bell <u>has rung</u> before. (past participle)
The bell <u>is rung</u>. (past participle)

sing	sang	(helper) sung

The choir <u>sang</u> yesterday. (past)
The choir <u>had sung</u> before. (past participle)
The hymns <u>are sung</u>. (past participle)

spring	sprang	(helper) sprung

The panther <u>sprang</u> yesterday. (past)

The panther <u>has</u> <u>sprung</u> before. (past participle)
The trap <u>will</u> <u>be</u> <u>sprung</u>. (past participle)

Underline each correct verb form.

1. Johnny Cash has (sing, sang, sung) prison songs.
2. The telephone has just (ring, rang, rung).
3. After she left, he (spring, sprang, sprung) a surprise.

ANSWERS

1. sung
2. rung
3. sprang

If you missed any, review the lesson and do the next exercise.

Underline each correct verb form.

1. The radiator has (spring, sprang, sprung) a leak.
2. He (ring, rang, rung) the bell at last year's fair.
3. The choir has (sing, sang, sung) that anthem many times.

ANSWERS

1. sprung
2. rang
3. sung

| begin | began | (helper) begun |

We <u>began</u> a game yesterday. (past)
We <u>have</u> <u>begun</u> games before. (past participle)
Games <u>were</u> <u>begun</u>. (past participle)

| swim | swam | (helper) swum |

He <u>swam</u> yesterday. (past)
He <u>had</u> <u>swum</u> before. (past participle)
The pool <u>was</u> <u>swum</u> twice. (past participle)

Underline each correct verb form.

1. He (begin, began, begun) to cry when I left.
2. They (swim, swam, swum) yesterday.

ANSWERS

1. began
2. swam

If you missed any, review the lesson and do the next exercise.

Underline each correct verb form.

1. My life (begin, began, begun) in 1923.
2. The dolphin had (swim, swam, swum) up to the window.

ANSWERS

1. began
2. swum

come	came	(helper) come

Spring came yesterday. (past)
Spring had not come before. (past participle)
Spring is come. (past participle)

become	became	(helper) become

He became afraid. (past)
He had never become afraid before. (past participle)

run	ran	(helper) run

She ran two laps yesterday. (past)
She had run five laps before. (past participle)
Seven laps were run. (past participle)

am, is, are	was, were	(helper) been

You were young. (past)
You have been young. (past participle)

Underline each correct verb form.

1. We have (come, came) to an understanding.
2. I (run, ran) home.
3. I (become, became) tired.
4. He (be, is, been) sleepy.

ANSWERS

1. come
2. ran
3. became
4. is

If you missed any, review the lesson and do the next exercise.

Underline each correct verb form.

1. They got up and (run, ran) four miles before breakfast.
2. She had (become, became) unhappy.
3. Whenever the mailman (come, came), she barked.
4. She has always (be, was, been) kind to everyong.

ANSWERS

1. ran
2. become
3. came
4. been

t for d on irregular verbs

PROBLEM

The sounds *t*, *d*, and *k* are very much alike. *T* and *d* sound especially alike. So *t* has replaced *d* as the sign of the past or past participle in some verbs. The vowel sound changes in these words, too. A writer may not know the correct forms of some of these irregular verbs.

SOLUTION

Study the following irregular verb forms using *t* instead of *d*. Cover up the past and past-participle forms and practice writing them until you know them. Study the examples using the different forms.

Present	Past	Past Participle
bring	brought	(helper) brought
catch	caught	(helper) caught
teach	taught	(helper) taught

You <u>bring</u> joy now. (present)

You <u>brought</u> joy yesterday. (past)

You <u>have</u> <u>brought</u> joy before. (past participle)

Joy <u>was</u> <u>brought</u>. (past participle)

You <u>catch</u> fish now. (present)

You <u>caught</u> fish yesterday. (past)

You <u>have</u> <u>caught</u> fish before. (past participle)

Fish <u>were</u> <u>caught</u>. (past participle)

You <u>teach</u> tennis now. (present)

You <u>taught</u> tennis yesterday. (past)

You have <u>taught</u> tennis before. (past participle)

Tennis was <u>taught</u>. (past participle)

Present	Past	Past Participle
deal	dealt	(helper) dealt
feel	felt	(helper) felt
keep	kept	(helper) kept
lose	lost	(helper) lost

You <u>deal</u> cards now. (present)

You <u>dealt</u> cards yesterday. (past)

You <u>had</u> <u>dealt</u> cards before. (past participle)

Cards <u>are</u> <u>dealt</u>. (past participle)

You <u>feel</u> velvet now. (present)

You <u>felt</u> velvet yesterday. (past)

You <u>had</u> <u>felt</u> velvet before. (past participle)

Velvet <u>is</u> <u>felt</u>. (past participle)

You <u>keep</u> score now. (present)

You <u>kept</u> score yesterday. (past)

You <u>had</u> <u>kept</u> score before. (past participle)

Score <u>is</u> <u>kept</u>. (past participle)

You <u>lose</u> points now. (present)

You <u>lost</u> points yesterday. (past)

You <u>had</u> <u>lost</u> points before. (past participle)

Points <u>are</u> <u>lost</u>. (past participle)

Write in each blank the correct form of the verb in parentheses at the beginning of that sentence.

1. (catch) In the spring the best fish are _____ .
2. (deal) The program _____ with drug abuse.
3. (keep) He has not _____ up with his piano-playing.
4. (teach) Before I graduated, he _____ all the music there.

ANSWERS

1. caught
2. dealt
3. kept
4. taught

If you missed any, review the lesson and do the next exercise. Follow the directions for the last exercise.

1. (bring) The judges perferred the dog that he had _____ to the show.
2. (lose) Valuable time was _____ .
3. (feel) I _____ unhappy after the test.
4. (keep) The girl was _____ in a cellar.

ANSWERS

1. brought
2. lost
3. felt
4. kept.

verbs already ending in d, t, or k

PROBLEM

Some verbs in the present form already end in sounds like the regular ending, *ed*. These sounds are *d*, *t*, and *k*. So adding *d* or *ed* or *t* to them would put two similar sounds together and make them hard to say. English has various solutions to this problem.

SOLUTION 1

Some verbs ending in *d*, *t*, or *k* are regular and add *ed* as a new syllable.

Present	Past	Past Participle
dread	dreaded	(helper) dreaded

See a dictionary to learn whether a verb ending in *t* or *d* is regular or not. After any verb that is regular, the dictionary will list nothing or its *ed* forms. See **33** for the uses of regular verbs.

SOLUTION 2

A few verbs ending in *t* or *d* do not change form to show time.

Present	Past	Past Participle
burst	burst	(helper) burst
put	put	(helper) put
set	set	(helper) set

Check the dictionary to see if a verb does not change. The dictionary will repeat these verbs after the present form to show that they do not change. The most common of these verbs are listed in **8**.

SOLUTION 3

Some verbs ending in *d* change their ending to *t* in the past and past participle. Study these.

Present	Past	Past Participle
bend	bent	(helper) bent
lend	lent	(helper) lent
send	sent	(helper) sent
spend	spent	(helper) spent

SOLUTION 4

Some verbs ending in *d*, *k*, or *t* keep the same ending but change their vowel sound. Study these.

Present	Past	Past Participle
find	found	(helper) found
get	got	(helper) got (or gotten)
lead	led	(helper) led
meet	met	(helper) met
shoot	shot	(helper) shot
sit	sat	(helper) sat
strike	struck	(helper) struck

Others like this are listed in 8.

Write in each blank the correct form of the verb in parentheses at the beginning of the sentence.

1. (shoot) In the movie he was _____ at many times.
2. (sit) He had _____ for hours trying to comfort her.
3. (get) I went to the bank and _____ the rest of the money.
4. (send) The Air Force _____ me to school for eight months.
5. (strike) This was clear when the union members _____ a few years ago.

ANSWERS

1. shot
2. sat
3. got
4. sent
5. struck.

If you missed any, review the lesson and do the next exercise. Follow the directions for the last exercise.

1. (meet) She has not _____ many people in Salt Lake City.
2. (find) It was _____ in two feet of water.
3. (bend) The axle was _____ beyond repair
4. (lead) After the game, Bob _____ us to Chaffs.
5. (get) We all had _____ tired of her.

ANSWERS

1. met
2. found
3. bent
4. led
5. got (or gotten)

The list of principal parts according to sound can be used as a review list of the most troublesome verbs. A more complete list is in 8.

Now take the post-test on the next page.

NAME

VERB TENSE FORMS
Post-Test A

Underline the accepted verb form in each sentence.

1. After I fed him, the dog (come, came) home with me.
2. She left cold meat and he (eat, ate, eaten) it.
3. Last year we (grow, grew, grown, growed) tomatoes.
4. The coupon had been (tear, tore, torn) out of the paper.
5. When he tightened the valve, the pipe (burst, busted).
6. She had (lie, lay, lain, laid) down on the bed.
7. He had (steal, stole, stolen) second base.
8. Tom had (choose, chose, chosen) Mary.
9. At the dance last night, Henry (give, gave, given) her his pin.
10. We have (drive, drove, driven) to Memphis.
11. Sara had (go, went, gone) to England.
12. Ernestine had (sing, sang, sung) with Elvis Presley.
13. The tank (run, ran, runned) over.
14. He was (suppose, supposed) to go.
15. I (use, used) to know him well.
16. Last year I (meet, met) new friends.
17. The players looked like (drown, drowned, drownded) dogs.
18. It took an hour to get the meal (cook, cooked).
19. Instead of apologizing, he just (laugh, laughed).
20. Footballs have a (point, pointed) oval shape.

Ask your instructor to check your answers, or turn them in.

See verbs in **2** and **8**, *lie/lay* and *sit/set* in **50**, Post-test B, or writing assignments in **54–56**.

NAME

VERB TENSE FORMS
Post-Test B

Underline the accepted verb form in each sentence.

1. He has never (do, did, done) the same thing for longer than two days.
2. I have the recipe (write, wrote, written) down at home.
3. That night we got (eat, ate, eaten) up by mosquitoes.
4. I have (ride, rode, ridden) through town about a million times.
5. I had (know, knew, known, knowed) a few people who had seen her.
6. He had to replace a (wear, wore, worn) water hose.
7. You should have (go, went, gone) to Denver with me.
8. He looked out into the deep water, and there (lie, lay, lain, laid) a medium-sized mink.
9. The bag (burst, busted) and spilled garbage all over him.
10. When I was a boy, I (learn, learned) this from my father.
11. Being born on a Monday is (suppose, supposed) to mean that the child will be fair of face.
12. He has (become, became) the most important thing in my life.
13. We had (break, broke, broken) Bradley High's ninety-nine game winning streak.
14. My grandfather is (use, used) to doing things the hard way.
15. Once a trapper (see, saw, seen, seed) him and tried to take the cubs away.
16. She took him for a canoe ride and (drown, drowned, drownded) him accidentally.
17. She had (spend, spent) all the money we had saved.
18. Running is not (use, used) just for hurrying along.
19. I never was good enough to start, so I (decide, decided) I would quit.
20. Both of them grew emotionally as time (pass, passed).

Ask your instructor to check your answers, or turn them in.

NAME

PRONOUN AGREEMENT
Pretest

A. Correct any pronouns in the following sentences that are not clear or are misleading.

Teenagers need to feel that they can talk to their parents and have them understand what they are going through. Parents feel what their children feel, and they need to know why they are going through it.

B. Underline the correct pronoun for each sentence.
1. A person needs to know (his, their) own mind.
2. If someone needs money, she will give it to (you, him, them).
3. The team has won every game that (it, they) played.
4. Any parent wants the best for (his, its, their, your) children.
5. The audience disagree about (its, their) reactions to the play.
6. Everybody tries to do (his, their) best when (he, they) can win.
7. A student works hard many times at (his, your, their) studies and at (his, your, their) job or home, too.
8. Who wants to wake up to water sprinkled on (his, their) face?
9. In classifying an entertainer, I would say (he, they) were good, unexciting, or vain.
10. Her family knows that (it, they) will have (its, their) turn.

ANSWERS

A. Corrections are italicized; other pronouns do not have to be changed.

Teenagers need to feel that they can talk to their parents and have *the parents* understand what *the children* are going through. Parents feel what their children feel, and *parents* need to know why *the children* are going through *problems*.

B.
1. his
2. him
3. it
4. his
5. their
6. his, he
7. his, his.
8. his
9. he
10. it, its.

35 Pronoun Agreement

Because a pronoun substitutes for a noun, it must be like that noun in some ways. This is called agreeing with the noun. Pronouns often change their forms to agree with nouns in sex, number, or person. This is discussed in 9 as well as in the lessons that follow.

PROBLEM

A pronoun substitutes for a noun. If a writer does not name the noun for which the pronoun substitutes, the reader will not know what the pronoun means.

CONFUSING: Children need discipline. They should not abuse children, though.

SOLUTION

Check each pronoun to be sure that the noun for which it is substituting is named. A coach cannot send a substitute in to play unless a player has already been filling the position for which the new player substitutes. You cannot send a pronoun into your writing unless a noun has been doing the job for which the pronoun will substitute. So be sure that you have named a noun before you use a pronoun to substitute for it.

CLEARER: Children need discipline. Parents should not abuse children, though.

Change any pronoun below that is not clear to a noun that makes it clear.

I like to watch football. They are exciting because of the fast action. They must be strong, but they must also think fast.

ANSWERS

The changes needed are italicized.
   I like to watch football. *Games* are exciting. *Players* must be strong, but they must also think fast.

If you missed any, review the lesson and do the next exercise. Follow the directions for the last exercise.

1. In Italy a guest is treated as a sacred person. They will offer a guest the best of the wine and food.
2. If you have some schooling and are looking for a job, they will talk to you before they would to some someone with no schooling.

ANSWERS

Only the italicized changes are necessary.
1. In Italy a guest is treated as a sacred person. *Italians* (or *People* or *His host*) will offer a guest the best of the wine and food.
2. If you have had some schooling and are looking for a job, *employers* (or *personnel managers*) will talk to you before they would to someone with no schooling.

PROBLEM

Sometimes a writer names two nouns a[...] tuting for either of the nouns. The reade[...] substitutes for.

CONFUSING: The doll was on the bed.[...]

SOLUTION

Check each pronoun to be sure that [...] substituting for.

CLEARER: The doll was on the bed. Th[...]
or
The doll was on the bed. Th[...]

Change any confusing pronoun to be sure that the reader knows w[...] for.

1. Jennifer toddled to her mother, and she tripped on a toy.
2. The Hawks beat the Lions. Then they were fourth in the league.
3. He brought the cake to the wedding. It was a catastrophe.

ANSWERS

1. Change *she* to *Jennifer* or *the child*.
2. Change *they* to *the Hawks* or *the Lions*.
3. Change *it* to *the cake* (or *the wedding*).

If you missed any, review the lesson and do the next exercise. Follow the directions for the last exercise.

1. In all nations, the threat of world destruction is in everybody's minds. If they would stop trying to destroy the world, we could live in peace.
2. My next-door neighbor shows the bargain plants to my mother, and if she likes them, she sells them to her cheap.
3. After Tom stole Jim's girl, he hit him the next time they met.

ANSWERS

Only these changes are necessary.
1. Sentence two should read: If *the nations* would stop trying . . . .
2. My next-door neighbor shows the bargain plants to my mother, and if *Mother* likes them, *the neighbor* sells them to her cheap.
3. After Tom stole Jim's girl, *Jim* hit him the next time they met.

PROBLEM

Sometimes a pronoun is used for "all people" or "people in general" or "people of the kind I have been talking about" which does not mean one of these. If a writer uses *you* the reader may be offended because the idea does not refer to him ... uses *they*, the reader looks for a noun for the pronoun to refer to.

NG: You study long hours.
They study long hours.

SOLUTION

The writer may correctly use any of the following when he or she means "all people" or "people in general" or "people of the kind I have been talking about."

A. *All people* or *people in general*
B. The name of the specific kind of people meant.
C. *Everyone, everybody, anybody, anyone*
D. *One*

A and B both mean more than one; the rest mean only one.

CLEARER: A. People study long hours.
B. Students study long hours.
C. Everyone studies long hours.
D. One studies long hours.

Underline the acceptable noun or pronoun to mean "people in general" in each of the sentences below.

1. When (you, they, people) get married, (you, they) take on great responsibility.
2. At a football game (everyone, you, they) will act more savagely than he or she would at a concert.
3. Without these three points (you, they, one) might as well not even try to break into racing.

ANSWERS

1. people, they
2. everyone
3. one

If you missed any, review the lesson and do the next exercise. Follow the directions for the last exercise.

1. Very few schools allow (you, them, people) to take a full course load for only eighty-four dollars.
2. (You, They, Everybody) should always look ahead and plan.
3. It is a very good exercise for (your, their, anyone's) body.

ANSWERS

   1. people
   2. Everybody
   3. anyone's

**agreement
of *which*
or *who***

PROBLEM

Sometimes a writer does not know whether to use *which* or *who* to substitute for a noun.

SOLUTION

Use *who* (or *whom* or *whose*) if you are talking about a person or people. Use *which* if you are talking about a thing or things. In talking about animals, you may use either. The word *that* may be used for either people or things. But it is not used unless the words that follow *that* have to be in the sentence to identify the thing that *that* stands for.

The chairs (things), *which* he bought cheaply, were antiques.

The leader (person), *who* was the youngest member, did an excellent job.

Underline the correct choice in each sentence.

1. The course, (who, which) was required, was dull.
2. The girls, (who, which) wanted to go, cried as we left.
3. He bought the red car, (whose price, the price of which) was lowest.
4. This person, (whom, which) I can't stand to be around, is so lazy that he would starve before he would work hard.

ANSWERS

   1. which
   2. who
   3. the price of which
   4. whom

If you missed any, review the lesson and do the next exercise. Follow the directions for the last exercise.

1. My best friend is a man (who, which) works with me in the ambulance service.
2. We visited my wife's aunt and uncle, (who, which) live in Indianapolis.
3. My children, (who, which) are five and six, keep me busy.
4. The problem (about whom, about which) I told you is solved.

ANSWERS

   1. who
   2. who
   3. who
   4. about which

Agreement in Number   A pronoun must agree with its noun in number. If a noun means only one thing, its pronoun must mean only one, also. If a noun means more than one, so must its pronoun.

> The boy likes his trumpet. (*Boy* means only one, so *his*, the pronoun substituting for *boy*, does, too.)
>
> The boys liked their trumpets. (*Boys* means more than one, so *their* is the correct pronoun.)

The handbook discusses this in 8.

PROBLEM

Sometimes a pronoun does not agree in number with a noun for which it is substituting.

> College *students* would not get into serious trouble if *he* was late once in a while. (*He* means one but is substituting for *students*, which means many. So they do not agree.)

SOLUTION

Change the noun or pronoun so that they are the same number.

> College *students* would not get into serious trouble if *they* were late once in a while. (The pronoun, like the noun, means many.)
>
> A college *student* would not get into serious trouble if *he* was late once in a while. (The noun, like the pronoun, means one.)

Underline the following pronouns that do not agree with the nouns they substitute for. Then change the pronouns so that they agree.

1. I hear noises so much that I do not pay any attention to it.
2. We keep hope chests or little tin boxes with all our most valuable things in it.
3. Seventy-five percent of all workers find it more convenient to drive his automobile to work.
4. Sam was, like all animals, dependent on their master.

ANSWERS

1. it—them
2. it—them
3. his—their
4. their—his (or its)

If you missed any, review the lesson and do the next exercise. Follow the directions for the last exercise.

1. Each prisoner may take a one-minute shower per day. This will help keep them cleaner.

2. Scouts can choose the areas of study he would like to enter.
3. He can take things that look like junk to me and make something out of it.
4. Every dog is special to their owner.

ANSWERS

1. them—him
2. he—they
3. it—them
4. their—his (or its)

PROBLEM

One kind of noun that gives trouble with pronoun agreement in number means only one person, but that person may be either male or female.

A parent needs to love _____ child.

If you write "A parent needs to love their child," you have used a pronoun (*their*) that is different in number from the noun (*parent*) for which it substitutes.

If you write "A parent needs to love its child," you are using nonstandard English, since *its* is used about only nonhuman things.

If you write either *his* or *her* to fill in the blank, you are leaving out half of all parents.

If you write both *his* and *her* in the form of "A parent must love his or her child," it is acceptable, but rather clumsy.

SOLUTION

Change the noun for which the pronoun substitutes so that the noun means more than one. Then *they*, *them*, *their*, amd *themselves* can correctly be used to substitute for the noun.

Parents need to love their children.

ALTERNATE SOLUTION

The accepted pronoun for a noun like this is the pronoun that means one: *he*, *him*, *his*, and *himself*, or *she*, *her*, *hers*, and *herself*.

Underline the pronoun that agrees in number with the word it substitutes for in each of the following sentences.

1. A manager has great influence on (her, their) department.
2. Good writers make (his, their) songs interesting to many people.
3. A poor salesperson may lose (his, their) job.
4. I diagnose a patient's problem so that (she, they) can be helped.

ANSWERS

1. her   2. their   3. his   4. she

If you missed any, review the lesson and do the next exercise. Follow the directions for the last exercise.

1. A college student has a planned program, but (he, they) may study and have lunch whenever (he wants, they want).
2. Every player will notice the coach doing that, and (she, they) will lose all respect for her.
3. A worker needs to have a feeling of pride in (his, their) work.
4. If drivers would watch (her, their) speed, there would be fewer accidents.

ANSWERS

1. he, he wants
2. she
3. his
4. their

PROBLEM

Another kind of noun giving trouble means no definite person but people in general.

A person likes to choose _____ own career.
(Here, the writer has the uneasy feeling that since he means all people, he needs a pronoun meaning more than one, but *person* means one, and its pronoun must, too.)

SOLUTION

Change words like *a person* or *one* to words meaning more than one like *people* so that your words are closer to your meaning. Then you may correctly use pronouns meaning more than one to substitute for the noun meaning more than one.

People like to choose *their* own careers.

ALTERNATE SOLUTION

Use *he, him, his,* and *himself* with words like "a person" that are talking about anyone but mean only one. The noun you use may name a particular kind of person, for example, *a student, a welder, a redhead*.

A *person* likes to choose *his* own career.

Underline the pronoun that agrees with the noun it substitutes for.

1. A person often forgets (his, their) debts of time to others.
2. Any person should be able to accept (herself, themselves, oneself).

3. People should read to know about (his, their) fellowman.
4. A person may let another know that (she is, they are) friendly by a smile, a nod, or a hello.

ANSWERS

1. his
2. herself
3. their
4. she is

If you missed any, review the lesson and do the next exercise. Follow the directions for the last exercise.

1. Every person needs someone that (she, they) can talk to when (her, their) emotions have been stirred.
2. Sometimes the person has a reason to go under the minimum speed limit, but (he, they) should be careful.
3. When a person gets some material object that (she wants, they want) very much, (her, their) excitement may show in (her, their) appearance.

ANSWERS

1. she, her
2. he
3. she wants, her, her

PROBLEM

A pronoun must sometimes substitute for another pronoun. If the first pronoun is one of the indefinite pronouns that always mean only one, the pronoun substituting for it must mean only one, also. These are indefinite pronouns always meaning one:

anyone	no one	each
anybody	nobody	either
anything	nothing	neither
everyone	someone	another
everybody	somebody	one
everything	something	none

SOLUTION

Change the indefinite pronoun to a plural noun that can agree with *they*, *them*, and *their*. If you do use any one of these pronouns, be sure that the pronouns referring to it mean only one.

CORRECT: Everybody took *his* date.
               Everything has *its* place.

Underline the pronoun that agrees with the indefinite pronoun it substitutes for.

1. Somebody wants to sell (her, their) car.
2. Everyone knows (his, their) own features.
3. If anyone feels like complaining about (his, their) problems, (he, they) should re-member Rose Kennedy's faith.
4. Everybody feels that way sometimes in (her, their) life.
5. Nobody would fish if (she, they) didn't enjoy it.

ANSWERS

1. her
2. his
3. his, he
4. her
5. she

If you missed any, review the lesson and do the next exercise. Follow the directions for the last exercise.

1. There would be fewer accidents if everyone would watch (his, their) speed.
2. If one cannot type, (she, they) must hire someone to type (her, their) paper for (her, them).
3. She always asked everybody how (he, they) felt.
4. I don't like someone to tell me (he, they) will do something and then not do it.
5. Each of us should remember (her, their) senior year.

ANSWERS

1. his
2. she, her, her
3. he
4. he
5. her

PROBLEM

Some nouns may mean either one or more than one, depending on the idea of the writer. These are called *collective* nouns. They collect several individual people or things into one group.

The *chorus* (meaning all the people in the chorus) went on tour.

If the writer means that all the things collected are acting together as one thing, he or she makes the verb and pronoun agree with one:

The <u>chorus</u> <u>sings</u> its part well.

(one) (one)

If the writer means that each individual thing collected is acting separately from the rest, the writer makes the verb and pronoun agree with more than one:

The chorus <u>sing</u> <u>their</u> part well

         (more) (more)

Either is grammatically acceptable. What the writer may not acceptably do is make the verb agree with one and the pronoun agree with more than one, or vice-versa.

WRONG: The <u>chorus</u> <u>sings</u> their part well.

             (one) (more)

WRONG: The <u>chorus</u> <u>sings</u>   its part well.

           (more) (one)

SOLUTION

When you have a collective-noun subject, be sure that the pronouns substituting for that noun mean the same number as the verb for that noun. The verb tells how many a collective-noun subject means. If it means only one, the present-time verb ends in s. If it means more than one, there is no s added to the end. You can study more about verbs agreeing with subjects in 7 and 27–32. Choose the pronoun that agrees with the number of the noun.

Write over the collective noun how many it means. Then underline the pronoun that agrees with that number.

1. The choir sings (its, their) final number best.
2. The baseball team have broken (its, their) contracts for this season.
3. The church is donating (its, their) time for the charity drive.
4. Society as a whole causes crime because (it does, they do) not discipline children.

ANSWERS
    one
1. choir—its
    more
2. team—their
    one
3. church—its
    one
4. society—it does

If you missed any, review the lesson and do the next exercise. Follow the directions for the last exercise.

1. My family has a good time and enjoys life in (its, their) own way.
2. The couple are bad neighbors because (it, they) always nose into everyone's business.

3. When the Sheriff's Department has a party, (it tries, they try) to make sure everyone enjoys it.

4. My class has gotten the most out of (its, their) school experience.

ANSWERS

1. family—its   *one*
2. couple—they   *more*
3. Department—it tries   *one*
4. class—its   *one*

Agreement in Person

PROBLEM

Personal pronouns talk about a first, second, or third person. The first person pronouns are *I, we,* and all their forms. We use them for ourselves, the person speaking or writing.

The second person pronouns are *you* and all its forms. We use them for the person to whom we are speaking or writing.

The third person pronouns are *he, she, it, they* and all their forms. They are used for the person or thing that we are writing or speaking about. The handbook discusses agreement in person in **9**.

When writers start writing about first or third person, they sometimes shift to *you* although they do not mean the person to whom they are writing.

CORRECT:	*I* love my parents. They give *me* everything they can, and *I* ought to be grateful.
WRONG:	*I* love my parents. They give *you* everything they can, and *you* ought to be grateful.
CORRECT:	Everyone should attend college to meet people and get *herself* ready to face the world.
WRONG:	Everyone should attend college to meet people and get *yourself* ready to face the world.
CORRECT:	A child should love his parents. They give *him* everything they can, and *he* ought to be grateful.
WRONG:	A child should love his parents. They give *you* everything they can, and *you* ought to be grateful.

SOLUTION

When you write *you,* be sure that you are writing to the reader and that you are not shifting from writing about yourself or about people in general.

Correct any pronouns that shift from one person to another without changing the real person they are talking about.

When I get in a down mood, a book helps me to understand my feelings. After you have read for a while, it is hard to stay moody because you become so interested in what your book is saying.

ANSWER

The passage should read: When I get in a down mood, a book helps me to understand my feelings. After *I* have read for a while, it is hard to stay moody because *I* become so interested in what *my* book is saying.

If you missed any, review the lesson and do the next exercise. Follow the directions for the last exercise.

The person that a girl first loves remains part of her life. You think of him when you see other men, and you may even choose a husband who reminds you of him.

ANSWER

The passage should read: The person that a girl first loves remains part of her life. *She* thinks of him when *she* sees other men, and *she* may even choose a husband who reminds *her* of him.

Now go on to the post-test.

NAME _____

35. PRONOUN AGREEMENT
Post-Test A

A. Correct any pronouns that are not clear or are misleading in the following sentences.

1. I like fancy jeans with fashionable tops, and I like the knickers that they wear with boots.

2. Everyone who plans to attend college should try to gather all the knowledge they can because once you get behind, it is hard to catch up.

3. In the float competition the seniors accused the sophomores of putting some of their material on their float.

B. Underline the correct choices for these sentences.

1. A person's possessions have nothing to do with (her, their) basic personality.
2. Everyone is always trying to find out who (he is, they are).
3. The government has increased juvenile delinquency because (they prevent, it prevents) teachers from disciplining students in public schools.
4. I really enjoy my weekends because (it gives, they give) me time to spend with my family.
5. Buying a car on time gets (your, a buyer's) credit record in order.
6. He is a young man of (which, whom) I am proud.
7. It is hard for a parent to put (himself, themselves) into a younger person's place.

Ask your instructor to check your answers, or turn them in.

See **9** about agreement, Post-test B, or writing assignments in **54–56**.

35. PRONOUN AGREEMENT
Post-Test B

A. Correct any pronouns in the following that are not clear or that are misleading.

1. When a person is playing softball, they get good exercise. They have to be running and moving around. That gives your whole body exercise.

2. All motorcyclists need to have one slight wreck just to let them know how dangerous they can be.

3. We are working on my son's problem now. They have to have a positive mental attitude.

B. Underline the correct pronouns for these sentences.

1. A person needs to have confidence in (herself, themselves).
2. A teacher may build or destroy confidence in (his, their) students.
3. One group doubts (its, their) ability to change (its, their) future.
4. A man wanting a woman to notice him will straighten his posture. Other times (he, they) will to pay any attention to (his, their) posture.
5. The movie made (you, the viewers) feel as if (you, they) were filming the movie with the actors.
6. Everybody needs to know (her, their) own telephone number and Social Security number.
7. I have two boys (which, whom) I did not take to church as babies.

Ask your instructor to check your answers, or turn them in.

NAME

36. PRONOUN CASE
Pretest

Underline the correct pronoun in each choice.

1. Being together is important to my boyfriend and (I, me).
2. The team in Jacksonville was composed mostly of officers (who, whom) had been college players.
3. Duke is the only one (who, whom) I went to with my problems.
4. Ten minutes later he has served (himself, himselves, hisself, hisselves).
5. My wife and (I, me, myself) usually get out of bed to quiet our playful children.
6. She knew that it was (he, him), but she was still scared.
7. (He, Him) and (I, me) get together to shoot our guns or to drink a few beers.
8. That was the case with (I, me, myself).
9. I looked to see (who, who's, whose) name was on it.
10. People value training for (themself, themselves, theirself, theirselves).

ANSWERS
1. me
2. who
3. whom
4. himself
5. I
6. he
7. He, I
8. me
9. whose
10. themselves

If you missed any, study the following unit.

36 Pronoun Case

Some pronouns change their forms for different uses in a sentence. This change of form is called *case*. The forms used most are subject and object. The following chart shows the forms of common pronouns used for subjects and for objects.

Subject Pronouns		Object Pronouns	
I	we	me	us
you	you	you	you
he, she, it	they	him, her, it	them
who	who	whom	whom

Notice that *m* often marks the object pronouns. The object pronouns *me*, *him*, *them*, and *whom* all have *m*. No subject pronoun has an *m*. The handbook discusses pronoun case in **10**.

Subjective Case

PROBLEM

When does a writer need to use a subject pronoun?

SOLUTION

Use a subject pronoun (*I, you, he, she, it, who we,* or *they*) when it is a subject for a verb or when a linking verb says that it is the same as a subject.

_____ like fish.

_____ likes fish.

These blanks show where a subject for the sentence must come. Any pronoun used there must be a subject. Any of the following subject pronouns make the sentence acceptable.

I like fish.   *It* likes fish.
You like fish.   *Who* likes fish?
He likes fish.   *We* like fish.
She likes fish.   *They* like fish.

Subjects are defined and discussed in **1** and **3**.
The other use for a subject pronoun is to rename the subject after a linking verb (usually a form of the verb *be*).

The guilty one was _____ .
      (subject)

The guilty ones were _____ .
      (subject)

These blanks must be filled with subject pronouns because the pronoun that goes in them is the same as the subject. It renames the subject and tells who it was. This pronoun is a subjective complement (or predicate pronoun). The following sentences correctly use the subject pronoun for the subjective complement.

The guilty one was *I*.   The guilty one was *it*.
The guilty one was *you*.   The guilty ones were *who*?
The guilty one was *he*.   The guilty ones were *we*.
The guilty one was *she*.   The guilty ones were *they*.

If you do not understand this, study the linking verb in **2** and subjective complements in **3**.

Practice choosing the subject pronoun in these sentences.

1. My sisters are all older than (I, me) am.
2. (He, Him) was my best friend.
3. (They, Them) left when (we, us) did.
4. It was (she, her) that tried to meet us.
5. The best players were (them, they).

ANSWERS

1. I   2. He   3. They, we   4. she   5. they

If you missed any, review the lesson and do the next exercise. Follow the directions for the last exercise.

1. The seniors did anything that (they, them) wanted to.
2. (He, Him) went swimming.
3. The one who got hurt was (she, her).
4. (We, Us) went to White Bear Lake.
5. (I, Me) lived in sight of Camelback Mountain.

ANSWERS

1. they   2. He   3. she   4. We   5. I

Objective Case

PROBLEM

When should the object pronoun be used?

SOLUTION

The object pronoun is used as an object of any sort in a sentence—as a direct object, an indirect object, or an object of a preposition. Study each of these kinds of objects carefully, and remember that *m* marks several of the most difficult object pronouns.

The direct object receives the action of an action verb. It answers the question *what?* after an action verb.

Jim hit _____ .

A pronoun filling this blank must be an object pronoun, for it is the direct object of the verb *hit*.

Jim hit *me*.   Jim hit *it*.
Jim hit *you*.   Jim hit *whom?*
Jim hit *him*.   Jim hit *us*.
Jim hit *her*.   Jim hit *them*.

You can study more about direct objects in **2** and **3**.

The indirect object also receives action from a verb, but it is not the thing acted upon. Instead, it is the thing to or for whom the action is done.

Sue sent _____ a letter.

The verb *sent* gives its action to *letter*, the direct object. But the blank indicates the place where we tell *to whom* the letter was sent. This is the place for the indirect object. Again, we must use the object form of the pronoun.

Sue sent *me* a letter.   Sue sent *it* a letter.
Sue sent *you* a letter.   Sue sent *whom* a letter?
Sue sent *him* a letter.   Sue sent *us* a letter
Sue sent *her* a letter.   Sue sent *them* a letter.

The handbook tells about the indirect object in **2** and **3**.

Finally, the object pronoun is used as object of the preposition.

Ellen went with _____ .
        (preposition)

A preposition is a word showing the relation of a noun or pronoun to the rest of the sentence. That noun or pronoun is its object. Any pronoun object must be in object form.

Ellen went with *me*.   Ellen went with *it*.
Ellen went with *you*.   Ellen went with *whom?*
Ellen went with *him*.   Ellen went with *us*.
Ellen went with *her*.   Ellen went with *them*.

A list of prepositions is in **2**, which also discusses objects of prepositions.

Practice choosing object pronouns in these sentences.

1. My relative gave (I, me) presents after graduation.

2. Hal asked (she, her) to the dance.
3. Pam needs (he, him) to help with her grammar.
4. I talked to (them, they).
5. The others went into the theater in front of (we, us).

ANSWERS

1. me   2. her   3. him   4. them   5. us

If you missed any, review the lesson and do the next exercise. Follow the directions for the last exercise.

1. They cruised around talking to (we, us).
2. The youth leader usually goes with (they, them).
3. Andy is very understanding about (I, me).
4. His son respects (he, him) very much.
5. Then Ann pitched (she, her) a slow ball.

ANSWERS

1. us   2. them   3. me   4. him   5. her

who/whom   **PROBLEM**

It is especially hard to choose between *who* and *whom*. This is partly because the sentences in which they are used often change the usual sentence word order. *Who* or *whom* may begin a sentence that asks a question.

Whom	do	you	want?
(object)	(verb)	(subject)	(verb)
Who	is going	with you?	
(subject)	(verb)		

They may show a relationship within a sentence:

I know	whom	you	mean.
	(object)	(subject)	(verb)
He is the one	who	is	angry.
	(subject)	(verb)	
I found out	for	whom	the letter was sent.
	(prep.)	(object)	(subject) (verb)

SOLUTION

Think about the use of *who* or *whom* in the whole sentence. Turn a question into an answer.

Whom do you want?
You do want *whom*?

Separate the relationship set up by *who* or *whom* from the rest of the sentence. Then turn the sentence around into subject-verb-complement order.

I know *whom you mean.*

you	mean	whom
(subject)	(verb)	(object)

Study word order in **3** if you have trouble with this.

He is the one *who is angry.*

who	is	angry
(subject)	(verb)	(predicate adjective)

Remember that the object form of this pronoun, *whom*, is marked by *m* like *him, them,* and *me*. Use *whom* where one of these other *m* pronouns fits.

You do want _____ .
You do want hi*m*, *me*, the*m*
            so
You do want who*m*?

Turn the sentence around into normal subject-verb-complement order if this helps you. Then underline the accepted form of the pronoun.

1. The students (who, whom) went were late.
2. The students (who, whom) he met seemed friendly.
3. (Who, Whom) did you see?
4. (Whom, Who) sent flowers?
5. She is the one (whom, who) you gave it to.

ANSWERS

1. who   2. whom   3. Whom   4. Who   5. whom

If you missed any, review the lesson and do the next exercise. Follow the directions for the last exercise.

1. When people call me Robin, I do not know (who, whom) they are speaking to.
2. Now I am sure about (who, whom) I want to spend my life with.
3. He wanted to know (who, whom) went.
4. (Who, Whom) were the losers?
5. He would never let (whoever, whomever) he was with out of his sight.

ANSWERS

1. whom   2. whom   3. who   4. Who   5. whomever

compounds   **PROBLEM**

In some sentences pronouns are joined to other pronouns and to nouns by *and*. This makes a correct choice harder.

Jerry and I went.

The ball hit Jerry and me.

SOLUTION

Think about how the pronoun you must decide about is used in the sentence without the noun or pronoun to which it is joined.

Jerry and I went.
(compound subject)

Jerry went, and I went.
(*not* Jerry went, and me went.
not Jerry and me went.)

You and I are selected.
(compound subject)

You are selected, and I am selected.
(*not* You are selected, and me am selected.
not You and me are selected.)

The ball hit Jerry and me.
            (compound subject)

The ball hit Jerry, and the ball hit me.
(*not* The ball hit Jerry, and the ball hit I.
(*not* The ball hit Jerry and I.)

This is between you and me.
        (compound object of preposition)

This is between you and between me.
(*not* This is between you, and this is between I.
not This is between you and I.)

Underline the correct pronoun for each of the following choices by asking how it is used. Do not think about the noun or pronoun to which it is joined by *and*. Cover the word joined if this helps you.

1. I would have the dog living with me if my father-in-law and (he, him) were not inseparable.
2. My family and (I, me) lived close to a little country store.
3. My father built my sisters and (I, me) a playhouse.
4. The environment here is healthier for my family and (I, me).
5. A child's parents direct (he, him) or (she, her) toward success.

ANSWERS

1. he   2. I   3. me   4. me   5. him, her

If you missed any, review the lesson above and do the next exercise. Follow the directions for the last exercise.

1. After the game is over, (she, her) and (I, me) throw the ball some.
2. It was important to me that (he, him) and my cousin liked each other.
3. On June 11, 1977, four friends and (I, me) went to Daytona.
4. My brother and (I, me) go deer hunting together.
5. No one cooks dinner for my roommate and (I, me).

ANSWERS

1. she, I   2. he   3. I   4. I   5. me

Possessive Case

PROBLEM

We add an apostrophe (') and *s* to the end of a noun or indefinite pronoun to show that it owns something, that it is possessive.

boy's book
anyone's book

But many pronouns have their own special form to show that they own something.

his book (not *he's* book)

These pronouns should *not* have an apostrophe and *s* added to show that they own things.

SOLUTION

Learn the possessive (owning) pronouns that do not add apostrophe and *s*, and use them to show ownership.

my book	our book
your book	your book
his book	their book
her book	whose book
its book	

If the thing owned is not named after the pronoun, some of the possessive pronouns have still another form.

The book is *mine*.	The book is *ours*.
The book is *yours*.	The book is *yours*.
The book is *hers*.	The book is *theirs*.

Do not use an apostrophe with any of these pronouns to show ownership. Study this in **10** if you need to.

Fill the blanks with the correct possessive form of the pronoun in parentheses.

1. (I) I said, "Is this _____ radio?"
2. (who) She has one brother, _____ name is Mark.
3. (she) That horse is _____ .
4. (they) _____ house burned to the ground in three hours.

ANSWERS

1. my   2. whose   3. hers   4. Their

If you missed any, review the lesson and do the next exercise. Follow the directions for the last exercise.

1. (he) That is the pride of _____ wardrobe.
2. (you) Don't forget _____ old friend.
3. (we) The winning side was _____ .
4. (who) _____ car is parked out front?

ANSWERS

1. his   2. your   3. ours   4. Whose

possessives versus contractions

COMPLICATION

Forms of these pronouns do use an apostrophe in contractions. A contraction is a shorter way of writing two words by putting them together and leaving out one or more letters.

it is = it's (contraction)

It is easy to confuse these contractions with the possessive pronouns of the same form.

SOLUTION

Study the most confusing of these pronouns.

Possessives	Contractions
your	you're (you are)
its	it's (it is, it has)
their	they're (they are)
whose	who's (who is, who has)

Notice that the contractions always mean two words—a subject and a verb. If you mean these two words, use the apostrophe or write the words out without contracting. But if you mean that the pronoun owns something, do not use the apostrophe.

> *Its* tail is striped. (possessive)
> *It's* a raccoon. (contraction for *it is*)

Write in the blank the correct form of the pronoun in parentheses.

1. (they) I am interested in stories about ghosts and _____ habits.
2. (it) After the song ended, she remembered _____ melody.
3. (who) I know the man _____ mother you met.
4. (you) Don't tell me that _____ leaving.

ANSWERS

1. their
2. its
3. whose
4. you're *or* you are

If you missed any, review the lesson and do the next exercise. Follow the directions for the last exercise.

1. (who) _____ your teacher?
2. (they) I like _____ style of singing.
3. (you) _____ a good friend.
4. (it) He studied the game and _____ tricks.

ANSWERS

1. Who's *or* Who is
2. their
3. You're *or* You are
4. its

possessives before gerunds

PROBLEM

A gerund is a verb form used as a noun.

> A *party* is fun.
>   (noun)

> *Going to parties* is fun.
>   (gerund)

Sometimes a pronoun is related to the gerund as a subject is to a verb and as a possessive is to the thing owned. What case is needed for the pronoun here?

SOLUTION

If a pronoun owns a gerund, the pronoun must be in possessive form, just as it would be for any noun.

His party is fun.
His going to parties is fun.

See **3** if you need to study more about gerunds.

Practice using the possessive before gerunds by writing in the blank the correct form of the pronoun in parentheses.

1. (I) The instructor praised _____ writing.
2. (he) _____ cracking his knuckles annoys me.
3. (you) I admire _____ dancing.

ANSWERS

1. my   2. His   3. your

If you missed any, review the lesson and do the next exercise. Follow the directions for the last exercise.

1. (they) We appreciated _____ giving us help.
2. (she) She practiced _____ swimming.
3. (it) The fan stopped _____ turning all at once.

ANSWERS

1. their   2. her   3. its

Reflexive Pronouns The reflexive form repeats or reflects the subject of a sentence. It ends in *self* or *selves* and always means the same as the subject just given. The handbook discusses it in **10**.

PROBLEM

Some writers incorrectly use *myself* when they mean *I* or *me*.

You could consider *myself* a settled family man.
    (incorrect)

Mary and *myself* were the only ones there.
    (incorrect)

The *self, selves* forms are always reflecting or repeating the subject. So they cannot correctly be subjects themselves. And they must always mean the same person as the subject.

SOLUTION

Say or write *myself* only when you have already just used *I* as the subject.

I hit *myself* with the bat.
I *myself* hit that home run.

If *I* was not the subject of the sentence, use *me*.

You could consider *me* a settled family man.

If the pronoun you need is the subject, use *I*.

Mary and *I* were the only ones there.

Underline the correct pronoun in each choice.

1. My wife and (I, me, myself) went to New Orleans, Louisiana, on our vacation this year.
2. Mechanical engineering will give (I, me, myself) and my family security.
3. (I, Me, Myself) along with everyone else in my group thought that he was a sissy.
4. Last, there is (I, me, myself).

ANSWERS

1. I (subject)
2. me (object)
3. I ((subject)
4. I (subjective complement)

If you missed any, review the lesson and do the exercise below. Underline the correct pronoun in each choice.

1. Today, he writes better than (I, me, myself).
2. I find (I, me, myself) a football game and a snack.
3. My boyfriend and (I, me, myself) will stay home and watch the movie together.

ANSWERS

1. I (subject of *write*, understood)
2. myself (repeating subject I)
3. I (subject)

PROBLEM

A writer sometimes does not know whether to say *self* or *selves* after a pronoun.

SOLUTION

The *self* form of the pronoun means one; *selves* means more than one. You need to write *self* if you are talking about or to only one (*myself, yourself, himself, herself, itself, oneself*). If you mean more than one, you need to write *selves* after the pronoun (*ourselves, yourselves, themselves*).

Underline the accepted pronoun forms for the following sentences

1. The baby birds taught (themself, themselves) to fly.
2. Mary, seat (yourself, yourselves) where you can see.
3. Students, seat (yourself, yourselves) where you like.

ANSWERS

1. themselves
2. yourself
3. yourselves

PROBLEM

Many people add *self* to the wrong forms of *he* and *they*. They say and write *hisself* and *theirselves*. But this is not accepted usage.

SOLUTION

Instead of *hisself* or *theirselves*, say and write *himself* and *themselves*.

Underline the accepted form of the pronoun in each choice.

1. He does not often let (hisself, himself) be open with others.
2. He always drives (hisself, himself).
3. They only hurt (theirselves, themselves).
4. They (theirselves, themselves) asked me to.

ANSWERS

1. himself
2. himself
3. themselves
4. themselves

If you missed any, review the lesson and do the next exercise. Follow the directions for the last exercise.

1. They tried to build their house (theirselves, themselves).
2. He was not happy about the job (hisself, himself).
3. He tired (hisself, himself) out on the first lap.
4. The family tried to keep it to (theirselves, themselves).

ANSWERS

1. themselves
2. himself
3. himself
4. themselves.

Now do the post-test on the next page.

<u>NAME</u>

36. PRONOUN CASE

Post-Test A

Underline the accepted pronoun for each choice.

1. She always stays with (whoever, whomever) she is with.
2. (He, Him) and his girlfriend had already left.
3. Many people confuse (theirself, themself, theirselves, themselves) about their daydreams and their memories.
4. The children bought it for my husband and (I, me).
5. Love of the wild makes this story and (I, me, myself) one and the same.
6. Being together is very important to (them, them).
7. Fred and (I, me, myself) skipped class when we had a substitute.
8. I don't know (who, whom) did it.
9. The dog knew (it, its, it's) own pup.
10. She was hurt by (me, my) lying to her.

Ask your instructor to check your post-test, or turn it in.

See sentence parts in **1**, pronouns in **2**, the sentence in **3**, pronoun forms in **10**, gerunds in **3**, contractions and possessives in **48** or **50**, Post-test B, or writing assignments in **54–56**.

NAME _____

36. PRONOUN CASE

Post-Test B

Underline the accepted pronoun for each choice.

1. My friend and (I, me, myself) are in the adult class.
2. (Who, Whom) do you call when you and your boyfriend break up?
3. I met a girl there, and (she, her) and (I, me, myself) became good friends.
4. Many of my friends (who, whom) have graduated before me are attending State College.
5. He carries (hisself, himself) so that people respect his size.
6. A young animal reflects the emotion of (it, its, it's) parents.
7. (She, Her) often invited us.
8. We bought it for (ourself, ourselves).
9. She grew up with (he, him).
10. They gave the test to Julie and (I, me, myself).

Ask your instructor to check your answers.

Punctuation

37. THE SEMICOLON

Pretest

Put semicolons in the following sentences where they are necessary. Some sentences may need none.

1. She caught a snook it weighed four pounds, seven ounces.
2. If I had left home to go to Tech, I might have lost my girlfriend.
3. I went to see who was banging on the door, I saw Bobby holding a little ground squirrel like a baby kitten.
4. I don't understand this since dogs are color-blind, however, he attacked anyone wearing blue.
5. I had planned to be a registered nurse now the field is hard to get into.
6. The second day was a little better, it was cloudy but without rain.
7. To me Roy Acuff is not only a star he is also a friend.
8. I drive a tow motor, some people call it a fork lift.
9. She has a big family, two sisters and five brothers.
10. They like to play football, many times they play till dark.

ANSWERS

Semicolons are correct *only* where shown here.

1. She caught a snook; it weighed four pounds, seven ounces.
2. Correct as written.
3. I went to see who was banging on the door; I saw Bobby . . . .
4. I don't understand this since dogs are color-blind; however, he attacked anyone wearing blue.
5. I had planned to be a registered nurse; now the field is hard to get into.
6. The second day was a little better; it was cloudy but without rain.
7. To me Roy Acuff is not only a star; he is also a friend.
8. I drive a tow motor; some people call it a fork lift.
9. Correct as written.
10. They like to play football; many times they play till dark.

If you missed any, study the following unit.

37 The Semicolon

Sometimes two complete statements are closely related to each other in thought and seem to belong in the same sentence. But they must still be separated from each other so that the reader knows where one statement stops and the next starts.

> In CB language a "Tijuana taxi" is a wrecker.
> "Hammer" refers to the accelerator. (two complete statements in separate sentences)

A semicolon between the two statements can separate them in the same way that a period and capital letter can separate.

> In CB language a "Tijuana taxi" is a wrecker; "hammer" refers to the accelerator. (complete statements separated by a semicolon)

The semicolon (;) is made up of a period on top of a comma. It may be helpful to think of the parts of the semicolon this way. The period separates the complete statements. The comma says that the statements are related to each other. Use a semicolon to separate two complete statements that are closely related. Do not use a capital letter to start the second statement unless it is a new sentence.

Note: It is also correct to separate these sentences with periods and capital letters.

> Do Not Use A Semicolon Unless You Could Use A Period.

Comma Splice

PROBLEM

A comma instead of a semicolon (or period) cannot separate complete statements. Using a comma between two complete statements makes a comma splice, a confusing error.

> I do like cold weather, it puts me in the Christmas spirit. (a comma splice)

SOLUTION

Use a semicolon (or a period and capital letter) between complete statements instead of a comma.

> I do like cold weather; it puts me in the Christmas spirit. (correct)

More work on comma splices is in **26**.

Put semicolons (or periods and capitals) between complete statements in the following.

1. It was a most enjoyable trip, we had good weather and beautiful beaches.
2. When people play tricks on Jake, he does not get angry, he just laughs with them.
3. The Marantz cost a hundred dollars more, theis was an important factor.

ANSWERS

Periods and capitals instead of semicolons are also correct. No changes except these shown should be made.

1. It was a most enjoyable <u>trip; we</u> had good weather and beautiful beaches.
2. When people play tricks on Jake, he does not get <u>angry; he</u> just laughs with them.
3. The Marantz cost a hundred dollars <u>more; this</u> was an important factor.

If you missed any, review the lesson and do the next exercise. Follow the directions for the last exercise.

1. I do not hate English, I just do not like it.
2. My name is Evelyn Anderson, I was born at Ogunquit, Maine.
3. The view is magnificent, I can see three counties from my front porch.

ANSWERS

1. I do not hate <u>English; I</u> just do not like it.
2. My name is Evelyn <u>Anderson; I</u> was born at Ogunquit, Maine.
3. The view is <u>magnificent; I</u> can see three counties from my front porch.

Fusion **PROBLEM**

Putting no separation at all between complete statements makes a more confusing error called a *fusion*.

This is how I get along with my best friends we try to be honest with each other all the time. (a fusion)

SOLUTION

Put a semicolon (or period and capital letter) between complete statements.

This is how I get along with my best friends<u>;</u> we try to be honest with each other all the time. (correct)

More work on fusions is in **25**.

Put semicolons (or periods and capital letters) between complete statements in the following.

1. I took a trip last year during the snow months it was a very good trip.
2. She already has a guitar book all she needs now is a guitar.
3. When pulling out, some drivers do not turn into the first lane they will turn out all the way into the second lane.

ANSWERS

Periods and capitals instead of semicolons are also correct. No changes except those shown should be made.

1. I took a trip last year during the snow <u>months; it</u> was a very good trip.
2. She already has a guitar <u>book; all</u> she needs now is a guitar.
3. When pulling out, some drivers do not turn into the first <u>lane; they</u> will turn . . . .

If you missed any, review the lesson and do the next exercise. Follow the directions for the last exercise.

1. Many young people are like me they get homesick when they leave home.
2. These people do not even know that they are tailgating that is what makes it so dangerous.
3. The gift itself is not important it is the love behind it.

ANSWERS

1. Many young people are like <u>me; they</u> get homesick when they leave home.
2. These people do not even know that they are <u>tailgating; that</u> is what makes it so dangerous.
3. The gift itself is not <u>important; it</u> is the love behind it.

Conjunctive Adverbs in Fusions and Comma Splices

COMPLICATION

Words such as *accordingly*, *also*, *besides*, *then*, *therefore*, and *however* are mistaken for conjunctions when they come between two main clauses. These words, which are called conjunctive adverbs, cannot separate complete statements. If a semicolon or a period is not used before them, they are fusions or comma splices.

WRONG: Fire coral makes painful welts wherever it scratches the skin however, cortisone soothes the pain. (a fusion)

WRONG: Fire coral makes painful welts wherever it scratches the skin, however, cortisone soothes the pain. (a comma splice)

SOLUTION

Put a semicolon (;) or a period and capital letter before the conjunctive adverb that comes between two complete statements.

CORRECT: Fire coral makes painful welts wherever it scratches the skin; however, cortisone soothes the pain.

Use the list that follows to learn some of the most commonly used conjunctive adverbs.

also	moreover	second (third, and so on)
besides	nevertheless	then (or another time word)
consequently	next	therefore
however	plus	

Be sure to put semicolons before each of these conjunctive adverbs when they are used between complete statements. Study this more in **25** and **26** if you need to.

Put semicolons where they are needed in the following sentences.

1. My friend was flying in from Philadelphia then we were to go to the all-star game.
2. I love my parents however, I don't want to stay at home the rest of my life.
3. We come home and eat a big dinner, after that, we play games or watch television.

ANSWERS

1. My friend planned to fly in from Philadelphia; then we were to go to the all-star game.
2. I love my parents; however, I don't want to stay at home the rest of my life.
3. We come home and eat a big dinner; after that, we play games or watch television.

If you missed any, review the lesson and do the next exercise. Follow the directions for the last exercise.

1. At first I was nervous about coming to college now I enjoy it.
2. Hugh worked alone, therefore, he could usually do as he pleased.
3. Chicago has many more advantages in recreation and education, however, I still prefer St. Charles for its living conditions.

ANSWERS

1. At first I was nervous about coming to college; now I enjoy it.
2. Hugh worked alone; therefore, he could usually do as he pleased.
3. Chicago has many more advantages in recreation and education; however, I still prefer St. Charles for its living conditions.

Now do the post-test on the next page.

37. THE SEMICOLON
Post-Test A

Put semicolons (or periods and capitals) between complete statements in the following. Some sentences may be correct as written.

1. Our record is 0–6 that means we have lost every game.
2. I saw many blackbirds fly up from the snow, they looked like oil spurting out.
3. I learned it was more fun to party than to study, consequently, I was placed on academic suspension.
4. Flash Cadillac does not write its own songs it uses hits of the past.
5. Before I knew it, I was standing up on the skis.
6. Riding a bike feels like complete freedom then someone pulls out in front of me and scares me half to death.
7. Some students major in playing cards others spend their time on the beach.
8. The movie had colorful scenery the plot was simple and to the point.
9. Our daughters were three years apart in age, consequently June gave me Phyllis's clothes for Brenda.
10. If God did appear to one of us, what would we do?

Ask your instructor to check this, or turn it in.

See the sentence core in **3**, phrases in **4**, clauses in **5**, compound sentences in **6**, semicolons in **14**, fusions in **25**, comma splices in **26**, Post-test B, and writing assignments in **54–56**.

NAME _____

37. THE SEMICOLON

Post-Test B

Put semicolons (or periods and capitals) between complete statements in the following.

1. He was a huge dog, many people were afraid of him.
2. The gas mileage is very reasonable, however, the oil changing is average.
3. My favorite team is the Green Bay Packers, they always play to win.
4. To know why someone acts a certain way, we must know something about his background.
5. Next quarter is going to be really hard I have more hours and more difficult subjects.
6. He means a great deal to me that is why I wrote the letter.
7. Al was a professional thief who was caught and put in jail then the government used him to steal for it.
8. This is where the fun begins, John is supposed to tell society that God has a message for them.
9. I am studying business administration I hope that someday I will own my own business.
10. When the rain starts, I get depressed.

Ask your instructor to check this, or turn it in.

NAME

38. THE COMMA

Pretest

In the following sentences, correct all errors in comma use, adding commas that are needed. Some sentences may need no commas.

1. My family is like the average family and we have our share of good and bad.
2. We live in the country and have a nice home which sits on an acre lot at the end of a dead-end street.
3. Its location is one thing that makes it desirable.
4. There are no houses behind us so we have a pleasant view.
5. Generally speaking Sundays are the best days at our house.
6. When you get up early on a spring morning and look out through the tall bright green trees at the cows grazing it's really beautiful.
7. Starting just a little later than other mornings Sundays are different all day.
8. We have a built-in alarm clock one about two feet tall.
9. She is thorough, not gentle.
10. The kids jump on the bed ride my back and scream in my ear.
11. We are sure to find almost everything for breakfast: eggs coffee juice home-made biscuits bacon and gravy.
12. My daughter Julie who is two usually spills her milk.
13. Then Jason complains that he doesn't like eggs.
14. "Turn down the stereo" my wife tells me "so that it won't sound like a 'honky-tonk' in here."
15. Then Julie gets down; consequently I scold her and tell her to finish her breakfast.
16. After supper I hunt for a relaxing entertaining television program.
17. Julie falls asleep and breathes so quietly that I feel her pulse to be sure she is alive.
18. My wife says "Who could believe she just hit her brother?"
19. When Sunday ends the feeling I have is regret.
20. Our address is 2130 Sunset Lane Hendersonville Tennessee 37075.
21. We moved here on August 30, 1972.
22. We have enjoyed the pleasant friendly neighborhood ever since.
23. I do however miss the bustle of city life.
24. I like a city's excitement not its stress.
25. If I could have both excitement and peace that would be perfect!

Check your answers. Mark the number at the end of any sentence that you missed.

ANSWERS

1. My family is like the average family, and we have our share of good and bad. **(38)**
2. We live in the country and have a nice home, which sits on an acre lot at the end of a dead-end street. **(43)**
3. Its location is one thing that makes it desirable. **(43)**
4. There are no houses behind us, so we have a pleasant view. **(38)**
5. Generally speaking, Sundays are the best days at our house. **(44)**
6. When you get up early on a spring morning and look out through the green trees at the cows grazing, it's really beautiful. **(39)**
7. Starting just a little later than other mornings, Sundays are different all day. **(40)**
8. We have a built-in alarm clock, one about two feet tall. **(43)**
9. She is thorough, not gentle. **(45)**
10. The kids jump on the bed, ride my back, and scream in my ear. **(41)**
11. We are sure to find almost everything for breakfast: eggs, coffee, juice, home-made biscuits, bacon, and gravy. **(41)**
12. My daughter Julie, who is two, usually spills her milk. **(43)**
13. Then Jason complains that he doesn't like eggs. **(46)**
14. "Turn down the stereo," my wife tells me, "so that it won't sound like a 'honky-tonk' in here." **(46)**
15. Then Julie gets down; consequently, I scold her and tell her to finish her breakfast. **(44)**
16. After supper I hunt for a relaxing, entertaining television program. **(42)**
17. Julie falls asleep and breathes so quietly that I feel her pulse to be sure she is alive. **(38)**
18. My wife says, "Who could believe she just hit her brother?" **(46)**
19. When Sunday ends, the feeling I have is regret. **(39)**
20. Our address is 2130 Sunset Lane, Hendersonville, Tennessee 37075. **(47)**
21. We moved here on August 30, 1972. **(47)**
22. We have enjoyed the pleasant, friendly neighborhood ever since. **(42)**
23. I do, however, miss the bustle of city life. **(44)**
24. I like a city's excitement, not its stress. **(45)**
25. If I could have both excitement and peace, that would be perfect! **(39)**

The numbers after the Pretest Answers are keyed to different lessons on comma use. Check in the block below beside the number or numbers that are at the end of any sentence that you missed above. Then do the lessons that have those numbers. For example, if you missed number 20 above, you should check number 2 in the Assignment Block and work lesson number 2.

If, in addition to the commas given in the Pretest Answers, you have added other commas, circle them and show them to your instructor.

Assignment Block

(38)_____   (39)_____   (40)_____

(41)_____   (42)_____   (43)_____

(44)_____   (45)_____   (46)_____

(47)_____

---

38 Commas Between Main Clauses

PROBLEM

Sometimes a sentence has two main clauses that are made up of two independent thoughts. These thoughts, though related, are independent in structure.

We like sports, and we plan to attend all the games.
(s) (v)   (s) (v)

We like sports. We plan to attend all the games.
(s) (v)   (s) (v)

SOLUTION

Two main clauses may be separated within one sentence by a comma and a coordinating conjunction. The coordinating conjunctions are *and, but, or, nor, for,* and sometimes *so* and *yet*. The first sentence above shows how the two main clauses may be separated this way within one sentence.

COMPLICATION

A coordinating conjunction may join structures that are not independent. Then no comma is needed.

We like sports and plan to attend all the games.

The verbs *like* and *plan* are joined by the coordinating conjunction *and* in the example. Because the verbs share the subject *we*, they are not independent main clauses. No comma is needed.
Study this model.

Independent thought	,	and but or nor for	Independent thought.

Write C before any of the following sentences that are punctuated correctly. Place a W before any that need commas; then add the commas.

_____ 1. She feels that Carter has been a good governor and has helped Georgia.

_____ 2. I know how to judge a good farm or a good house and I enjoy selling.

_____ 3. I like to research the records and find out who has owned the property.

_____ 4. He enjoys farming, and he finds it profitable.

ANSWERS

1. C
2. W—I know how to judge a good farm or a good house, and I enjoy selling.
3. C
4. C

If you missed any, review the lesson and do the next exercise. Follow the directions for the last exercise.

_____ 1. We now raise corn, beans, and tobacco and we hope to start a dairy herd.

_____ 2. I am married but have no children.

_____ 3. We have enjoyed the location and the neighbors.

_____ 4. He joined the service for all the wrong reasons.

ANSWERS

1. W—We now raise corn, beans, and tobacco, and we hope to start a dairy herd.
2. C
3. C
4. C

Now do the post-test.

NAME

38. COMMAS BETWEEN MAIN CLAUSES
Post-Test

Place commas between coordinating conjunctions in the sentences that need them.

1. We have been married four years and have two children.
2. The interior is a solid blue and is decorated with small plastic balls.
3. Some people think Mr. Johnson is hard on them but they find out he is just doing his job.
4. She has had this cat a long time and loves it very much.
5. He is only three years old but counts to ten very well.
6. He has short black hair and black mustache.
7. I have no clothes to change for the airline lost my luggage.
8. Sometimes she wears eye shadow and a bit of lipstick.
9. Carver found a tiny cottage on the edge of town and he opened a small hand laundry.
10. Using an electric mixer is easier and saves time.

Ask your instructor to check these answers, or turn them in.

See the sentence core in **3**, compound sentences in **5** and **6**, the general post-test after **47**, and writing assignments in **54–56**.

39 Commas After Introductory Clauses

PROBLEM

Some sentences have an independent structure (main clause) and a dependent structure (a structure that cannot stand alone as a sentence and, therefore, depends on the main clause to make sense).

Because we like sports, we plan to attend all the games.

This sentence is made up of one independent thought (main clause) and one dependent thought (dependent clause).

We plan to attend all the games.
(independent thought—main clause)

because we like sports
(dependent thought—dependent clause)

SOLUTION

The independent thought (main clause) is separated from the dependent thought (dependent clause) with a comma if the dependent thought is introductory (comes first). The comma is placed where the dependent thought ends and the independent thought begins. Words like *if, because, when, as, while,* and *after* introduce dependent clauses. A fuller list of these is in **2**.

Dependent clause	,	Independent clause.

Apply this solution to the following sentences by placing commas after introductory dependent clauses.

1. Because it rained so hard I was late getting to class.
2. When the earthquake hit we were asleep.
3. As the lightning crackled red fire danced around the pole.
4. While I was in high school I was a member of the Future Farmers of America.

ANSWERS

1. Because it rained so hard, I was late getting to class.
2. When the earthquake hit, we were asleep.
3. As the lightning crackled, red fire danced around the pole.
4. While I was in high school, I was a member of the Future Farmers of America.

If you missed any, review the lesson and do the next exercise. Follow the directions for the last exercise.

1. If Linda had had any sense she would have dropped him.

2. After he died he was buried in a borrowed grave.
3. If you do your camping trip will be much more trouble free.
4. As soon as he lands he starts to chatter.

ANSWERS

1. If Linda had had any sense, she would have dropped him.
2. After he died, he was buried in a borrowed grave.
3. If you do, your camping trip will be much more trouble-free.
4. As soon as he lands, he starts to chatter.

COMPLICATION

In some sentences, the dependent clause is not introductory. It comes after the main idea, and no comma is needed to separate. The word introducing the dependent clause separates it from the main idea.

We plan to attend all games   because   we like sports.

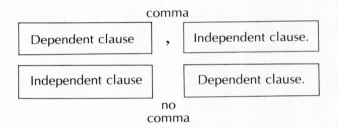

Write C before the following sentences that are correct. Write W before any that need commas, and add the needed commas.

_____ 1. My mind stopped wandering as they called my name.

_____ 2. Since we moved in we have had nothing but trouble.

_____ 3. We went to eat after we all rested a little

_____ 4. If she does not get that fixed it will wear out.

ANSWERS

1. C
2. W—Since we moved in, we have had nothing but trouble.
3. C
4. W—If she does not get that fixed, it will wear out.

If you missed any, review the lesson and do the next exercise. Follow the directions for the last exercise.

_____ 1. A golfer will hit a bad shot if he loses his concentration.

_____ 2. I need to work during the day although I have not found a job yet.

———— 3. I do not mind composition because I enjoy writing.

———— 4. When we are late we must go to the office for a note.

ANSWERS

1. C
2. C
3. C
4. W—When we are late, we must go to the office for a note.

Now do the post-test.

NAME

39. COMMAS AFTER INTRODUCTORY CLAUSES
Post-Test

Place commas where they are needed to set off an introductory adverb clause.

1. If he gets in we have a hard time getting him out.
2. When I walk in the yard Toby jumps up on me.
3. Malcolm is sometimes late for class because he does not have a car.
4. After Christie left Bob called his friends to get advice.
5. Anytime I needed her she was there.
6. Although we begged Mother refused to change her mind.
7. You are educated in some way even if you never went to school.
8. Uncle would freshen up the conversation if it ever turned stale.
9. Because he enjoys children he really does not mind the baby-sitting.
10. When they roughhouse his grandmother gets alarmed.

Ask your instructor to check this, or turn it in.

See clauses in **5**, comma charts in **15**, the general post-test after **47**, and writing assignments in **54–56**.

40 Commas After Introductory Phrases

PROBLEM

Sometimes a phrase (a group of words without a subject and predicate) begins a sentence. A phrase is always dependent.

From the hardwood forests of the Cumberland Mountains in Tennessee, state rangers report a rumor about the existence of a strange animal called the "whirling whimpus."

When the phrase is long like the one above, a comma before the main clause makes reading easier. Sometimes a comma before the main clause is *necessary* to prevent misreading.

For something without sex life presents unique problems.

For something without sex, life presents unique problems.

SOLUTION

After a long introductory phrase, use a comma before the main clause.

In the sentences below, place commas after the introductory phrases.

1. Along a walk of singular beauty bath houses were constructed.
2. In the first New England duel servants of the same master fought.
3. After the very long winter with its bitter storms we were glad to see spring.

ANSWERS

1. Along a walk of singular beauty, bath houses were constructed.
2. In the first New England duel, servants of the same master fought.
3. After the very long winter with its bitter storms, we were glad to see spring.

If you missed any, review the lesson and do the next exercise.

Place commas after the introductory phrases.

1. At the house of my mother's cousin and his wife I found the runaways.
2. With all of this trouble out of one small car it seems to be a genuine lemon.
3. At the very last possible minute before take-off we boarded the plane.

ANSWERS

1. At the house of my mother's cousin and his wife, I found the runaways.
2. With all of this trouble out of one small car, it seems to be a genuine lemon.
3. At the very last possible minute before take-off, we boarded the plane.

PROBLEM

Certain kinds of introductory phrases are especially confusing. These are phrases that have verbals in them (gerunds, participles, and infinitives). A verbal is a verb form used as some other part of speech. These are discussed in **3**. A comma is always needed after an introductory verbal modifying phrase to separate it from the main clause.

> After *leaving* the camp, woodsmen disappear and are never seen again.   (gerund)
>
> *Making* a droning sound, the whimpus whirls on its hind legs until it becomes invisible.   (participle)
>
> *To obtain* food, the whimpus stations himself on the trail and traps his victims.   (infinitive)

SOLUTION

After an introductory modifying phrase that has a verb form, use a comma before the main clause.

Put commas where they are needed in these sentences.

1. In a little village known as Rix Mills Agnes Morehead was born.
2. Disapproving of modern machines the Amish still live simple lives.
3. Scarred by the fire the warehouse reminded me of the arsonist's threats.

ANSWERS

1. In a little village known as Rix Mills, Agnes Morehead was born.
2. Disapproving of modern machines, the Amish still live simple lives.
3. Scarred by the fire, the warehouse reminded me of the arsonist's threats.

If you missed any, review the lesson, study **3**, and do the next exercise. Follow the directions for the last exercise.

1. Carrying the eggs in a box she walked carefully up the steps.
2. Burdened by the wet snow the limbs of the hemlock bent to the ground.
3. To get to the big rock ledges we climbed for hours.

ANSWERS

1. Carrying the eggs in a box, she walked carefully up the steps.
2. Burdened by the wet snow, the limbs of the hemlock bent to the ground.
3. To get to the big rock ledges, we climbed for hours.

COMPLICATION

Sometimes phrases coming at the beginnings of sentences are not modifiers. They act as subjects of the sentence. Compare the two sentences below.

| PHRASE AS SUBJECT: | *Walking to school every day* is good exercise. |
| PHRASE AS MODIFIER: | *Walking to school every day*, he found time to think. |

The comma is used only when the phrase modifies. When the phrase is a necessary part of the main idea of the sentence, do not set it off with commas.

If a sentence needs a comma to set off a verbal phrase that modifies, write W and put in the comma. If the sentence is correct without the comma, write C.

_____ 1. To achieve her aim she would lie.

_____ 2. To achieve her aim is first with Sue.

_____ 3. Wanting the best he refused the job.

_____ 4. Wanting the best is not wrong.

ANSWERS

1. W—To achieve her aim, she would lie.
2. C
3. W—Wanting the best, he refused the job.
4. C

If you missed any, review the lesson, study **3** about the parts of a sentence and **4** about phrases used as parts, and do the next exercise. Follow the directions for the last exercise.

_____ 1. Putting on a false Southern colonial front they ruined the style of their Pennsylvania farmhouse.

_____ 2. Putting on a false Southern colonial front ruined the style of their Pennsylvania farmhouse.

_____ 3. To clean up the block is a good project.

_____ 4. To clean up the block the teenagers worked three weekends.

ANSWERS

1. W—Putting on a false Southern colonial front, they ruined the style of their Pennsylvania farmhouse.
2. C
3. C
4. W—To clean up the block, the teenagers worked three weekends.

COMPLICATION

Short phrases that do not have verbs or verbals are often used at the beginnings of sentences.

1. After awhile Adam awoke.
        or
   After awhile, Adam awoke.

2. In the long run, you were lucky.

3. In accounting, math skills are essential.

4. About Sarah, Jane was uncertain.

5. In the next room John waited.

or

In the next room, John waited.

SOLUTIONS

When no danger of unclear meaning exists, no comma is necessary, but one may be used (see numbers 1 and 5). Sometimes the phrase is not modifying anything in the sentence so much as it is showing the relation between this sentence and something else that has been said. Such transitional phrases are set off with a comma. (See number 2.) Always use a comma if it is necessary to prevent confusion. (See numbers 3 and 4.)

Place commas in these sentences where they are needed.

_____ 1. By looking up the bystander could always see the clock.

_____ 2. On the other hand is a ring.

_____ 3. Looking anxious Maria demanded that we tell her.

_____ 4. To our knowledge this had not happened before.

ANSWERS

1. W—By looking up, the bystander could always see the clock.
2. C
3. W—Looking anxious, Maria demanded that we tell her.
4. C or W—To our knowledge this had not happened before *or* To our knowledge, this had not happened before. Either is correct.

If you missed any, review the lesson and do the next exercise. Follow the directions for the last exercise.

_____ 1. After two months I got the promotion I was hoping for.

_____ 2. After the last game play picks up.

_____ 3. To sum up the situation is good.

_____ 4. Having posted grades by each classroom door the teacher went home.

ANSWERS

1. C or W—After two months, I got the promotion I was hoping for.
2. W—After the last game, play picks up.
3. W—To sum up, the situation is good.
4. W—Having posted grades by each classroom door, the teacher went home.

Now do the post-test.

40. COMMAS AFTER INTRODUCTORY PHRASES
Post-Test

Place commas after the introductory phrases in the following sentences if you think they are needed.

1. During the afternoon our time is our own.
2. While washing up in the bathroom I hear about how unsafe the water supply is.
3. On the other hand Percy is very courteous.
4. To look my best every day is important to me.
5. To change her many methods were employed.
6. After getting out on the highway I found out that it was easier than I had thought it would be.
7. In summary I prefer the atmosphere, the pay, and the goals.
8. Being a middle-aged woman she felt good about learning to play the piano.
9. Most of all Taurus is known for stubbornness.
10. Despite this she manages to find her socks when needed.

Ask your instructor to check this, or turn it in.

See verbals in **3**, phrases in **4**, comma charts in **15**, the general post-test after **47**, or writing assignments in **54–56**.

41 Commas in a List

PROBLEM

Often two or more items are listed in a sentence. These lists may be made up of words, phrases, or clauses.

LISTING WORDS:	We cleaned the swimming <u>pool</u>, the dressing <u>rooms</u>, and the main <u>office</u>.
LISTING PHRASES:	Mordecai enjoyed <u>traveling in his pink hearse</u>, <u>picking up hitchhikers</u>, and <u>talking them to death</u>.
LISTING CLAUSES:	We read that Monday's <u>child</u> <u>is</u> fair of face, that Tuesday's <u>child</u> <u>is</u> full of grace, and that Wednesday's <u>child</u> <u>is</u> loving and giving.

SOLUTION

A comma is placed between words, phrases, or clauses when more than two items are listed. A comma is used before the conjunction (*and, or*) that separates the last two in order to make reading easier and to prevent misreading.

COMPLICATION

When only two items or thoughts are listed, no comma is needed.

We discovered that the grocery had milk and cheese.   (two words)

We packed for the formal affairs and for our own relaxation.   (two phrases)

We know which you like and which you dislike.   (two clauses)

Write C if the following lists need no commas. Write W and put in commas if they are needed.

_____ 1. Jimmie Rogers introduced novel techniques and attracted a lot of followers.

_____ 2. Jimmie Rogers introduced novel techniques styles and variations.

_____ 3. The blues arose out of the miseries of poverty and the injustice of oppression.

_____ 4. The blues arose out of the miseries the injustice and the oppression of the blacks.

ANSWERS:

1. C
2. Jimmie Rogers introduced novel techniques, styles, and variations.
3. C
4. The blues arose out of the miseries, the injustice, and the oppression of the blacks.

If you missed any, review the lesson and do the next exercise. Follow the directions for the last exercise.

_____ 1. Puritan naming practices have been carried over in names such as Charity Prudence Patience Faith and Constance.

_____ 2. The Puritans searched every nook and cranny of the Bible for these names.

_____ 3. I live in the country in a very small neighborhood.

_____ 4. Stories about space adventure show a fantastic world of passage through time robot armies and thought communication.

ANSWERS

1. Puritan naming practices have been carried over in names such as Charity, Prudence, Patience, Faith, and Constance.
2. C
3. C
4. Stories about space adventure show a fantastic world of passage through time, robot armies, and thought communication.

Now do the post-test.

NAME

41. COMMAS IN A LIST
Post-Test

Place commas in the sentences in which *more than two* items, phrases, or clauses are listed.

1. His favorite people were his hair stylist his tailor and the elevator man in his office building.
2. John worked at the rug factory and in the bus depot.
3. We searched in the laundry room in the hall closet and in the attic.
4. He was a protestor who wrote to editors who called senators and who marched in demonstrations.
5. He works in the winter at the ski lodge and in the summer at the beach.
6. Food tools sleeping equipment and a tent are musts in camping.
7. Dr. Ortega has taught practiced medicine and worked for the government.
8. We have to put up with splinters and chips of wood coming off both the desks and the chairs.
9. I went through hollows woods and places I never would have walked.
10. We go visiting have guests in or watch television.

Ask your instructor to check this, or turn it in.

See phrases in **4**, clauses in **5**, comma charts in **15**, the general post-test after **47**, or writing assignments in **54–56**.

42 Commas Between Adjectives

PROBLEM

Sometimes two adjectives modify the same word equally but are not linked by *and*.

She was a tall, stately model.

This sentence means:

She was a tall *and* stately model.

COMPLICATION

Sometimes the two words only seem to modify equally the same word. One word may really modify the other.

I bought a bright red Chevrolet.

Bright really modifies *red*, so you cannot translate to a bright *and* red Chevrolet.

SOLUTION

Place a comma between two or more adjectives that modify equally the same word or word group. They are equal if *and* can be placed between them before reading the word modified.

Mark the sentences that need no commas C. If a sentence contains adjectives that could be joined by *and*, mark it W and put in the needed commas.

_____ 1. She was a small-boned pretty brunette.

_____ 2. The large soggy muddy pawprints tracked the clean waxed floor.

_____ 3. He wore a blue velvet tux.

ANSWERS

1. W—She was a small-boned, pretty brunette.
2. W—The large, soggy, muddy pawprints tracked the clean, waxed floor.
3. C

If you missed any, review the lesson and do the next exercise. Follow the directions for the last exercise.

_____ 1. He ate a delicious nutritious lunch.

_____ 2. She has a crinkled cotton sundress.

_____ 3. They are happy healthy children.

ANSWERS

1. W—He ate a delicious, nutritious lunch.
2. C
3. W—They are happy, healthy children.

Now do the post-test.

42. COMMAS BETWEEN ADJECTIVES
Post-Test

Put in commas where they are needed.

1. They have a dark blue car.
2. The short pink-faced man reminds me of a cherub in a painting by Reubens.
3. The Smiths are an active intelligent good-looking family.
4. Mary writes with smooth even strokes.
5. She sang a really long song next.
6. Mother paid a huge price for red juicy apples.
7. A street bike gives fast cheap transportation.
8. Discolored flannel shirts are his usual tops.
9. She really likes a monotonous daily routine.
10. He uses a seven-bladed Barlow knife.

Ask your instructor to check this, or turn it in.

See adjectives in **2**, the general post-test after **47**, or writing assignments in **54–56**.

43 Commas Setting Off Modifiers

PROBLEM

Sometimes words are renamed or described by a word, phrase, or clause that follows.

Mary Jones, a neighbor, is a Seventh-Day Adventist.
(The word neighbor tells about Mary Jones.)

At Lake Aster we relaxed, swimming every day.
(The underlined phrase tells about swimming.)

He is a man that is sure to succeed. (The underlined clause tells about man.)

The problem is knowing when to use a comma to set off these modifiers.

SOLUTION 1

Set off loose (nonrestrictive) modifiers with commas. A loose modifier tells more about a word, but it is not necessary to identify the word that it modifies.

James, my son, is healthy.

"My son" is the modifier in that sentence. It is set off on both sides by commas because it is not necessary to explain that James is "my son" in order to say that James "is healthy." So, this is a loose modifier that adds to the meaning of "James" but is not necessary to identify "James" in that sentence.

The following sentences have loose modifiers. Place the commas where they are needed.

1. He played his own composition "Walking the Floor over You."
2. Ernest Tubb one of the first country performers to feature an electric guitar was an early success.
3. The electric guitar which was not available in the pioneer period is a suitable addition for today's music.

ANSWERS

1. He played his own composition, "Walking the Floor over You."
2. Ernest Tubb, one of the first country performers to feature an electric guitar, was an early success.
3. The electric guitar, which was not available in the pioneer period, is a suitable addition for today's music.

If you missed any, review the lesson and do the next exercise. Follow the directions for the last exercise.

1. Roy Acuff and Little Jimmie Dickens early country-music stars played anywhere fairs, school programs or church gatherings.

2. They stayed wherever they could sleeping in the homes of friends.

3. Wilma Jones who grew up in Carthage recalls having to sleep with her sister when Roy Acuff stayed with her family.

ANSWERS

1. Roy Acuff and Little Jimmie Dickens, early country-music stars, played anywhere, fairs, school programs, or church gatherings.
2. They stayed wherever they could, sleeping in the homes of friends.
3. Wilma Jones, who grew up in Carthage, recalls having to sleep with her sister when Roy Acuff stayed with her family.

SOLUTION 2

Use no commas with close (restrictive) modifiers. A close modifier is necessary to identify the word that it modifies.

My son James is healthy.

"James" is the modifier now, explaining who "my son" is. This explanation is necessary because the speaker might have other sons, some not "healthy." So "James" is singled out as "my son" who is "healthy." No commas are used in order to show how *close* the explanation is to the word it modifies. The explanation identifies which son, so it could not be left out of the sentence without changing the meaning. Do not use commas to set off such close modifiers.

Practice the two solutions. Place commas to set off loose modifiers. Some sentences have close modifiers, which need no commas; mark these C.

_____ 1. Fay Smith the staff guitarist at KGKO in Fort Worth played the electric guitar at a recording for Ernest Tubb.

_____ 2. The event that caused country music performers to amplify their instruments was the introduction of the tavern jukebox.

_____ 3. Uncle Dave Macon a popular performer was applauded strongly.

_____ 4. These songs extremely sad and sorrowful have been loved for generations.

ANSWERS

1. Fay Smith, the staff guitarist at KGKO in Fort Worth, played the electric guitar at a recording for Earnest Tubb.
2. C
3. Uncle Dave Macon, a popular performer, was applauded strongly.
4. These songs, extremely sad and sorrowful, have been loved for generations.

If you missed any, review the lesson and do the next exercise. Follow the directions for the last exercise.

_____ 1. Southern country music working from a definite solo style changed.

———— 2. The dulcimer an ancient instrument of Germanic origin was popular in remote mountain areas.

———— 3. The change that made the banjo popular was the addition of the fifth or drone string.

———— 4. The source of the song "Wabash Cannonball" was tradition.

ANSWERS

1. Southern country music, working from a definite solo style, changed.
2. The dulcimer, an ancient instrument of Germanic origin, was popular in remote mountain areas.
3. C
4. C

Now do the post-test.

43. COMMAS SETTING OFF MODIFIERS
Post-Test

Use commas to set off modifiers that are loose (nonrestrictive).

1. Weight-watching which had become Betsy's newest cult began to interest me.
2. I ate a salad made of kiwi a strange little tropical fruit from New Zealand.
3. The present that you gave me is one I shall always cherish.
4. Airline stewards that are discourteous to passengers should be replaced.
5. Charlotte the girl next door has become my friend.
6. The students who were absent will not be able to take the test.
7. Her Aunt Mary is extremely curious about other people's affairs.
8. The candidate who wore casual clothes joined in the picnic fun.
9. Another factor is the reasons women want abortions which can be as varied as the women themselves.
10. Then the driver adjusts the rear-view mirror that is attached to the windshield.

Ask your instructor to check this, or turn it in.

See adverbs in **2**, clauses in **5**, comma charts in **15**, the general post-test after **47**, or writing assignments in **54–56**.

44 Commas Setting Off Conjunctive Adverbs

PROBLEM

Words like "therefore," "however," and "on the other hand" often tie sentences together and show the relation of one thought to another. Such words are not themselves part of the main idea. They show the relation of the main idea of the sentence to something else the writer has said. They are set off from the main idea in different ways, depending on where they come in the sentence.

SOLUTION 1

Set off conjunctive adverbs with commas when they come at the beginning or the end of one thought.

> He assured us that he was loyal. *However*, we learned not to trust him. (adverb at beginning of sentence)

> He assured us that he was loyal. We learned not to trust him, *however*. (adverb at end of sentence)

In each of these examples, the adverb joins the thought of its sentence to the thought in the sentence that comes before it. The adverb is set off from its sentence with a comma.

SOLUTION 2

Set off a conjunctive adverb with commas on both sides when it interrupts a sentence. This sets it off from the thought of the sentence.

> He assured us that he was loyal. We learned, *however*, not to trust him. (adverb interrupting sentence)

COMPLICATION

When two complete thoughts are joined into one sentence by one of these adverbs, both a comma and a semicolon (;) are used. The semicolon substitutes for the period.

> He assured us that he was loyal; *however*, we learned not to trust him. (The semicolon separates one complete statement from another; the comma separates the adverb from the sentence.)

Practice with adverbs by punctuating these sentences.

1. She wore unbecoming clothes. Consequently she was overlooked by the judges.
2. He challenged us to a game. He demanded that we play him as a matter of fact.
3. We liked the view; on the other hand we did not like the price.
4. In all the holidays are my favorite times of the year.

ANSWERS

1. She wore unbecoming clothes. Consequently, she was overlooked by the judges.
2. He challenged us to a game. He demanded that we play him, as a matter of fact.
3. We liked the view; on the other hand, we did not like the price.
4. In all, the holidays are my favorite times of the year.

If you missed any, review the lesson and do the next exercise. Follow the directions for the last exercise.

1. Well, enough of that let's start from the beginning.
2. For one thing he has never been fair to me.
3. He never washes his hands; therefore everything he touches gets dirty.
4. Sarnoff believes on the other hand that the computer is like a person's right arm.

ANSWERS

1. Well, enough of that, let's start from the beginning.
2. For one thing, he has never been fair to me.
3. He never washes his hands; therefore, everything he touches gets dirty.
4. Sarnoff believes, on the other hand, that the computer is like a person's right arm.

Now take the post-test.

NAME

44. COMMAS SETTING OFF CONJUNCTIVE ADVERBS
Post-Test

Place commas to set off any conjunctive adverbs in these sentences.

1. Consequently we did not arrive in time.
2. We did not as a matter of fact have any reason to trust him.
3. These are not our only reasons however.
4. We were told we could have the day off; however here we are!
5. However hard we tried, we could not win.
6. In addition it helps couples to deal with problems of sex and money.
7. When I get my paycheck therefore I list necessities and spend only for those.
8. Evelyn will get along somehow.
9. Steve enjoys his work; therefore he creates a positive atmosphere.
10. Consequently she did not know that the horse was going lame.

Ask your instructor to check this, or turn it in.

See conjunctive adverbs in **25, 26,** or **37,** the sentence core in **3,** the general post-test after **47,** or writing assignments in **54–56.**

45 Commas Before *Not*

PROBLEM

A modifier often emphasizes a word or a thought by saying what it is *not*. This modifier will be loose; that is, it is not a necessary part of the sentence. Such modifiers only add more information.

This is a Volkswagen, not a pregnant skate.

SOLUTION

Use a comma before *not* when *not* introduces a loose modifier.

In these sentences, place commas before *not* when they are needed.

1. It is my fault not yours.
2. That was not the idea at all.
3. I picked the winner not that it matters.
4. I know that not everyone has such a chance.
5. You are an employee not the boss.

ANSWERS

1. It is my fault, not yours.
2. C
3. I picked the winner, not that it matters.
4. C
5. You are an employee, not the boss.

Now take the post-test.

NAME

45. COMMAS BEFORE *NOT*

Post-Test

Put a comma before *not* when *not* begins a loose modifier. Some sentences may need no comma.

1. He liked the quality not the price.
2. Electricity is a servant not a master.
3. Not only the girl but also her mother went.
4. He died of kidney failure not a heart attack.
5. Some salespeople are considerate of their own time not the customer's.
6. Dayton is called Sinus Valley because it is not the healthiest place to live.
7. Dogs protect not only cattle but people.
8. Parenthood is responsibility not just fun.
9. My popular husband is a Pisces not a Leo.
10. The most dangerous drivers are sometimes old not young.

Ask your instructor to check this, or turn it in.

See *not* as fragment additions in **24**, the general post-test after **47**, or writing assignments in **54–56**.

46 Commas with Speaker Tags

PROBLEM

In a sentence that quotes the direct words of a speaker, the speaker is identified by a speaker tag such as "he said," "they shouted," or "she protested." These tags appear in different sentence positions and must be separated from the the direct words that were spoken.

> He said, "I don't believe it."
> "Get out of here," they shouted.

SOLUTION 1

Place a comma between the speaker tag and the speaker's direct words in these two positions:

1. Speaker tag before direct words:
She said, "I don't believe that you meant to threaten him."

2. Speaker tag following direct words:
"I don't believe that you meant to threaten him," she said.

In both examples, commas separate the speaker tag from the words of the direct quotation. Notice that the comma is placed inside the quotation marks in number 2.

COMPLICATION

Sometimes the speaker tag is placed within the direct words, breaking them up.

1. "I don't believe," she said, "that you meant to threaten him."
2. "You are wrong," she said. "That color does fade."

SOLUTION 2

Place commas before and after the speaker tag when the tag breaks up the direct words of the speaker's sentence (number 1). When the speaker tag comes between two complete sentences, a period must be used (number 2).

Apply the solution to the sentences below.

1. "Clean up the whole area" the officer told Buckskin.
2. Buckskin replied "I never used a machine like that."
3. "You'd better learn how" the officer threatened "or you'll be out of circulation."
4. "I'd like to be out of circulation" Buckskin muttered. "Then I could rest."

ANSWERS

1. "Clean up the whole area," the officer told Buckskin.
2. Buckskin replied, "I never used a machine like that."
3. "You'd better learn how," the officer threatened, "or you'll be out of circulation."
4. "I'd like to be out of circulation," Buckskin muttered. "Then I could rest."

If you missed any, review the lesson and do the next exercise. Follow the directions for the last exercise.

1. "Those napkins are on sale for fifty-nine cents" said Mrs. Emerson.
2. "No" the checker replied "that was the luncheon size."
3. Mrs. Emerson insisted "The sign advertised the dinner size for fifty-nine."
4. "I'm sorry" the checker responded. "I must charge what the tag says."

ANSWERS

1. "Those napkins are on sale for fifty-nine cents," said Mrs. Emerson.
2. "No," the checker replied, "that was the luncheon size."
3. Mrs. Emerson insisted, "The sign advertised the dinner size for fifty-nine."
4. "I'm sorry," the checker responded. "I must charge what the tag says."

PROBLEM

Speaker tags are used with indirect quotations, too. An indirect quotation reports about what a speaker said but does not use his or her exact words. In an indirect quotation, the word *that* often follows the speaker tag. No quotation marks are used with an indirect quotation.

DIRECT: She said, "I don't want to live with him."
INDIRECT: She said that she did not want to live with him.
                        or
              She said she did not want to live with him.

SOLUTION

Do *not* put a comma after a speaker tag when it introduces an indirect quotation.

If each of the following needs a comma, put it in. If it does not, write C for correct.

_____ 1. Mark reported "The systems are all go."

_____ 2. Mark reported that the systems are all go.

_____ 3. Sheryl wrote that she was homesick.

_____ 4. The teacher remarked that his class was working hard.

ANSWERS

1. Marked reported, "The systems are all go."
2. C
3. C
4. C

If you missed any, review the lesson and do the next exercise. Follow the directions for the last exercise.

_____ 1. The judge ruled that the evidence was in Ellis's favor.

———— 2. I said "I am not interested."

———— 3. I said I was not interested.

———— 4. She replied "Brains are not everything."

ANSWERS

1. C
2. I said, "I am not interested."
3. C
4. She replied, "Brains are not everything."

Now take the post-test.

NAME _____

46. COMMAS WITH SPEAKER TAGS

Post-Test

Place commas where they are needed in the following sentences.

1. I said "You should not worry."
2. He told me that I was lucky.
3. "Josephine" he cried "don't leave me!"
4. "You should not have come here" she said.
5. She asked what was wrong.
6. "I have broken my arm" Ruby called. "You must help me."
7. The warning states that smoking cigarettes can cause cancer.
8. God says to John "Tell your world that it has everything it needs, but it needs to use it better."
9. I have asked people for part-time jobs, but they say that they have all the help they need.
10. She enjoyed the dance, and he said that he had a good time, too.

Ask your instructor to check your answers, or turn them in.

See comma charts in **15**, the general post-test after **47**, or writing assignments in **54–56**.

47 Commas with Dates and Addresses

PROBLEM

Some sentences refer to towns, cities, and countries or mention dates or addresses. In these sentences, use commas to make the references clear.

SOLUTION 1

Use commas between the city and the state to which you are referring *and* between the state and the remainder of the sentence if the sentence continues.

We are moving to Madison, Wisconsin, in July.

Any other geographical references added to such a sentence will be separated in the same way.

We are moving to Madison, Dane County, Wisconsin, in July.

SOLUTION 2

Use commas between the items in dates and after the last of several items in the date if the sentence continues.

We moved here on Tuesday, August 22, 1968.
We moved here on Tuesday, August 22, 1968, with great hopes.

SOLUTION 3

Use commas between the items in addresses except for the ZIP code number.

I addressed the letter to Erma Bombeck, Field Enterprises, Inc., Chicago, Illinois 60603.

COMPLICATION

The items in geographical references, dates, and addresses are not separated by commas when words come between the items.

I addressed the letter to Erma Bombeck at Field Enterprises, Inc., Chicago, Illinois 60603. (*at* substitutes for a comma)

Put commas in the following sentences where they are needed.

1. The family arrived in Huntsville Alabama on June 19 1971 with thirteen hamsters and a canary.
2. His address is Route 7 Box 23 Cambridge Ohio 43725.
3. I was born on February 9 1959 in Fort Bragg North Carolina.

ANSWERS

Only these commas are needed.

1. The family arrived in Huntsville, Alabama, on June 19, 1971, with thirteen hamsters and a canary.
2. His address is Route 7, Box 23, Cambridge, Ohio 43725.
3. I was born on February 9, 1959, in Fort Bragg, North Carolina.

If you missed any, review the lesson and do the next exercise. Follow the directions for the last exercise.

1. She lives at 947 Broadway New Orleans Louisiana 70118.
2. I lived in Silver Spring Maryland until 1956 and liked it very much.
3. She finished her tour of duty at Fort Hood Texas on May 27 1967.

ANSWERS

1. She lives at 947 Broadway, New Orleans, Louisiana 70118.
2. I lived in Silver Spring, Maryland, until 1956 and liked it very much.
3. She finished her tour of duty at Fort Hood, Texas, on May 27, 1967.

Now do the post-test.

NAME _____

47. COMMAS WITH DATES AND ADDRESSES

Post-Test

Place commas where they are needed to separate items in geographical names, addresses, or dates.

1. He can be reached at 280 Bride Path Mountainside New Jersey 07092.
2. My birthday is May 15 1958 and I am a Taurus.
3. We left Bullitt County and went to Jefferson County Louisville Kentucky.
4. His wife studied pediatrics at Boston University Boston Massachusetts.
5. In Birmingham Alabama Tom woke up and asked where we were.
6. They went to Lincoln High School Newton New Jersey.
7. We saw the Lost River New Braunfels Texas in June 1945.
8. He drives between St. Louis Missouri and Des Moines Iowa.
9. His business opened December 3 1971 and closed July 10.
10. The meeting was at Grambling College Grambling Louisiana.

Ask your instructor to check your answers, or turn them in.

See comma charts in **15**, the general post-test on the next page, or writing assignments in **54–56**.

NAME _____

COMMAS

General Post-Test

In the following sentences, put commas where they are needed.

1. The Pinto has more horsepower than the Vega but it gets fewer miles per gallon. (**38**)

2. In the cafe I noticed a man who reminded me of my father in the way he walked. (**40**)

3. The manager went to her for advice when he could not handle the situation. (**39**)

4. Parked by a maple the orange and brown Firebird looked like the tree's autumn leaves. (**40**)

5. When we went to the park to play basketball John always coached the smaller boys. (**39**)

6. The kitchen has a dishwasher and the water heater is directly under it. (**38**)

7. Prisons should be made a place to reform people not just to lock them up. (**45**)

8. Mr. Griffen the principal led us in the national anthem. (**43**)

9. My son Jesse however is full of energy. (**44**)

10 Our new address is Apartment 3-D 2113 South Ames Avenue Terre Haute Indiana 47802. (**47**)

11. I moved to Atlanta and worked for Jim Tobias who was the best carpenter I ever saw. (**43**)

12. I always enjoy a tasty filling lunch. (**42**)

13. They have lived in a tent a camper and an abandoned trailer. (**41**)

14. The surgeon expects a long operation not a dangerous one. (**45**)

15. Melvin told the police he had called some friends bought four cases of beer and thrown a colossal blast. (**41**)

16. "Where" asked my mother "have you been?" (**46**)

17. However these bears are not really tame. (**44**)

18. On April 7 1976 I was discharged from the Navy. (**47**)

19. He lives in a beautiful modern inexpensive apartment in Madison. (**42**)

20. Ted replied "If we ever get to Houston, you won't need it." (**46**)

Ask your instructor to check your answers, or turn them in.

See phrases in **4**, clauses in **5**, sentence core in **3**, comma charts in **15**, or writing assignments in **54–56**.

NAME _____

48. THE APOSTROPHE

Pretest

Use an accepted possessive form in filling in these blanks.

1. A house belonging to a family named Jones is the _____ house.
2. A house belonging to a family named Riley is the _____ house.
3. A car belonging to Robert Burns is _____ car.
4. A car belonging jointly to Frank and Penelope is _____ car.
5. Clothes belonging to George and clothes belonging to Jeff are _____ clothes.
6. A plant belonging to a mother-in-law is a _____ plant.
7. A desk belonging to Charles is _____ desk.
8. A name belonging to no one is _____ name.

Use an accepted plural form to fill in these blanks.

9. More than one 8 is referred to as _____ .
10. Two people, each with a Ph.D., could be referred to as those _____ .
11. Repetition of the word *then* could be referred to as many _____ .
12. If a word uses the letter *L* too many times, you could say it has too many _____ .

ANSWERS

1. Joneses'
2. Rileys'
3. Burns's or Burns'
4. Frank and Penelope's
5. George's and Jeff's
6. mother-in-law's
7. Charles's or Charles'
8. no one's (not any one's)
9. 8's
10. Ph.D.'s
11. *then*'s
12. *L*'s

48 The Apostrophe

**Apostrophe with
Possessives**

**possessive
of singular
nouns**

PROBLEM

Either the apostrophe (') or the apostrophe and an *s* ('s) is used to show that one person or thing owns another. The word that owns is called possessive.

the girl's   hat
(owner)   (owned)

Moses'   sister
(owner)   (owned)

SOLUTION 1

Use 's to form the possessive of most singular nouns.

The leader's uniform fits well. (singular—one leader)
   (owner) (owned)

The waitress's uniform fits well. (singular—one waitress)
   (owner) (owned)

Use the solution to correct these sentences

1. The man   jacket is brown.
2. The boss   son was hired.
3. We eat at grandmother   house.
4. Greg   best friend is David.
5. New Year   Eve is a happy time.
6. Our landlord   wife brought the kitten.

ANSWERS

1. man's
2. boss's
3. grandmother's
4. Greg's
5. Year's
6. landlord's

SOLUTION 2

When the addition of another -*s* sound to a name ending in -*s* would make saying the word difficult, you may add the apostrophe only.

Charles' appearance

possessive of plural nouns   **PROBLEM**

Plural nouns form possessives in two ways according to whether or not they end in -s.

SOLUTION 1

Add only the apostrophe to show possession with most plural nouns. Most nouns form their plurals in a regular way by adding s to their singular form. The apostrophe comes after the s to show possession for these nouns.

leaders' courage (plural—more than one leader)
cars' fenders (plural—more than one car)

Two steps are involved in showing possession correctly with these plural nouns. The first step is to add the s to change its form from singular to plural. The second step is to add the mark of possession, the apostrophe.

Step 1 boy (singular) to boys (plural)	Step 2 boys (plural) to boys' (plural possessive)

Practice what you have learned so far about forming possessives by filling in the columns below. Review the lessons if they help. The first is done for you.

Singular	Singular Possessive	Plural	Plural Possessive
1. student	student's	students	students'
2. girl			
3. hour			
4. Robert			
5. Jones			
6. Brown			

ANSWERS

1. student	student's	students	students'
2. girl	girl's	girls	girls'
3. hour	hour's	hours	hours'
4. Robert	Robert's	Roberts	Roberts'
5. Jones	Jones's	Joneses	Joneses'
6. Brown	Brown's	Browns	Browns'

SOLUTION 2

Some nouns do not form their plurals in the regular way, adding s. Some other changes in these words show that they are plural, or the same form is used for singular and plural.

Singular	Plural
child	children
ox	oxen
woman	women
fish	fish

When nouns are made plural without an added s, you must add 's to form their plural possessive.

Singular Possessive	Plural Possessive
child's	children's
ox's	oxen's
woman's	women's
fish's	fish's

Practice forming these possessives by filling in the columns below. The first is done for you.

Singular	Singular Possessive	Plural	Plural Possessive
1. mouse	mouse's	mice	mice's
2. woman			
3. deer			
4. child			
5. man			
6. goose			

ANSWERS

2. woman	woman's	women	women's
3. deer	deer's	deer	deer's
4. child	child's	children	children's
5. man	man's	men	men's
6. goose	goose's	geese	geese's

possessive pronouns

PROBLEM

Many pronouns have a possessive form.

Subject Form	Possessive Form
I	my, mine
you	your, yours
she	her, hers
it	its
we	our, ours
they	their, theirs
who	whose

SOLUTION

This form is understood to show ownership and does not require an apostrophe. The possessive form of these pronouns is shown more fully in **10** and in **36**.

This is *my* aunt. She is on *her* honeymoon with *her* new husband. *He* is driving *his* new car, which is now *their* new car.

possessive in indefinite pronouns

PROBLEM

Indefinite pronouns, unlike the pronouns above, do not have a different form to show possession.

It is anybody's guess.
(anyone's, everybody's, another's)

SOLUTION

Use 's to form the plural of indefinite pronouns, just as you do for singular nouns.

joint possession

PROBLEM

Sometimes two nouns are joint owners; both together own something. How is this shown?

Helen and Joseph own a horse.
It is Helen and Joseph's horse.

SOLUTION

In showing joint possession, add the signs for possession only after the last owning noun.

individual ownership in nouns joined by *and*

PROBLEM

Sometimes individual ownership must be expressed even though the nouns are joined by *and*. If the nouns separately own separate things, both nouns must have the signs of possession added to show this correctly.

Jack's and John's clothes.

Practice showing the difference between the use of the possessive in joint ownership and in individual ownership. How would you write about the following?

1. A cigar store owned by two brothers, Moses and Sam: _____ and _____ store.
2. A play presented by teachers and students: _____ and _____ play.
3. Two wardrobes, one owned by Doris and one by Sarah: _____ and _____ wardrobes.
4. The cooperation of the driver and pit crew: _____ and _____ cooperation.
5. The motions of the defense lawyer and of the prosecutor: the _____ and _____ motions.

ANSWERS

1. Moses and Sam's cigar store
2. teachers and students' play
3. Doris' or Doris's and Sarah's wardrobes
4. the driver and pit crew's cooperation
5. defense lawyer's and prosecutor's motions

possessive form in compound nouns

PROBLEM

Compound nouns show ownership in a particular way.

My brother-in-law's house is on this street.

SOLUTION

Show possession only on the last word of compound nouns.

Show possession where it is needed.

1. the King of Poland crown
2. my sister-in-law cake
3. the three-toed stump-sitter song
4. the bride-elect mother

ANSWERS

1. King of Poland's
2. sister-in-law's
3. stump-sitter's
4. bride-elect's

Apostrophes in Contractions

PROBLEM

The apostrophe has another use completely different from its use as a mark of ownership.

It is used to show that words or numerals have been left out in contractions. A contraction makes something shorter by leaving out letters or numbers.

> he will = he'll
> will not = won't
> should have = should've
> of the clock = o'clock
> class of 1976 = class of '76

SOLUTION

Use the apostrophe to show that numbers or letters have been omitted. The apostrophe is placed where the omitted letters or numbers would have been. Or do not use contractions and avoid trouble with this use of the apostrophe.

Apostrophes to Show Plurals

PROBLEM

Another use of the apostrophe is to form the plurals of letters, of numbers, of abbreviations, and of words referred to as words.

> Mind your *P*'s and *Q*'s.
> That happened in the 1970's.

SOLUTION

Add 's after the end of the letter, number, abbreviation, or word referred to as a word to make it plural.

Now do the post-test.

NAME _____

48. THE APOSTROPHE

Post-Test A

A. For each of the following fill in the blank with the correct possessive.

1. A car belonging to a family named Burns is the _____ car.
2. A car belonging to Robert Burns is Robert _____ car.
3. A car belonging to Richard and Joe jointly is _____ and _____ car.
4. Two cars, one belonging to Mary and one belonging to Alice, are _____ and _____ cars.
5. A car belonging to your brother-in-law is your _____ car.
6. A toy belonging to a child is a _____ toy.
7. A gift prepared by the children is the _____ gift.
8. A hat belonging to a woman is the _____ hat.
9. Messages to be given to the men are the _____ messages.
10. The end of today is _____ end.
11. The work of the last two weeks is _____ work.

B. Place the apostrophe to show possession, contraction, or plurals of numbers or words.

1. I dont care at all.
2. I will make my choice.
3. This is anybodys game.
4. Clothes in the style of 1960–1969 are said to date from the _____ .

Ask your instructor to check this, or turn it in.

See apostrophe charts in **18**, plurals in **52**, possessive pronouns in **10** and **36**, contractions confused with possessive pronouns in **50**, Post-test B, or writing assignments in **54–56**.

NAME _____

48. THE APOSTROPHE
Post-Test B

A. For each of the following, fill in the blank with the correct possessive.

1. The aide belonging to a nurse is a _____ aide.
2. The house belonging to his parents is his _____ house.
3. The hard work belonging to a day is a hard _____ work.
4. The arms belonging to men are _____ arms.
5. The coat belonging to my mother-in-law is my _____ coat.
6. The horses belonging to the James family are the _____ horses.
7. The grades belonging to a student are the _____ grades.
8. The marriage of Martha and Albert is _____ and _____ marriage.
9. The marriages of Martha and Myrtle are _____ and _____ marriages.
10. A car that belongs to somebody is _____ car.
11. A car that belongs to him is _____ car.

B. Use the apostrophe where needed to show contraction or plurals of numbers or words.

1. He wont go with us.
2. He bought a 67 Corvette.
3. They met in the 1950s.
4. I like your style.

Ask your instructor to check your answers.

Mechanics

49. CAPITALIZATION

Pretest

Capitalize all words that need to be capitalized in the following sentences.

1. the miami dolphins are the only team to win the superbowl two years in a row.
2. in arkansas there is enough snow to make winter fun, but in the north there is too much snow.
3. i started college at wheaton college, wheaton, illinois, after i finished high school.
4. shirley majored in french and history.
5. her mother asked ann, "do you really want to be a doctor?"
6. the children begged, "please, daddy, take us to see *star wars*."
7. my saturdays in july and august are for relaxing but my saturdays in november and december are for preparing for christmas and fighting the problems of winter.
8. henry got an idea that he told father about.
9. we lived south of little masterson lake.
10. aunt alice asked if we took chemistry.

ANSWERS

Only the following should be capitalized:
1. The Miami Dolphins, Superbowl.
2. In, Arkansas, North.
3. I, Wheaton College, Wheaton, Illinois, I.
4. Shirley, French.
5. Her, Ann, Do.
6. The, Please, Daddy, *Star Wars*.
7. My, Saturdays, July, August, Saturdays, November, December, Christmas.
8. Henry, Father.
9. We, Little Masterson Lake.
10. Aunt Alice

If you missed any, study this unit.

49 Capitalization

Capitals Beginning Sentences

PROBLEM

It is important to have a clear break between sentences so that the reader does not confuse the end of one sentence with the beginning of another.

It is raining cats and dogs stay inside.

SOLUTION

A period (or question mark or exclamation point) ends the old sentence, and the new sentence begins with a capital letter, which shows that something important is coming. This makes the meaning clearer.

It is raining. Cats and dogs stay inside.
or
It is raining cats and dogs. Stay inside.

COMPLICATION

Sometimes a sentence quotes another sentence, so one sentence is inside the other. How are they capitalized?

SOLUTION

Capitalize both the beginning of the whole sentence and the beginning of the quoted sentence.

He said, "The snow will not stop me."

If the beginning of the sentence is the beginning of the quotation, only one capital begins both.

"The snow will not stop me," he said.

Only one capital—the one beginning the sentence—is needed if you do not quote but just tell the meaning of the sentence said or written before your sentence. A quotation is the exact words spoken, not just the meaning.

He said that the snow would not stop him. (These are not his exact words.)

For the punctuation of quotations, see 17 on quotation marks and 15 and 38–47 on commas.

Capital for the Pronoun *I*

PROBLEM

Only one pronoun, *I*, is capitalized, so sometimes writers forget to capitalize it.

SOLUTION

Always capitalize the word *I*.

Practice the problems studied so far by capitalizing in the following sentences when it is necessary. Review the lessons above if you need to.

1. since i was a child, i have enjoyed the colorful ways some people talk.
2. once she said, "that man is so wild he'll never be tamed."
3. another is that some angry person could have a calf with a crocheted tail.
4. the strangest i know is "they were as happy as dead pigs lying in the sunshine."

ANSWERS

Only the following capitals are correct:

1. Since, I, I.
2. Once, That.
3. Another.
4. The, I, They.

Capitals for Names of Particular Persons, Places, or Things

PROBLEM

Many nouns (names of persons, places, or things) are capitalized sometimes and not capitalized others.

I went to *Sieg School* in Detroit.
I went to a *school* in Detroit.

SOLUTION

Nouns are capitalized when they are the particular names of particular persons, places, and things.

Sieg School	(a particular place)
a *school*	(a general kind of place)
the *Titanic*	(a particular ship)
a *luxury liner*	(a general kind of ship)

In these sentences, place capitals where they are needed.

1. After graduating from stuart elementary school, mark went to three different high schools.
2. Take a right turn at the first street past the light.
3. Take a right turn at first street.
4. charleston is the home of franklin furniture company, run by don greer.
5. My gremlin rides as smoothly as a ford granada or a mercedes-benz or some other expensive car.

ANSWERS

Only the following capitals should be added:

1. Stuart Elementary School, Mark.
2. none.
3. First Street.
4. Charleston, Franklin Furniture Company, Don Greer.
5. Gremlin, Ford, Granada, Mercedes-Benz.

Capitals for Titles of People

PROBLEM

Titles of jobs or positions are sometimes capitalized and sometimes not.

SOLUTION

Titles are capitalized when they are particular names of people. They are not capitalized when they are a general description of the occupation of the person.

> *Dr. S*pragg practices family medicine.
> The *d*octor practices in a small town.

A title is a particular name if it is used as part of the person's name.

> *Professor Eccles* is an interesting woman.

It is also a particular name if it is used instead of his name.

> Yes, Commander, I have the charts ready.

PROBLEM

Titles of relatives are sometimes capitalized and sometimes not.

SOLUTION

Capitalize the title of a relative when it is the particular name of that relative, not a general description of the relationship.

> Her aunt was innocent. (description of the relationship)
>
> She thought *Aunt Opal* was innocent. (part of a particular name)
>
> She said, "I believe that *Aunt* could not do such a thing." (used instead of particular name)

In the following, capitalize when necessary.

1. By now, mother knows when to expect my letters.
2. I call my uncle early each morning.
3. The foreman began his shift late.
4. We asked rabbi Roth to drive with us.

5. My best enemy is cousin James.

6. The best policeman was officer Andrews.

ANSWERS

Only the following capitals should be added:

1. Mother.
2. none.
3. none.
4. Rabbi.
5. Cousin.
6. Officer.

Capitals for Titles of Works

PROBLEM

The first letters of some words in a title are capitalized.

SOLUTION

Capitalize the first letters of the first and last words, all important words, and any other words at least five letters long.

A Comparison of Town and Country Life (a title on a student essay)

"September in the Rain" (a song)

The Family (a painting)

Crisis in the Classroom (book title)

"Because I Could Not Stop for Death" (a poem)

Happy Days (a television show)

Notice that the first letters of articles (a, an, the), conjunctions (and, but, or), and short prepositions (for, in) are not capitalized unless they begin the first word in the title. For the punctuation of titles, see **16** on underlining and **17** on quotation marks.

Place capitals where they are needed in these sentences.

1. The family sang songs like "white christmas."
2. who painted the picture *harps in the wind?*
3. We read *one flew over the cuckoo's nest.*
4. Robert Frost wrote "stopping by woods on a snowy evening."
5. We listened to "still crazy after all these years."

ANSWERS

Only the following should be capitalized:

1. White Christmas.
2. Harps, Wind.

3. One Flew, Cuckoo's Nest.
4. Stopping, Woods, Snowy Evening.
5. Still Crazy After All These Years.

Capitals for Names of Places

PROBLEM

Sometimes place-names begin with capital letters.

SOLUTION

The particular names of nations, states or provinces, counties, cities or towns, streets, districts, buildings, rivers, mountains, and other political or geographic names begin with capitals. A general reference to a place does not begin with a capital.

> We waited in the *Terminal Tower* in *Cleveland, Ohio*. (names of particular places)
>
> The *building* was cold. The *city* was lonely.
> One *state* is like another. (general references to places)

Adjectives and other nouns made from the names of particular places are also capitalized.

> They are both native *Iowans*.
> It is an *Iowan* tradition.

Capitals for Names of Directions

PROBLEM

Many writers do not know when to capitalize *north*, *south*, *east*, and *west*.

SOLUTION

Capitalize the names of a direction only when it is used instead of the names of particular states or countries.

> He has lived in the *Deep South* (used instead of the particular names of Georgia, Alabama, Mississippi, and others).
>
> He lives *south* of here (used to name a general direction).
>
> Most of the world's wealth is in the *West* (used instead of the particular names of North American countries).

Capitalize when needed in the following sentences.

1. I like to read about cowboys in the west.
2. The university of minnesota in minneapolis has one of the strongest american studies programs in the midwest.
3. We met in brown chapel.
4. We drove thirty miles north of odessa, texas.
5. Joe went to india and japan because of his interest in eastern philosophies.

ANSWERS

Only the following should be capitalized:

1. West.
2. University, Minnesota, Minneapolis, American, Midwest.
3. Brown Chapel.
4. Odessa, Texas.
5. India, Japan, Eastern.

Capitals for the Names of Languages

COMPLICATION

The names of languages are forms of the names of particular nations or tribes. So they, too, are always capitalized.

My *Russian* friend Maria speaks *Russian*, *Greek*, *German*, and *English* and also reads *Italian* and a little *French*.

Capitals for the Names of School Subjects

PROBLEM

The first letters in the names of school subjects are not always capitalized.

SOLUTION

Capitalize the names of a language or a particular course. Do not capitalize the name of a general field of study. If the field includes a particular name, capitalize the particular name but not the field.

I study *Spanish*. (language)
I study *History* I. (particular course)
I study *history*. (general field)
I study *Spanish* history. (general field including particular name)

Capitalize when necessary in the following sentences.

1. Tim met Amy in their french class, conversation and composition in french.
2. Both had already taken french I and french II.
3. She is majoring in political science and plans to use her french as a diplomat.
4. He is a psychology major who wants to translate psychology textbooks into french.

ANSWERS

Only the following changes are correct:

1. French, Conversation, Composition, French.
2. French I, French II.
3. French.
4. French.

Capitals for Time

PROBLEM

Some references to time are capitalized, and some are not.

months, days of the week, and holidays

SOLUTION 1

The first letters of the names of months of the year, days of the week, and holidays are always capitalized. The first letter of *day* or *eve* is capitalized when used as part of the name of a holiday.

> School began in *September*. (month)
>
> We met on the first *Tuesday*. (day of the week)
>
> Lise's birthday is the *Fourth of July*. (holidays)
>   *but*
> He wrote on the *fourth of August*. (date not a holiday)
>
> I don't like April Fool's Day. (word as part of the name of a holiday)

seasons

SOLUTION 2

Names of seasons are not usually capitalized. Use a capital letter to begin the name of a season only if you are talking about it as if it were a person.

> The autumn was late. (time)
>
> Tardy *Autumn* tried to sneak into his seat, but the shuffling of his moccasins through the dry leaves gave him away. (person)

Capitalize when necessary in the following

1. I like the springtime best; it includes the months of march, april, and may here.
2. We threw a big new year's eve party.
3. We moved on memorial day.
4. The hardest days of the week for me are mondays.
5. The only days to brighten up february are lincoln's birthday, washington's birthday, and valentine's day.

ANSWERS

Only the following changes are correct:

1. March, April, May.
2. New Year's Eve.
3. Memorial Day.
4. Mondays.
5. February, Lincoln's Birthday, Washington's Birthday, Valentine's Day.

Now take the post-test on the next page.

NAME _____

49. CAPITALIZATION

Post-Test A

Capitalize when necessary in the following sentences.

1. I find colorful sayings whether I travel north or south.
2. cousin tim always said, "i can eat four miles of chitt'lin's with a maw at every mile-post."
3. a student swears that his doctor is so tight he will ruin a dollar knife to skin a flea for his hide and tallow.
4. "plenty of fellows are walking around with ten-gallon hats and no cattle," says a friend, "and i don't just mean in the west."
5. "i felt so low I could crawl under a caterpillar with a top-hat on," says my mother.
6. when dr. smith bought a cadillac, grandmother said that he was boring with a mighty big auger.
7. in minnesota, they say summer is the best season—both days of it.
8. if i publish these sayings, i will call them "a collection of colors."
9. the first people who said them probably hadn't studied much english, but they knew their psychology.
10. they expressed themselves well by looking clearly at life and, as the song title says, "doin' what comes natcherly."

Ask your instructor to check this, or turn it in.

See capitalization in **21**, proper nouns in **2**, Post-test B, or writing assignments in **54–56**.

49. CAPITALIZATION
Post-Test B

Capitalize when necessary in the following sentences.

1. buford pusser in *walking tall* was a very lawful sheriff who tried to clear up macon county, tennessee.
2. my father tends two small flower gardens that have different kinds of flowers to bloom all spring, summer, and fall.
3. it was saturday night, and earth, fire, and water had just given a concert in san bernardino, california.
4. rita speaks with an eastern or northern accent.
5. everyone who spoke at grandfather's funeral said, "he was really an honest man."
6. in conclusion, i think my sundays are very special.
7. in my monday-wednesday english class, i met this great guy who is studying mathematics.
8. on thanksgiving day i always stuff myself with turkey dressing.
9. helga studies psychology, german, and biology i.
10. Then mother asked pastor edmonds to conduct the marriage ceremony.

Ask your instructor to check this, or turn it in.

Spelling

50. PROBLEM WORDS

Pretest

Choose from the words at the left the correct word for each blank.

a
an
and

1. Thermal heat transfer provides _____ extremely cheap source of fuel.

He was driving _____ M.G.

_____ apple a day keeps the doctor away.

_____ onion a day keeps everybody away.

You _____ I are just like a couple of kids.

accept
except

2. _____ a compliment.

Everybody _____ me went.

It was difficult to_____.

affect
effect

3. Smoking can _____ your growth.

One _____ of the act was his being fired.

allowed
aloud

4. Talking _____ can disturb others.

We were _____ to help.

all ready
already

5. We are _____ to go.

He has _____ left.

alone
along

6. We traveled _____ the river.

After he left, I finished _____.

altar
alter

7. They married before the church _____.

_____ the suit that's too big.

are
or

8. Fido's mouth is large and holds many teeth that _____ good for biting, for chewing, _____ for tearing off a person's arm. Fido has bushy ears that _____ always full of burrs from his hunting trips after rabbits _____ gophers.

bare
bear

9. That _____ walked through the _____ winter forest.

I will explain if you will _____ with me.

brake
break

10. _____ an egg.

It is best not to _____ your car on an icy road.

buy
by

11. I will _____ the next round of drinks.

She sat _____ me.

cents
scents
sense
since

12. _____ you are unhappy, why don't you leave?

He has common _____.

It costs thirty _____.

The _____ of the flowers were strong.

chews
choose

13. I want to _____ sides.

He _____ his food carefully.

cite
sight
site

14. It was a _____ to see.

We chose a building _____ that was in

_____ of the Pacific.

He can _____ you chapter and verse.

close
clothes

15. If you move _____ to the front, you can see the

colorful _____ the group are wearing.

coarse
course

16. He took a _____ in real estate.

_____ gravel hit the car.

Of _____, I will go.

desert
dessert

17. We were lost in the _____.

Carl likes ice cream for _____.

doing
during

18. She is now _____ her nails.

The rope broke _____ the act.

ever
every

19. He came to see me _____ day.

I don't think I will _____ see him again.

father
farther
further

20. I want to _____ my education.

We went _____ down the road.

My _____ taught me hunting.

feel
fell
fill

21. I do _____ that you are right.

Please _____ the tank with regular.

The skater _____ three times.

half
have
of

22. Please accept _____ my lunch.

We should _____ waited.

He drank a pint _____ milk.

hear
here

23. It's hard to _____ her.

I live _____.

hole
whole

24. A good fishing _____ is worth a lot.

He ate the _____ thing.

hour
our

25. One _____ of my time is worth a lot.

_____ long-lost friend showed up.

its
it's

26. _____ a good show.

_____ not the same kind.

The tree shed _____ leaves.

know
no
now

27 I don't _____ you.

_____ is the time.

Working leaves _____ time for living.

_____ your neighbor, but not too well.

lead
led
lead

28. He _____ her a dog's life while they were married.

You can _____ a horse to water.

Get the _____ out.

The shot gun pellets were made of _____.

lie
lay
laid
lain

29. I will _____ down to rest.

He _____ there all day yesterday.

He has _____ down for an hour.

He will _____ there all day.

He has _____ the package down.

loose
lose

30. On a warm summer night, I like to _____ a little time with a large group who are _____ and ready for fun. Sometimes around a campfire, a party like that can cause me to _____ all sense of time.

meat
meet
met

31. We have _____ there before.

He will _____ me at the station.

This _____ is tough.

on
own

32. When you're _____ your _____ time, you're less likely to take coffee breaks.

They _____ a fleet of trucks and keep them _____ the road twenty-four hours a day.

one
won

33. I _____ the game.

_____ of the boys left early.

passed
past

34. Time _____ slowly.

My troubles are _____.

He lives in the _____.

patience
patients

35. She becomes angry easily and has little _____.

The dentist treats his _____ well.

peace
piece

36. _____ that "passeth understanding" is rare.

I would like a _____ of pie.

quit
quiet
quite

37. He wants everything to be _____ spotless, and he won't let you _____ work at night until it is. Although he is _____ and easygoing, he's a mean person to work for. He's _____ capable.

raise
rise

38. _____ early with the chickens.

_____ the window.

right
write

39. _____ a letter to your friend.

He will win, _____ or wrong.

sit
set

40. _____ on the floor.

_____ the box down somewhere.

than
then

41. Bowie took the flowers a young lady handed him and _____ handed them to a man playing a keyboard. He took and smelled them, _____ threw them to the drummer. Bowie is better at making the crowd like him _____ any other entertainer I have watched.

thank
think

42. I want to _____ you for the help.

Do not _____ about the problem anymore.

their
there
they're

43. It was _____ choice.

_____ goes John.

_____ not asking the right questions.

We left them _____ in the rain.

theirs
there's

44. The best poker hands were _____.

_____ a bear outside who wants to see you.

threw
through

45. He _____ a slow ball.

It went _____ the air.

I am _____ now.

to
too
two

46. I learned one big lesson in college, and that's _____ stay ahead and not _____ get behind.

Going _____ the lake one summer morning, the _____ of us decided it was _____ far _____ walk.

I like you, _____, but not _____ much.

waist
waste

47. _____ makes want.

The girl's _____ was small.

want
won't

48. If you do not understand how they _____ a particular job done, they _____ act impatient. Instead, they will come over and show you how they _____ it done. Then they'll correct any mistakes

that you have made and _____ leave until they watch you do it correctly.

weather
whether

49. Fair _____ is predicted.
_____ you like it or not, I will.

went
when

50. He left home _____ he graduated.
He _____ to the East Coast.

were
where

51. Several of my friends _____ coming from the Gulf Coast to Nashville, _____ the David Bowie concert was being held. David Bowie was great; he had moves that _____ so smooth they made me feel like a million dollars.

who's
whose

52. He is a friend _____ been working with me at Opryland since 1973. He is someone _____ able to get along with everybody. However, he expects perfection from everyone _____ under him. I don't know _____ friend he is.

your
you're

53. When you decide that _____ going to lose weight, the first thing to do is to check with _____ doctor. He may say _____ a person who needs exercise. On the other hand, _____ physical condition may allow for exercise and a low-calorie diet.

ANSWERS

1. an, an, an, an, and.
2. Accept, except, accept.
3. affect, effect.
4. aloud, allowed.
5. all ready, already.
6. along, alone.
7. altar, Alter.
8. are, or, are, or.
9. bear, bare, bear.
10. Break, brake.
11. buy, by.
12. Since, sense, cents, scents.
13. choose, chews
14. sight, site, sight, cite.
15. close, clothes.
16. course, Coarse, course.
17. desert, dessert.
18. doing, during.
19. every, ever.
20. further, farther, father.

21. feel, fill, fell.
22. half, have, of.
23. hear, here.
24. hole, whole.
25. hour, Our.
26. It's, It's, its.
27. know, now, no, know.
28. led, lead, lead, lead.
29. lie, lay, lain, lay, laid.
30. lose, loose, lose.
31. met, meet, meat.
32. on, own, own, on.
33. won, One.
34. passed, past, past.
35. patience, patients.
36. Peace, piece.
37. quite, quit, quiet, quite.
38. Rise, Raise.
39. Write, right.
40. Sit, Set.
41. then, then, than.
42. thank, think.
43. their, There, They're, there.
44. theirs, There's.
45. threw, through, through.
46. to, to; to, two, too, to; too, too.
47. Waste, waist.
48. want, won't, want, won't.
49. weather, Whether.
50. when, went.
51. were, where, were.
52. who's; who's, who's; whose.
53. you're, your; you're; your.

In the Review Practice, the numbers of the lessons that follow match those in the pretest above. Study all that you missed. Then take the post-test on all words.

Notice that the words are arranged alphabetically. When you are writing, you can use the Review Practice to check on the use of a word that you are unsure about.

50 Problem Words

Review practice

a
an
and

1. Use *a* before any word that does not begin with a vowel *sound*. Use *an* before any word that does begin with a vowel *sound* (a, e, i, o, u *sound*). Remember that the spelling and the sound may be different.

an umpire (um' pire), but *a* universe (yoo' ni verse)

Remember that we say letter names with sounds that are not the same as the letter.

Artoo–Detoo was *an* R2 unit.

Consonants (letters that are not vowels) whose names begin with vowel sounds need *an* before them when we use the letter as an initial.

She is *an* R.N. (ar—en).

These consonants are F (ef), H (aitch), L (el), M (em), N (en), R (ar), S (es), and X (eks). On the other hand, the vowel U begins with a consonant sound (yoo), so we say *a* before the initial U.

We went to *a* U.N. session.

Use *and* to join things together.

you *and* I

1. This is _____ disturbing issue.
2. We are looking for _____ electrical outlet.
3. The noise _____ smells of the place are offensive.
4. Their set is _____ RCA.

ANSWERS

1. a   2. an   3. and   4. an

---

accept 2. Use *accept* when you mean taking.
except   Use *except* when someone or something has been left out.

Everyone goes except you. You have been crossed off the list.

1. They all left _____ Larry.
2. Please _____ his apologies.
3. Lisa was the only one _____ Mary who cried.

ANSWERS

1. except.   2. accept.   3. except

---

affect 3. *Affect* is always a verb showing action.
effect Men like Napoleon *affect* the course of history.

Effect is usually a noun.

The decorator achieved an unusual *effect* with zebra-striped walls.

Use *effect* if *the* or *a* could be put before it.

The decorator achieved the effect.
NOT
Men like Napoleon the effect . . . .

1. He had a pleasant _____ on the crowd.

2. What you do will _____ his life.

ANSWERS

1. effect.   2. affect.

---

allowed   **4.** You are sometimes *allowed* to speak *aloud*.
aloud

> Speak out loud = speak aloud

1. I am not _____ to leave work before four o'clock.
2. She spoke her thoughts _____.

ANSWERS

1. allowed.   2. aloud.

---

all ready   **5.** Use *all ready* when you mean all (of them are) ready.
already   Use *already* to show something has finished happening (or has been decided).

We are all ready.
We are all (of us) ready.

1. We are _____ to go.
2. They had _____ heard the news.

ANSWERS

1. all ready.   2. already.

---

alone   **6.** Spell *alone* as you would spell a part of *lonely*.
along

> I am *lone*ly when I am a*lone*.

Spell *along* as you would *long*, which describes length.

> I walked a*long* a *long* road.

Also use *along* when you mean *also with*.

I went *along with* them.

1. He left me _____.
2. Please go _____ with me.

ANSWERS

1. alone.   2. along.

---

altar   **7.** Use *altar* when you are referring to a church interior.
alter   Use *alter* when you mean "to change."

> Awe at the altAr

1. The years will _____ anyone's appearance.
2. They stood together before the _____.
3. You will need to _____ the trousers.

ANSWERS

1. alter.   2. altar.   3. alter.

---

are
or

8. Use *or* when you're presenting a choice (you *or* I).

Use *are* when you're making a statement (you *are* the one).

> The sound of *or* is made with the mouth rounded and the lips pushed forward into an O shape.

1. Together they _____ invincible.
2. Choose now _____ you lose.
3. What _____ your reasons?

ANSWERS

1. are.   2. or.   3. are.

---

bear
bare

9. Use *bear* to name the animal or to mean "to endure, to stand" or "to bring to birth" or "to convey."

Use *bare* to mean naked.

B A R E
N A K E D

Daniel Boone could shoot better than he could spell.
It's bEar, not *bar* or *barE*. I cannot *bear* misspellings on trees.

1. The new look in clothing is the _____ midriff.
2. An animal that hibernates is the _____.
3. I'd appreciate hearing only the _____ facts.
4. Please _____ this in mind.

ANSWERS

1. bare.   2. bear.   3. bare.   4. bear.

---

break 10. You *break* eggs (*break* as in breaking a fast—*breakfast*).
brake   You *brake* a car.

> Break—Breakfast

1. _____ the window and you may get cut.
2. The serviceman replaced a left _____ shoe.
3. You should not _____ when you hit a slick spot.

ANSWERS

1. Break.   2. brake.   3. brake.

by 11. Use *by* in phrases like "by the sea" or "by the way."
buy   Use *buy* to indicate purchasing.

> by the way—buy the best.

1. He passed _____ the open door.
2. I like to _____ clothes.

ANSWERS

1. by.   2. buy.

cents 12. *Since* I had the good *sense* to pay only six *cents* for these *scents*, I have been
scents   congratulating myself.
sense
since   *Since* means *time*.   S⌐NCE
           Cents means money.   T⌐ME
           Scents means smells.

           Sense means reason or understanding or five senses (seeing, etc.)

1. Too many strong _____ make me sick.
2. I came here _____ you.
3. He had seventy _____.
4. I left _____ you came.
5. She had a good _____ of humor.

ANSWERS

1. scents.   2. since.   3. cents.   4. since.   5. sense.

chews 13. Use *chews* for the action with the teeth.
choose   Use *choose* for the action of choice.

che W s with teeth

ch⌐ws
te⌐th

1. Jake will always _____ the largest piece of pie.
2. Jake _____ his pie with enjoyment.

ANSWERS

1. choose.   2. chews.

---

cite 14. *Site* is a location.
sight   *Sight* is the act of seeing or something seen.
site   *Cite* is to quote or to summon to court.

⎛IGHT
⎝EE

1. You are a _____ to see.
2. The officer will be glad to _____ the charges.
3. He will _____ the Bible to prove anything.
4. He looked at the building _____.

ANSWERS

1. sight.   2. cite.   3. cite.   4. site.

---

clothes 15. Use *clothes* for writing about what you wear—garments.
close   Use *close* when you mean nearness (close to me) or "to shut"
                  (close the door).

Clothes are made from *cloth*.

1. Please _____ the door after you.
2. Put your _____ on, Jack.
3. This afternoon they will _____ the deal.

ANSWERS

1. close.   2. clothes.   3. close.

---

course 16. Use *course* to say "of course," or to write about a special road (race course), or to
coarse   refer to study of a course in school.
                  Use *coarse* to say something is rough and possibly hard.

Coarse is hard.

1. Of _____, he is not the only applicant.
2. The _____ texture of the material is not pleasing.
3. The cars were on the last mile of the _____.
4. I took that _____ last semester.

ANSWERS

1. course.   2. coarse.   3. course.   4. course.

---

desert 17. Soldiers of the French Foreign Legion fight natives in the *desert* unless they *desert*.
dessert   You eat *dessert*.

> desSert is sweet

1. The Sahara is a _____.
2. Ice cream is a _____.

ANSWERS

1. desert.   2. dessert.

---

doing 18. Use *doing* as you use *do*.
during   We are *doing* all right.

Use *during* when showing time passing. An event is always named after *during*: during the *war* . . . during the *show*.

During the intermission, we drank a coke.
1. How are you _____?
2. She left _____ the intermission.
3. Howard came _____ the test.
4. He is _____ well.

ANSWERS

1. doing.   2. during.   3. during.   4. doing.

---

ever 19. Use *ever* if you could use *never*.
every   We do *not ever* go. We *never* go.

Use *every* if you mean *each*.

We go *every* day. We go *each* day.
1. She saw us _____ week.
2. I wondered if he would _____ come.
3. He did not _____ write.
4. _____ month, we have a meeting.

ANSWERS

1. every.   2. ever.   3. ever.   4. Every.

---

farther
father
further

20. Use *farther* for *far*.

We drove *far*. They drove *farther*.

Use *further* for more when talking about something not measured.

We studied the problem *further*.
We wanted to *further* our understanding.

Use *father* for a male parent.

Please show me, *Father*.

1. I want to _____ my education.
2. I asked my _____.
3. New Bedford is _____ from Boston than I knew.
4. We shall talk _____ about it.

ANSWERS

1. further.   2. father.   3. farther.   4. further.

---

feel
fell
fill

21. Use *feel* for health or emotions or touch.

I *feel* good.

Use *fell* for the past of *fall*: fall, fell, fallen.

I *fell* off the roof.

Use *fill* to the brim.

I *fill* a glass of water to the brim.

F T LL
BR L M

1. How do you _____ about it?
2. Don't _____ bad.
3. We did not _____ the tank.
4. She _____ down the stairs.

ANSWERS

1. feel.   2. feel.   3. fill.   4. fell.

---

half
have
of

22. A *half* is a part of something.

I ate *half* the food.

Have is a verb or a helping verb.

I should *have* gone.
I *have* a new shirt.

"Should've" or "could've" or "would've" means "should *have*," "would *have*," or "could *have*," NOT "should of," "would of," or "could of."

A thing will always be named after the preposition *of*: a deck *of cards*, a moment *of quiet*.

1. I need a piece _____ paper.
2. We should not _____ waited.
3. They _____ a sled.
4. Here is _____ a piece.
5. We could _____ gotten lost.

ANSWERS

1. of.   2. have.   3. have.   4. half.   5. have.

---

hear 23. Use *hear* for what happens when you listen with your ear.
here Use *here* as you do the following: W(here) is she? She is (here). W(here) is she? She is t(here).

> *here*   *ear*
> *there*   *hear*
> *where*

1. I _____ the sound of bells.
2. _____ is the story I read first.
3. The best place for a picnic is _____.

ANSWERS

1. hear.   2. Here.   3. here.

---

hole 24. Use *hole* to write about what you fall into when someone has been digging.
whole Use *whole* to mean "all of it."

Fill up the hole with a *W* to make the landscape level—whole.

1. The dog dug a _____ to bury the bone.
2. I want the _____ truth.

ANSWERS

1. hole.   2. whole.

hour 25. Use *hour* to write about time.

our   Use *our* to show possession.

1. These are _____ plans.

2. _____ love is stong.

3. At what _____ do you get up?

ANSWERS

1. our.   2. Our.   3. hour.

---

its 26. *It's* means *it is* or *it has*. The apostrophe in *it's* stands for the letter or letters left out

it's   when the contraction was made: It's my turn. *It is* my turn.

It's been a long day. *It has* been a long day.

> Avoid mistakes by avoiding contractions.
> Write out *it is* or *it has*. Then never use an apostrophe with *its*.

Use *its* when you are showing ownership.

The dog chased *its* tail.

1. _____ a long way to Tipperary.

2. The horse lost _____ shoe.

3. _____ love you're searching for.

4. I know _____ been hard for you.

ANSWERS

1. It is (It's).   2. its.   3. It is (it's).   4. it has (it's).

---

know 27. Use *no* for a negative answer. Use *now* for "right now." Use *know* for "I under-

no   stand"—what you have *know*ledge about.

now

Now comes between the *no* and the *knowing*.

1. The customer needs help _____.

2. I _____ the customer needs help.

3. She gave _____ indication of her preference.

4. The answer is, "_____, you may not."

ANSWERS

1. now.   2. know.   3. no.   4. No.

lead 28. Use the verb *lead* when you mean the action of leading (Jane leads and Tarzan
led   follows).
lead   Use the verb *led* when you mean that Jane led Tarzan through the jungle yesterday.
             Use the noun *lead* when you mean the dark grey metal.

Present lead	Past led

Get the   lead   out!

1. You should follow where I _____.
2. They _____ me to the table.
3. You're heavier than _____.
4. He is the _____ horse in the parade.

ANSWERS

1. lead.   2. led.   3. lead.   4. lead.

lie 29.
lay
laid
lain

	Present	Past	Perfect	Meaning

Tense and meaning for *lie*:
  Today I lie down.
  Yesterday I lay down.
  I have lain down before.
	lie	lay	lain	to recline

Tense and meaning for *lay*:
  Today I lay it down.
  Yesterday I laid it down.
  I have laid it down before.
	lay	laid	laid	to place

Shared tenses and meanings for *lay*: The "to recline" *lay* is past tense. Yesterday I lay down.		lay		to recline
The "to place" *lay* is present tense. Today I lay it down.	lay			to place
Tenses and meanings for both *lie* and *lay*:	lie	lay	lain	to recline
	lay	laid	laid	to place

1. Please _____ the books down here.
2. I _____ down each day at noon now.
3. I _____ down yesterday.

4. I have _____ down every day at noon for three months.
5. Yesterday the newspaper _____ in the rain all day.
6. The paper boy _____ the paper inside our door.

ANSWERS

1. lay.   2. lie.   3. lay.   4. lain.   5. lay.   6. laid.

---

lose   30. Use *lose* to refer to something you have *lost*. Notice: *Lose* and *lost* each have one
loose   *o*. Use *loose* to refer to something which is rattling or not tight.

Something is L O *o* S E .

L◯SE
L◯ST

1. You _____ when you hesitate.
2. Something is _____ in the engine.
3. When I play him, I always _____.
4. He wore a _____ top.

ANSWERS

1. lose.   2. loose.   3. lose.   4. loose.

---

meat   31. *Meat* is what we *eat*.
meet   *Meet* and *met* are verbs in two forms, one present tense and one past tense.
met
I *meet* him on this corner.
I *met* him there yesterday.

1. Will they _____ each other again?
2. Cheese is as expensive as _____.
3. He has _____ his match.
4. We _____ every day for a week.

ANSWERS

1. meet.   2. meat.   3. met   4. met.

---

on   32. Use *on* to tell where something is (*on* the floor).
own   Use *own* to show *own*ership.

own—owner

1. I live in a house _____ that hill.

2. You _____ the largest farm.

3. The wreck occurred _____ the way to the airport.

ANSWERS

1. on.   2. own.   3. on.

---

one 33.   Use *one* when counting.

won   Use *won* to describe victory.

> I won one!

1. Who is the _____ you described?

2. Who _____ the game?

ANSWERS

1. one.   2. won.

---

past 34.   Use *past* to describe something that is "over with" or "gone by."

passed   When I walk *past* your house, I remember the happy days of the *past*.

Use *passed* as the *past* tense of the verb *pass*.

He *passed* the other runner.

> Days that have *passed* become the *past*.

1. My _____ life is my affair.

2. Life has _____ me by.

ANSWERS

1. past.   2. passed.

---

patience 35.   The people that we can *see* are patients.

patients   The thing that we cannot see is patience.

The *patients* waited with *patience*.

1. The teacher did not have enough _____.

2. The doctor had too many _____.

3. The _____ paid their bills slowly.

4. The doctor waited with _____.

ANSWERS

1. patience.   2. patients.   3. patients.   4. patience.

peace 36. Use *peace* when you write about war.
piece   Use *piece* when you mean "a part of."

1. The work is paid for by the _____.
2. We hope to see a _____ settlement soon.
3. I cut him a _____ of cake.
4. It is important to be at _____.

ANSWERS

1. piece.   2. peace.   3. piece.   4. peace.

---

quit 37. Use *quit* to mean *stop*. Use *quiet* for "*quiet* as a whisper."
quiet   Use *quite* for "*quite* enough."
quite

The "whisper quiet" has two syllables, qui'et, as does whis'per.

1. The library expects visitors to be _____.
2. I have had _____ enough of your behavior.
3. You'd better _____ while you are ahead.
4. They were _____ tired.

ANSWERS

1. quiet.   2. quite.   3. quit.   4. quite.

---

raise 38. Use *rise* when you mean "to move upward." (They rise to applaud the singer.)
rise   Use *raise* when you mean "to lift." (Please raise a window.)

Rising is something moving up.
Raising is something being moved up.

1. If you _____ the window, I'll jump.
2. Prices are sure to _____.
3. Don't _____ that issue again.
4. Gentlemen, please _____.

ANSWERS

1. raise.   2. rise.   3. raise.   4. rise.

write 39. Use *write* to refer to writing letters.

right　　Use *right* to indicate correct or the opposite of left.

　　Right, not Wrong! *Right* does not begin with a *W*, as wrong does.

1. You cannot ＿＿＿＿＿＿＿ on my book.

2. You have no ＿＿＿＿＿＿＿ to call me names.

3. She likes to ＿＿＿＿＿＿＿ letters.

4. My ＿＿＿＿＿＿＿ hand is stronger than my left.

ANSWERS

　　1. write.　　2. right.　　3. write.　　4. right.

set 40. Use *sit* when you mean to "sit upon" or to "sit down."

sit　　Use *set* when you mean "to place."

　　It sits, once you have set it somewhere.

1. Will you ＿＿＿＿＿＿＿ here?

2. I'd like for you to ＿＿＿＿＿＿＿ the package down.

3. ＿＿＿＿＿＿＿ the container down.

4. The container ＿＿＿＿＿＿＿ there.

ANSWERS

　　1. sit.　　2. set.　　3. set.　　4. sits.

thank 41. Use *thank* when you are grateful.

think　　Use *think* when you use your mind.

1. I do not ＿＿＿＿＿＿＿ she's here.

2. They ＿＿＿＿＿＿＿ about the problem

3. Do not forget to ＿＿＿＿＿＿＿ her.

ANSWERS

　　1. think.　　2. think.　　3. thank.

than 42. Use *then* like *when* for showing time. (He went *then*.)

then　　Use *than* to compare: better than I.

when—then

1. He is taller ＿＿＿＿＿＿＿ Jack.

2. I intended to go until ＿＿＿＿＿＿＿.

3. ＿＿＿＿＿＿＿ he fell from the balcony.

4. I like you better ＿＿＿＿＿＿＿ I do Mary.

ANSWERS

1. than.   2. then.   3. Then.   4. than.

---

their
there
they're

43. Use *their* to show possession (*their* house). Use *there*, as you use *here*, to point out the place of someone or something. (He lives *there*. She lives *here*.)

Use *there* to begin a sentence. (*There* are two choices.)

They're is a contraction for *they are*. The apostrophe stands for a letter left out when the contraction was made.

they + r =

theyr =

their

| Avoid mistakes by avoiding the use of contractions. Write out "they are." |

here
t\here
w\here

1. The sentry called, "Who goes _____?"
2. _____ the best.
3. We asked for _____ identifications.
4. The group improved _____ performance.
5. I guess _____ ready.

ANSWERS

1. there.   2. They are (They're).   3. their.   4. their.   5. they are (they're).

---

theirs
there's

44. Use *theirs* to show that something belongs to them.

The game was *theirs*.

Use *there's* to mean *there is*, or avoid trouble by writing out *there is*.

There's a new bird on the feeder.
There is a new bird on the feeder.

1. Is that child _____?
2. Do you think _____ enough spaghetti?
3. _____ too much here.

ANSWERS

1. theirs.
2. there's or there is.
3. There's or There is.

---

threw
through

45. Use *threw* to mean pitched. It tells what was done to something.

He *threw* a ball into a window.

Use *through* to tell where something went, or to mean *finished*.

The ball went *through* the air.
The team was *through*.

1. Are you _____ with your homework?
2. The umpire _____ him out.
3. We crawled _____ the cave.
4. She _____ a fit.

ANSWERS

1. through.   2. threw.   3. through.   4. threw.

---

two **46.** Use *two* for the number 2. Use *too* for *also* and for "too much of.'"

too

to   t o o o o o o   much—t o o o o o o   many

Use *to* for all other choices you have to make.

More than *two* are *too* many *to* send.

1. He wants _____ be noticed.
2. I have _____ jobs.
3. This last act was _____ much.
4. I'd like to go, _____.
5. Eliza said, "That is _____ bad."

ANSWERS

1. to.   2. two.   3. too.   4. too.   5. too.

---

waste **47.** Use *waste* when you mean what Benjamin Franklin was against.

waist   Use *waist* for a reference to human anatomy.

Waste no food, and your *waist* will grow.

1. To _____ not is to want not.
2. She measured his _____.
3. Don't _____ that food.

ANSWERS

1. waste.   2. waist.   3. waste.

---

won't **48.** Use *want* to show desire or need. *Won't* is a contraction for *will not*.

want

| Avoid contractions. Use "will not." |

1. I _____ things to go right.
2. You _____ tell on me.

ANSWERS

1. want.   2. won't or will not.

---

weather 49. Use *weather* when you write about climate.
whether   Use *whether* for "whether . . . or not" meanings.

Whether you like it or not!

1. _____or not I go is unimportant.
2. The _____ is beautiful today.
3. I don't know _____ he is coming.

ANSWERS

1. Whether.   2. weather.   3. whether.

---

went 50. Use *went* for going through space:
when
We *go* now.   We *went* yesterday.   We *have gone* before.

Use *when* to tell about time.

I will go *when* you do.

| when—then |

1. _____ will you be ready?
2. They _____ to the game together.
3. The candy _____ fast.

ANSWERS

1. When.   2. went.   3. went.

---

were 51. Use *were* when you need a verb (We *were*.) Use *where* when you ask for directions.
where

Here is in *w(here)*. They both say *where*.

1. _____ are you going?
2. We _____ going to the pool.
3. I don't know _____ they went.

ANSWERS

1. Where.   2. were.   3. where.

who's 52. Use *whose* to show possession. (Whose child is this?)
whose   *Who's* means *who is*.

> Avoid contractions. Write out "who is."

1. Besides us, _____ going?
2. John is the person _____ responsible.
3. We don't know _____ car we'll take.

   ANSWERS

   1. who is (who's).   2. who is (who's).   3. whose.

your 53. Use *your* to show possession (*your* friend). *You're* means "you are."
you're

> Avoid contractions. Write out "you are."

1. Let me try to understand _____ position.
2. I like _____ friend.
3. I know _____ the one for the job.

   ANSWERS

   1. your.   2. your.   3. you are (you're).

NAME

50. WORDS

Post-Test A

Underline the correct word for each choice.

1. That's (a, an) orange from Texas.
2. Our team would not (accept, except) defeat.
3. The newspaper had a strong (affect, effect) on the community.
4. The hospital has not (aloud, allowed) visitors.
5. We have (all ready, already) decided.
6. When the children moved, he was (alone, along) in the house.
7. Don't (alter, altar) the plans.
8. Either you (or, are) I will go.
9. I cannot (bare, bear) to let you go.
10. That boy will live to (brake, break) laws.
11. He will (by, buy) my lunch Tuesday.
12. That idea doesn't make (cents, scents, sense, since).
    You may stay up late (cents, scents, sense, since) you don't have school tomorrow.
13. She will (choose, chews) her own school.
14. We hurried to keep the car in (cite, sight, site).
15. I like the (clothes, close) she wears.
16. The gravel where he fell was (coarse, course).
17. Eat your (desert, dessert), Frankenstein.
18. She washes dishes (doing, during) commercials.
19. I see her (ever, every) day.
20. She will advance (father, farther, further) in her job.
21. I (feel, fell, fill) blue today.
22. You should (half, have, of) seen it.
23. Daniel Boone could (hear, here) well.
24. That's the (whole, hole) story.
25. This is (our, hour) sponsor.
26. The dog shook (its, it's) head.
27. I am sure (no, now, know) that he meant it.
28. Martha (lead, led) George a dog's life.
29. (Lie, Lay) the book on the chair.
    I (lie, lay) down every day now.
    He has (lain, laid) down for a nap.
    She has (lain, laid) the heavy package in the hall.

30. Something is (loose, lose) in the engine.
31. I want to (meat, meet, met) him.
    We almost (meat, meet, met) last fall.
32. Mind your (on, own) business.
33. That's (one, won) game I'll miss.
34. What is (past, passed) is behind.
35. She has great (patience, patients) with my children.
36. A (peace, piece) of pie is my choice for dessert.
37. I enjoy a (quiet, quit, quite) evening at home.
38. They (raise, rise) early in the morning.
39. She discussed the way I (write, right).
40. Won't you (sit, set) here?
41. I (thank, think) that this was important for me.
42. She knew more (then, than) anyone else.
43. They lost (their, there) place in line.
44. Is that car (theirs, there's)?
45. I zipped (threw, through) my work in two hours.
46. He has had (to, too, two) many chances.
47. Put the (waist, waste) paper here.
48. They (want, won't) to know your reasons.
49. I shall ask (weather, whether) he is going.
50. I almost (went, when) to the state university.
51. Be careful (were, where) you go.
52. Do you know (who's, whose) song that is?
53. (You're, Your) grandmother is beautiful.

Ask your instructor to check this, or turn it in.

See Post-test B, which follows, or writing assignments in **54–56**.

NAME _____

50. WORDS

Post-Test B

Underline the correct word for each choice.

1. I bought (a, an, and) IBM Selectric second-hand.
2. Everyone sang (accept, except) Ted.
3. She has a great (affect, effect) on me.
4. She objected (allowed, aloud).
5. The car is (all ready, already).
6. Will you take me (alone, along) with you?
7. He paid to (altar, alter) the fit.
8. They (are, or) sick of the mess.
9. (Bare, Bear) the fact in mind that he was new at the job.
10. I would like to (brake, break) his neck.
11. The Jenkins plan to (buy, by) a new car.
12. (Cents, Scents, Sense, Since) you ask, yes, I did.
    He has shown good (cents, scents, sense, since) in choosing a career.
13. Don't try to (chews, choose) for me.
14. The river is a (cite, sight, site) to behold.
15. We find great (clothes, close) at Good Will.
16. This is my first (coarse, course) in college.
17. Chocolate anything is my favorite (desert, dessert).
18. I met him (doing, during) the holidays.
19. Will this program (ever, every) end?
20. Read (farther, father, further) in the fine print.
21. Mother broke her hip when she (feel, fell, fill) down.
22. We could (half, have, of) left an hour earlier.
23. Put the washer in (hear, here).
24. I want you to tell the (hole, whole) truth.
25. Each class lasts about an (hour, our).
26. Most of the time, (its, it's) my fault.
27. I do not (know, no, now) what to do (know, no, now).
28. He (lead, led) the parade.
29. The doctor told me to (lie, lay) down.
    He (lay, laid) down.
    He (lay, laid) the book down.
    He has (laid, lain) down.
    He has (laid, lain) the cornerstone.

30. They tried to (loose, lose) the car following them.
31. Will you (meat, meet, met) me after work?
32. I want to (on, own) my (on, own) business.
33. He ordered (one, won) dozen roses.
34. She lived in the (passed, past).
35. I need more (patience, patients) with other people.
36. They learned to live in (peace, piece).
37. Please be (quiet, quit, quite) while I study.
38. We (raise, rise) corn.
39. That is the (right, write) answer.
40. We (set, sit) at the table and talk.
41. She did not (thank, think) about the others.
42. I paid the check; (than, then) I left.
43. It was (their, there) farm.
44. (Theirs, There's) a new model out.
45. She was (threw, through) with him.
46. It was just (to, too, two) cold for me.
47. His (waist, waste) is too inches bigger.
48. It (want, won't) be long.
49. He asked (weather, whether) we knew.
50. They (went, when) to every game.
51. I wondered (were, where) you (were, where).
52. She had many friends (who's, whose) names she forgot.
53. (You're, Your) anger showed when he ruined (you're, your) joke.

Ask your instructor to check these answers, or turn them in.

NAME _____

51. BASIC SPELLING RULES
Pretest

A. Write the correct form these words take when the base word and the suffix (the ending) are put together.

1. prefer + ing	11. begin + ing
2. university + es	12. omit + ed
3. gossip + ed	13. journey + ed
4. desire + ing	14. lose + ing
5. rely + es	15. dim + ing
6. judge + ing	16. try + ed
7. day + s	17. deny + al
8. instil + ing	18. write + ing
9. come + ing	19. lay + ing
10. nine + ty	20. study + ing

B. Choose the correct form from each pair of words below. Circle your choice.

1. believe	2. frieght	3. decieve	4. weigh	5. rien
beleive	freight	deceive	wiegh	rein

ANSWERS
1. preferring (1).
2. universities (4).
3. gossiped (1).
4. desiring (2).
5. relies (4).
6. judging (2).
7. days (4).
8. instilling (1).
9. coming (2).
10. ninety (2)
11. beginning (1).
12. omitted (1).
13. journeyed (4).
14. losing (2).
15. dimming (1).
16. tried (4).
17. denial (4).
18. writing (2).
19. laying (4).
20. studying (4).

B.
1. believe (3).
2. freight (3).
3. deceive (3).
4. weigh (3).
5. rein (3).

The Pretest Answers are keyed to instructions in spelling that follow. In the assignment block below, place a check by any numbers like those that follow words you missed.

Assignment Block

Rule 1   _____   Rule 2   _____

Rule 3   _____   Rule 4   _____

In using the instructions, do this: If you made any errors under Rule 1, turn to Rule 1. If you missed none in 1, you understand this spelling use. Skip to another numbered area in which you did make an error. Work all areas you have checked. Then take the post-test.

51 Basic Spelling Rules

Rule 1

Doubling the Final Consonant

PROBLEM

When do you need to double the final letter of a word before adding a suffix (an ending added to a word to change its use)?

SOLUTION

This is a long rule that sets up four conditions to consider when adding a suffix to a base word. A consonant is any letter other than *a*, *e*, *i*, *o*, or *u*; these are vowels. *Y* counts as a vowel when it sounds like *i* or *e*.

CONDITIONS

Double the final consonant when

admi (t)   1. The base word ends in a single consonant.

adm (i) t   2. A single vowel comes before the consonant.

(i) ng   3. The suffix begins with a vowel.

ad-mit′   4. The base word has only one syllable or is accented on the last syllable.

Study these examples.

Base Word	Consonant to Double	Single Vowel	Suffix	One Syllable or Accent on Last Syllable	Correct Spelling
admit	admit (t)	adm (i) t	(i) ng	ad-mit′	admitting
begin	begi (n)	beg (i) n	(i) ng	be-gin′	beginning
stop	sto (p)	st (o) p	(e) d	stop	stopped

Fill in the chart below, doubling the final consonants when the rule above applies.

Base Word (mark accent)	Consonant to Double	Single Vowel	Suffix	Correct Spelling
1. fog′	*g*	*o*	-y	*foggy*
2. compel			-ing	
3. defer			-ment	
4. confer			-ing	
5. dim			-ed	

Base Word (mark accent)	Consonant to Double	Single Vowel	Suffix	Correct Spelling
6. drop			-ing	
7. occur			-ence	
8. log			-ing	
9. refer			-ed	
10. get			-ing	

ANSWERS

Base Word (mark accent)	Consonant to Double	Single Vowel	Suffix	Correct Spelling
2. compel'	l	e	- (i) ng	compelling
3. defer'	r	e	- m ent	deferment
4. confer'	r	e	- (i) ng	conferring
5. dim'	m	i	- (e) d	dimmed
6. drop'	p	o	- (i) ng	dropping
7. occur'	r	u	- (e) nce	occurrence
8. log'	g	o	- (i) ng	logging
9. refer'	r	e	- (e) d	referred
10. get'	t	e	- (i) ng	getting

Rule 2

Dropping the Final e

PROBLEM

Many words end in silent *e* (an *e* that we do not pronounce or hear). Sometimes the silent *e* is dropped and sometimes the *e* is kept when a suffix is added.

SOLUTION

Drop the silent *e* when adding a suffix that begins with a vowel. Keep the silent *e* when adding a suffix that begins with a consonant.

Study these examples.

Base Word	Silent *e*	Suffix	Correct Spelling
make	mak (e)	(i) ng	making
use	us (e)	(i) ng	using
use	us (e)	l ess	useless
surprise	surpris (e)	(i) ng	surprising
surprise	surpris (e)	(e) d	surprised
judge	judg (e)	(i) ng	judging

For practice of this rule, fill in the chart as Number 1 is done.

Base Word	Silent e	Suffix	Correct Spelling
1. fame	*fame*	- (o) us	*famous*
2. receive		-ing	
3. hope		-ing	
4. hope		-less	
5. use		-ing	
6. awe		-some	
7. suppose		-ing	
8. desire		-ing	
9. guide		-ing	
10. use		-less	
11. excite		-ment	

ANSWERS

2. receive	receiv (e)	- (i) ng	receiving
3. hope	hop (e)	- (i)ng	hoping
4. hope	hop (e)	- l ess	hopeless
5. use	us (e)	- (i) ng	using
6. awe	aw (e)	- s ome	awesome
7. suppose	suppos (e)	- (i) ng	supposing
8. desire	desir (e)	- s	desires
9. guide	guid (e)	- (i) ng	guiding
10. use	us (e)	- l ess	useless
11. excite	excit (e)	- m ent	excitement

Rule 3

i Before

e

PROBLEM

When does *i* come before *e*, and when does *e* come before *i*?

SOLUTION

Write *i* before *e*/ except after *c*,/ or if sounded like *a*/ as in *neighbor* and *weigh*.

i before *e* belief	except after *c* perceive	except sounded like a freight (frayt)

Indicate the parts of the rule that apply to the spelling of these words: (a) *i* before *e* (b) except after *c* (c) except sounding like *a*.

1. weighed	6. believe
2. piece	7. receive
3. conceit	8. weight
4. eight	9. achieve
5. chief	10. neighbor

ANSWERS

1. c   2. a   3. b   4. c   5. a   6. a   7. b   8. c   9. a
10. c

Rule 4

Changing y to i

PROBLEM

When do you change the *y* to *i* before adding a suffix?

SOLUTION

When a word ends in a consonant + *y* combination, change *y* to *i* before adding the suffix, *unless* the suffix begins with an *i*. A consonant is any letter other than *a, e, i, o,* or *u*.

CONDITIONS

Change *y* to *i* when

1. The base word ends in *y*.
2. A consonant comes before the *y*.
3. The suffix does not begin with *i*.

Note: To add *s* to a word that fits these conditions, change the *y* to *i* and add *es*, not just *s*.

Study these examples.

Base Word	Consonant + *y*	Suffix	Suffix Begins with *i*	Correct Spelling
study	stu (dy)	-es		studies
study	stu (dy)	-ing	(i) ng	studying
baby	bab (by)	-es		babies
baby	ba (by)	-ing	(i) ng	babying
try	t (ry)	-es		tries
try	t (ry)	-ing	(i) ng	trying

Fill in the following columns as Number 1 is done.

Base Word	Consonant + *y*	Suffix	Suffix Begins with *i*	Correct Spelling
1. happy	*py*	-ly		*happily*
2. story		-es		
3. bury		-al		
4. carry		-ed		
5. study		-ing		
6. try		-al		
7. pity		-ing		
8. society		-es		
9. industry		-es		
10. busy		-ness		
11. easy		-ly		
12. dry		-est		

ANSWERS

	Base Word	Consonant + *y*	Suffix Begins with *i*	Correct Spelling
2.	story	ry	no	stories
3.	bury	ry	no	burial
4.	carry	ry	no	carried
5.	study	dy	- (i) ng	studying
6.	try	ry	no	trial
7.	pity	ty	- (i) ng	pitying
8.	society	ty	no	societies
9.	industry	ry	no	industries
10.	busy	sy	no	business
11.	easy	sy	no	easily
12.	dry	ry	no	driest

Now take the post-test.

NAME _____

51. BASIC SPELLING RULES
Post-Test A

A. Use the rules you have learned, looking back at them if necessary, and add the base word to the suffix correctly.

1. refer + ed
2. buy + ing
3. family + es
4. try + ing
5. offer + ed
6. write + ing
7. hope + ing
8. try + al
9. cry + s
10. fry + ing
11. trim + ed
12. begin + ing
13. hope + ful
14. notice + ing
15. come + ing
16. drip + ed
17. fry + s
18. sit + ing
19. reject + ing
20. change + less

B. Put a circle around the correct spelling in each pair below.

1. riendeer   2. relieve   3. receive   4. neice   5. weight
   reindeer   releive   recieve   niece   wieght

Ask your instructor to check your answers, or turn them in.

See Post-test B or writing assignments in **55** and **56**.

NAME _____

51. BASIC SPELLING RULES
Post-Test B

A. Use the rules you have learned, looking back at them if necessary, and add the base word to the suffix correctly.

1. happy + ness		11. stop + ed	
2. include + ing		12. advise + er	
3. equip + ment		13. come + ing	
4. city + s		14. activity + ies	
5. study + ed		15. manage + ment	
6. begin + ing		16. study + ing	
7. party + s		17. state + ment	
8. swim + ing		18. cram + ed	
9. give + ing		19. keep + ing	
10. dine + ing		20. make + shift	

B. Put a circle around the correct spelling in each pair below.

1. believe	2. frieght	3. decieve	4. friend	5. their
beleive	freight	deceive	freind	thier

Ask your instructor to check your answers, or turn them in.

NAME

52. PLURALS

Pretest

Write the plurals for these nouns.

1. attorney	9. Henry	17. fuzz
2. knife	10. tomato	18. display
3. epoch	11. switch	19. deputy
4. compress	12. gulch	20. tax
5. life	13. Burns	21. Thomas
6. echo	14. proof	22. night
7. monarch	15. year	23. thing
8. stereo	16. family	

ANSWERS

1. attorneys (4).
2. knives (7).
3. epochs (3).
4. compresses (2).
5. lives (7).
6. echoes (6).
7. monarchs (3).
8. stereos (6).
9. Henrys (5).
10. tomatoes (6).
11. switches (3).
12. gulches (3).
13. Burnses (2).
14. proofs (7).
15. years (1).
16. families (4).
17. fuzzes (2).
18. displays (4).
19. deputies (4).
20. taxes (2).
21. Thomases (2).
22. nights (1).
23. things (1).

The pretest answers are keyed to instructions in spelling that follow. In the assignment block below, place a check by any numbers like those that follow words you missed.

Assignment Block

Rule 1 _____   Rule 5 _____

Rule 2 _____   Rule 6 _____

Rule 3 _____   Rule 7 _____

Rule 4 _____

In using the instructions, do this: If you made any errors under Rule 1, turn to Rule 1. If you missed none in 1, you understand this plural ending. Skip to another numbered area in which you did make an error. Work all areas you have checked. Then take the post-test.

52 Plurals

A noun shows whether it is singular (means only one) or plural (means more than one) by its form. Most nouns add *s* or *es* at the end to show that they mean more than one. But there are some special rules for spelling many nouns when *s* or *es* is added.

Rule 1

s on Most Nouns

PROBLEM

Most nouns just add *s* to show that they mean more than one. But a writer must know what words are nouns before he or she can know whether to add an *s*, and many speakers and writers leave *s* off the ends of words in general.

SOLUTION

A noun is the name of a person, place, or thing. If you write about more than one of these, be sure to put an *s* at the end of the word meaning persons, places, or things.

Practice learning to recognize nouns that need plurals. In the following sentences, underline every word that names a person, place, or thing. If it means more than one person, place, or thing, add an *s* to the end.

1. Many thing happened to the boy at the fair.
2. The woman cooked several kind.
3. One of my highest aim is to get a degree.
4. These gift are the best present Sue ever received.
5. Two teacher taught twenty-four student, who ranged from five to thirteen year of age.
6. James is the closest of her friend.
7. The parent get tired of television program and wish for more change in scheduling.

ANSWERS

1. thing(s), boy, fair.
2. woman, kind(s).
3. one, aim(s), degree.
4. gift(s), present(s), Sue.
5. teacher(s), student(s), year(s), age.
6. James, friend(s).
7. parent(s), program(s), change(s), scheduling.

Rule 2

Plural for s, sh, x, and z Endings

PROBLEM

Although most plurals are formed with a simple *s*, others are formed with an *es* because of the ending sound of the base word. Words ending in *s*, *sh*, *x*, and *z* will generally require an *es* plural because they need an extra syllable to make their pronunciation easier.

kiss—kisses (not kiss—kisss)
swish—swishes (not swish—swishs)
box—boxes (not box—boxs)
ax—axes (not ax—axs)

SOLUTION

To form the plurals of words ending in *s*, *sh*, *x*, and *z*, add *es*.

Add plural endings to the following words. Some form plurals through the addition of the *s*; some through the addition of *es*.

1. strap	4. box	7. leave	10. bash
2. miss	5. splash	8. six	11. mush
3. play	6. fox	9. wax	12. floor

ANSWERS

1. straps	4. boxes	7. leaves	10. bashes
2. misses	5. splashes	8. sixes	11. mushes
3. plays	6. foxes	9. waxes	12. floors

Rule 3

Plural for *ch* Sound in Endings

PROBLEM

The plural of a word ending in *ch* may take an *s* or an *es* plural, depending on the sound of the *ch* in the ending of the base word.

Churches has a soft *ch* sound, so the *es* ending is used (soft *ch* sound as in *cheese*).

Monarchs has a hard *ch* sound, so the *s* ending is used (hard *ch* sound like *k* as in *character*).

SOLUTION

Use *es* if the *ch* sound is soft (hisses at the end). Use *s* if the *ch* sound is hard (*k*).

Fill in the correct columns below with the plurals of the nouns given.

	Hard (k)	Soft (ch)
1. peach		
2. arch		
3. attach		
4. church		
5. epoch		
6. witch		

ANSWERS

	Hard (k)	Soft (ch)
1. peach		peaches
2. arch		arches
3. attach		attaches
4. church		churches
5. epoch	epochs	
6. witch		witches

Rule 4

Plurals and Vowel + y Endings

PROBLEM

Basic Spelling Rules, Rule 3, tells about adding an ending to a word ending in a *consonant + y*. You are to drop the *y* and add *i + es* to spell the plural correctly. This rule that you already know applies to plurals as well as to other endings.

deputy + s = deputies

Now you need to know how to add *s* to a noun ending in a *vowel + y*.

pays   keys   chimneys

SOLUTION

A *vowel + y combination* at the end of a word forms a plural by adding only *s*.

If a word ends in a vowel + *y*, add only *s* to form its plural.

key	keys
chimney	chimneys

Write the plurals of the following words. Look back at **51**, Rule 3, if you need help on the words that end in a consonant + *y*.

1. activity	7. toy
2. way	8. company
3. journey	9. buy
4. holiday	10. Saturday
5. responsibility	11. lay
6. cranberry	12. country

ANSWERS

1. activities	7. toys
2. ways	8. companies
3. journeys	9. buys
4. holidays	10. Saturdays
5. responsibilities	11. lays
6. cranberries	12. countries

Rule 5

Plurals and Proper Names

PROBLEM

First and last proper names ending in a consonant + *y* take only an *s* plural to keep from changing the name.

More than one Kennedy—the Kennedys
More than one Libby—the Libbys

Most proper names, in fact, require only an *s*; but some must have an *es* added because of the sound. (See Rule 2 above.)

More than one Jones—the Joneses
More than one Charles—the Charleses

SOLUTION

For first and last names ending in *s*, add *es* to form the plural. For proper names ending in a consonant + *y*, add only an *s* so that the name is not changed.

Write plurals for these proper names.

1. Tyler
2. Lesly
3. Gladys
4. Johnson
5. Fries
6. James
7. Alexis
8. Guy
9. Story

ANSWERS

1. Tylers
2. Leslys
3. Gladyses
4. Johnsons
5. Frieses
6. Jameses
7. Alexises
8. Guys
9. Storys

Rule 6

Plurals of Nouns Ending in *o*

PROBLEM

Most nouns ending in *o* form plurals through the addition of *s*. There are six nouns to which *es* must be added to form the plural.

veto — vetoes	potato — potatoes
echo — echoes	tomato — tomatoes
hero — heroes	torpedo — torpedoes

SOLUTION

Memorize these nonsense sentences.

The *hero* cast a *veto*.
The *echo* of the *torpedo* shriveled the *tomato* and the *potato*.

Remember that all other words ending in *o* take an *s* plural.

Work this exercise. Without looking at the nonsense sentences, write in the plurals.

1. torpedo
2. zoo
3. tomato
4. silo
5. veto
6. boo
7. echo
8. potato
9. radio
10. memo
11. hero
12. photo

ANSWERS

1. torpedoes
2. zoos
3. tomatoes
4. silos

5. vetoes
6. boos
7. echoes
8. potatoes

9. radios
10. memos
11. heroes
12. photos

Rule 7

Plurals of Nouns Ending in f, fe, or ff

PROBLEM

Most nouns ending in *f*, *fe*, or *ff* form plurals through the addition of *s* only.

turf—turfs   strife—strifes   cliff—cliffs

Some words ending in *f* or *fe*, however, change their ending to *ves* to form their plurals. These are:

elf — elves
half — halves
knife — knives
leaf — leaves
life — lives

self — selves
shelf — shelves
thief — thieves
wife — wives
wolf — wolves

SOLUTION

Learn these nonsense sentences.

The *thieves* hired *elves* to cut the *wolves* in *halves*, put them on *shelves*, and cover them with *leaves*.

The *wives* feared for their *lives* when they lost their *knives*.

Remember the nine words in them are are the only words ending in *f* or *fe* that must form the plural by changing the *f* to *v* and adding *es*. To the other words ending in *f*, you may simply add *s* to form the plural.

Write the correct plurals of the following words.

1. thief
2. chief
3. wife
4. self

5. wolf
6. half
7. leaf
8. chef

9. life
10. shelf
11. elf
12. knife

ANSWERS

1. thieves
2. chiefs
3. wives
4. selves

5. wolves
6. halves
7. leaves
8. chefs

9. lives
10. shelves
11. elves
12. knives

Now take the post-test.

52. PLURALS

Post-Test A

Write the plurals for these nouns.

1. journey	10. potato	19. ax
2. life	11. witch	20. James
3. monarch	12. church	21. reason
4. dress	13. Williams	22. housewife
5. wife	14. roof	23. proof
6. veto	15. family	24. thing
7. study	16. buzz	25. friend
8. vireo	17. day	26. curl
9. Amy	18. patriarch	27. gulf

Ask your instructor to check your answers, or turn them in.

See Post-test B or writing assignments in **55** and **56**.

NAME

52. PLURALS
Post-Test B

Write the plurals for these nouns.

1. epoch	10. chance	19. Jones
2. cliff	11. leaf	20. buy
3. Sunday	12. Smitty	21. hero
4. photo	13. present	22. church
5. tornado	14. strife	23. kind
6. box	15. key	24. arch
7. life	16. way	25. study
8. peach	17. thief	26. potato
9. year	18. buzz	27. holiday

Ask your instructor to check your answers, or turn them in.

53. WRITING NUMBERS

Pretest

Write correctly the numbers in the following list. If the numbers are written correctly, write *C* for correct. If they are not, make changes.

1. 381 _____
2. sixty-one _____
3. 3000 _____
4. six hundred and one _____
5. six hundred one _____
6. 6/7 _____
7. 15 _____
8. thirty five _____
9. one-fourth _____
10. 6 _____

ANSWERS

1. C
2. C
3. three thousand
4. 601
5. 601
6. six-sevenths
7. fifteen
8. thirty-five
9. C
10. six

If you missed any of these, study the lesson that follows.

53 Writing Numbers

PROBLEM

Numbers are written in two forms: words and numerals. The different forms are used for different situations.

I watched the entertainer swallow *two* swords.
We hatched *158* baby chicks in an incubator.

SOLUTION 1

Write in words a number that can be written in one or two words.

one   six million   thirty thousand   one-third

All the numbers from one to one hundred can be written in one or two words and should be spelled out.

seven   seventeen   seventy

SOLUTION 2

Write in numerals (figures) a number that takes more than two words to write out.

  130 (NOT one hundred thirty, three words)
1717 (NOT one thousand seven hundred seventeen, five words)

Write correct (C) or incorrect (I) before the following sentences. Correct the incorrect ones.

_____ 1. Ed worked on a tramp steamer 287 days last year.

_____ 2. Exactly 1075 bankers will be present.

_____ 3. We received sixteen applicants.

_____ 4. I have three thousand one rubber bands.

_____ 5. Charlie the Tuna has appeared on television 11,000 times.

_____ 6. He is 50 years old.

_____ 7. We saw 123 kinds of roses.

ANSWERS

1. *C*   2. *C*   3. *C*   4. *I*—3001   5. *I* eleven thousand   6. *I*—fifty   7. *C*

EXCEPTION 1

Be consistent in spelling numbers within a sentence. If you must use numerals for one number because it takes more than two words to write out, use numerals for all numbers in that sentence.

The nuclear plant will have 18 buildings and will require 3670 acres.

EXCEPTION 2

If the first word of a sentence is a number, it must be written in words even if it takes more than two words. It is sometimes better to rewrite the sentence so that the number is not the first word.

One hundred one of our fighters never returned.
or
We lost 101 fighters.

Change any numbers in the following sentences that are not correctly written.

1. He was stuck in an elevator with 13 people for 20 minutes.
2. She is five feet, nine inches tall and weighs 139 pounds.
3. The team has a record of 165 wins and 94 losses in the last eleven years.
4. 117 of the workers went on strike last night.
5. 250 congressmen voted for the bill.

ANSWERS

Only the following changes should be made:
1. thirteen, twenty.
2. 5 feet, 9 inches.
3. 11.
4. One hundred seventeen *or* Last night, 117 of the workers . . . .
5. Two hundred fifty *or* Voting for the bill were 250 congressmen.

PROBLEM

Hyphens are needed to spell some numbers because they are made up of two words.

SOLUTION 1

Most of the numbers from twenty-one through ninety-nine are made up of two numbers, and a hyphen is needed between the words. The one-word numbers (thirty, forty, and so on) need no hyphens.

sixty-one   thirty-seven
              but
  sixty   thirty

SOLUTION 2

Fractions are made up of two numbers, a numerator and a denominator. A hyphen is placed between the two.

one-fourth   thirteen-sixteenths

Place hyphens where they belong in the following numbers

1. eighty three
2. twenty five
3. four fifths
4. sixty
5. sixty three
6. nineteen twentieths
7. one hundred

ANSWERS

1. eighty-three
2. twenty-five
3. four-fifths
4. no hyphen
5. sixty-three
6. nineteen-twentieths
7. no hyphen

Now take the post-test.

53. WRITING NUMBERS

Post-Test A

A. Write correctly the numbers in the following list. Change only the numbers that are incorrect.

1. 410 _____
2. seventy four _____
3. eight hundred forty-seven _____
4. 1000 _____
5. 1595 _____
6. 27 _____
7. forty-two _____
8. seven tenths _____
9. four million _____
10. one third _____

B. In the following sentences, change any numbers that should be changed.

1. 16,024 people live in Landmark, Delaware.
2. Gwaltney signed a contract for thirty-seven thousand, five hundred dollars for each of the next two years.
3. 163 technicals have been called against the team since it began playing.
4. The plant will employ 342 people working two shifts.
5. Three thousand dollars would buy the land.

Ask your instructor to check your answers, or turn them in.

See Post-test B or writing assignments in **55** and **56**.

<u>NAME</u> _____

53. WRITING NUMBERS
Post-Test B

A. Write correctly the numbers in the following list. Change only the numbers that are incorrect.

1. 236 _____
2. fifty-four _____
3. 13 _____
4. two thousand five _____
5. six hundred one _____
6. two thousand _____
7. twenty five _____
8. 2/3 _____
9. 5000 _____
10. one sixth _____

B. In the following sentences, change any numbers that should be changed.

1. 2043 coal miners went on strike for better health care.
2. The teacher graded 27 essays of five hundred words each.
3. They packed two hundred forty-five cans of rations and three cases of beverages.
4. One hundred thirty-two cases have been reported in Madison County.
5. I ordered 300 cases.

Ask your instructor to check your answers, or turn them in.

WRITING ASSIGNMENTS

PART

The assignments on the following pages will give you practice in using your knowledge about writing. Your instructor will assign sentences, paragraphs, or essays for you to write. The sentence assignments (54) are keyed to particular lessons in the lab manual. The paragraph and essay assignments will show how you can use all of your language skills together. The paragraph assignments (55) will also help you develop ideas in your writing, and the essay assignments (56) will teach you an order for writing your ideas.

SENTENCES

54 Sentence Assignments

After you have finished a lesson in the manual, look through these assignments for a writing exercise about the same problem. Look back at the lesson if you need to.

24.
Fragments
Use each of the following groups of words in a sentence. Remember that each sentence must make a complete statement.

1. that will pay well
2. a neighbor whom I like
3. to decide what I want to do
4. the best being my child
5. after the snow melts
6. in one big, sticky mess
7. trying to start the car
8. especially my father
9. because she was kind
10. not just the salary

Ask your instructor to check your sentences.

25.
Fused
Sentences
Write two sentences for each of the following. Be sure that the first complete statement (A) is separated from the second complete statement (B).

1. (A) something you like
   (B) something you don't like
2. (A) something you like
   (B) why you like it
3. (A) how something has made you feel
   (B) why it made you feel that way
4. (A) something exciting that happened
   (B) something else exciting that happened just after (A)
5. (A) a question
   (B) its answer

Ask your instructor to check your sentences.

26.
Comma
Splices
Write two sentences about each of the following. Be sure that the first complete statement (A) is separated from the second complete statement (B).

1. (A) something your job is
   (B) something it is not
2. (A) something that upsets you
   (B) why it upsets you
3. (A) a question
   (B) its answer
4. (A) the worst thing anyone ever did to you
   (B) how you feel about this
5. (A) something you want to do
   (B) whether you think you will do it or not

Ask your instructor to check your sentences.

27.
General
Subject-
Verb
Agreement
Write five sentences using each of the following as a predicate (verb).

1. buys
2. ask
3. sloshes
4. interests
5. hop

Now write five sentences using each of the following as a subject.

1. people
2. "Silver Bells"
3. patience
4. a person
5. *Sixty Minutes*

Ask your instructor to check your sentences.

28.
Agreement
with
Irregular
Verbs
Write sentences using each of the following as a verb.

1. do	6. were
2. is	7. are
3. was	8. have
4. has	9. isn't
5. doesn't	10. does

Ask your instructor to check your answers.

29. Write sentences using each of the following in the subject.

Agreement with Compound Subjects

1. Mary and Ted
2. My husband or my parents
3. My son and his dog
4. My wife and I
5. Their cheerfulness and loyalty
6. Not only the sandwich but also the soup
7. The snow or the ice
8. Elvis or the Beatles
9. Either my car or my motorcycle
10. Arts and crafts

Ask your instructor to check your sentences.

30. Complete the following sentences by adding a verb to agree with the subject.

Agreement of Separated Subjects and Verbs

1. The car that has those options
2. The people working the late shift
3. My father, who slept through the songs,
4. The girl on the stairs
5. One of the singers
6. The policemen stopping our car
7. Ryman, converted by an evangelist,
8. The bus that runs this route
9. We work there and
10. He drives carefully and

Ask your instructor to check your sentences.

31. Complete the following sentences by adding a subject to agree with the verb.

Agreement When the Verb Comes Before the Subject

1. There is
2. There are
3. There was
4. There were
5. Seldom were
6. Have
7. Does
8. Next was
9. Here are
10. Doesn't

Ask your instructor to check your answers.

32. Write sentences using each of the following as a subject.

Agreement with Pronoun Subjects

1. I
2. I
3. The elevator, which
4. An animal that
5. The boys, who
6. Everybody
7. Some
8. Anyone
9. The weather that
10. Somebody

Ask your instructor to check your answers.

33. Write sentences using the correct form of each of the following as a *past-tense* verb.

Regular Verbs

1. meet
2. burst
3. catch
4. lie
5. use
6. do, does

34. Write sentences using the correct form of each of the following as a *past-participle* verb.

Irregular Verbs

1. suppose
2. froze
3. give
4. know

Ask your instructor to check your sentences.

35. Write sentences using each of the following subjects *and* at least one pronoun that agrees with it.

Pronoun Agreement

1. people
2. the committee
3. everyone
4. a person
5. our team
6. an employer
7. the group
8. a student
9. someone
10. a flu victim

Ask your instructor to check your sentences.

36. Write sentences using each of the following correctly.

Pronoun Case

1. myself
2. who
3. whom
4. him and me
5. themselves
6. she and they
7. your
8. mine
9. him
10. we

Ask your instructor to check your sentences.

37. Write five sentences using the semicolon correctly.

The
Semicolon Ask your instructor to check your sentences.

38. Write five sentences following the pattern below.

Commas
Between
Main Clauses

| Independent clause | , | and but or | independent clause. |
| | | nor for | |

Ask your instructor to check your sentences.

39. Write three sentences following the pattern below.

Commas
After
Introductory

| Dependent clause | , | independent clause. |

Clauses Now write three sentences following this pattern

| Independent clause | no comma | dependent clause. |

Ask your instructor to check your sentences.

40. Begin sentences with the following phrases. Separate the phrases from the rest of the

Commas sentences with commas where this is necessary.

After
Introductory 1. To buy a house   4. Being tired

Phrases 2. In the spring   5. To sum it all up
3. At the present

Ask your instructor to check your sentences.

41. Write three sentences linking two things with *and* or *or*. Write three sentences linking

Commas three or more things with *and* or *or*.

in a List
Ask your instructor to check your answers.

42. Write five sentences, each using two of the following words to describe one thing.

Commas
Between 1. sad lonely   4. slick slimy

Adjectives 2. fast smooth   5. light purple
3. very old

Ask your instructor to check your sentences.

43.   Write five sentences, each using one of the following to describe something or someone
Commas   in the sentence.
Setting Off
Modifiers   1. who was tired
2. fighting off the girls
3. that I know
4. my friend
5. the best one

Ask your instructor to check your sentences.

44.   Write five sentences, each using one of the following words or phrases.
Commas
Setting Off   1. therefore   4. all in all
Conjunctive   2. in conclusion   5. however
Adverbs   3. of course

Ask your instructor to check your sentences.

45.   Write five sentences using *not*, putting in commas where necessary.
Commas
Before *Not*   Ask your instructor to check your sentences.

46.   Write five sentences telling what someone said and who said it. Put in commas where
Commas with   necessary.
Speaker Tags
Ask your instructor to check your answers.

47.   Write two sentences naming places.
Commas with   Write two sentences naming addresses.
Dates and   Write two sentences naming dates.
Addresses
Ask your instructor to check your answers.

48.   Write five sentences, each making one of the following own a thing that is named right
The   after it.
Apostrophe
1. children   6. day
2. friend   7. boys
3. you   8. they
4. anyone   9. the Queen of England
5. Charles   10. Jim and Bob

Ask your instructor to check your answers.

49. Write sentences to tell about each of the following.
Capitalization

1. two doctors that you have known
2. two of your relatives
3. two holidays, seasons, days of the week, or months
4. four school subjects
5. two names of directions.

Ask your instructor to check your answers.

50. Write sentences using each of the following.
Problem Words

1. an
2. effect
3. along
4. sense
5. ever
6. fill

7. meet
8. patients
9. quiet
10. there
11. to
12. your

Ask your instructor to check your answers.

53. Write five sentences using two numbers in each.
Writing Numbers Ask your instructor to check your answers.

PARAGRAPHS

55 Paragraph Assignments

The following paragraph assignments tell you about two ways of ordering or arranging the sentences in a paragraph. There are also several other ways of ordering sentences for other purposes.

Read below about space ordering and time ordering, and write one of the practice paragraphs. Then read it to see if its sentences are in the best order. Finally, check it for errors.

SPACE ORDERING The sentences in a paragraph are sometimes ordered according to the way in which objects or persons are placed in space. Details may be given in the order of near to far, far to near, left to right, right to left, up to down, or down to up.

Practice 1. Think of a museum, amusement park, old house, or some other tourist attraction that you have visited. Imagine that you are again in one room or interesting part of the place. In your first sentence, tell where you are standing in that room or area. Then tell what you see. Use one of the orders above to help the reader understand the relation of one thing you describe to another.

Practice 2. Using one of the orders above, describe a street you know well. In your first sentence, tell what kind of street it is. Then describe the buildings, plants, vehicles, and/or activities on the street.

Practice 3. Describe a place outdoors where you like to be or a landscape that you remember well. It might be a corner of your campus, a scene in a park, or some wild spot that impressed you. In your first sentence, tell what the place is and how it makes you feel. Then give details that show why you feel that way. Be sure that the details are ordered in space so that the reader understands their relation to each other.

Practice 4. Describe the looks of a person you know well. The first sentence should tell how you know the person (friend, relative, boss) and the person's age. Then begin with the person's head and describe him or her in detail down to the feet. You may want to tell about the clothes the person is wearing, too.

TIME ORDERING Several kinds of paragraphs usually order sentences in time. The first thing that happens is told about first, the second thing next, and so on. Getting things out of their order in time may confuse the reader.

Practice 1. Tell about getting ready for a trip that you have taken. In the first sentence, tell where you were going. Then give details about your getting ready. Arrange the details by time.

Practice 2. Tell how to do something that takes a short time, like getting a stuck lid off a bottle, filling a hot-water bottle, warming a can of soup, or some other simple task.

The first sentence should tell what the task is. Be sure not to leave out any necessary step, and be sure to put the steps in their right order in time.

Practice 3. Tell something funny that happened to you lately. The first sentence should tell where you were and when. Then tell what happened in the order of the time that it happened.

Practice 4. Tell what happened at a meeting you have been to lately. First, name the time, place, and people there. Then tell in order of time what happened.

PAPERS

56 Paper Assignments

All essays should be written with blue or black ball-point pens on 8″ × 10″ white, lined paper which does not have rough edges. The first page should be the title page. In the middle of the page, write the title of the paper. Capitalize words in the title correctly, and do *not* put quotation marks around the title. In the lower right-hand corner, write your name on one line, the course identification numbers below it, and the date on a third line. Your title page should look like this:

Do not repeat your title on the first page. Your papers should all be about four pages long. You should write only on every other line. Leave blank lines between all the lines of your writing so that there is room for your instructor to make comments and for you to make corrections.

All corrections are to be made above the errors marked. Correct errors with a red ball-point pen.

Each paper should be written here, in your classroom, unless your instructor assigns it as homework. Unless you are told otherwise, you may use a dictionary, refer to any book (including this one), or ask the instructor about something that you are not sure of.

PAPER 1   INTRODUCING MYSELF

Purpose. To tell the important things about yourself.

Paragraph 1. Give your name and the general facts about yourself that you want us to know. These might include your age, appearance, family situation, education, and/or job.

Paragraph 2. Tell briefly about your chief interests. What things do you enjoy doing most?

Paragraph 3. Tell about what you are doing in school. You might want to tell about your reasons for coming here or about your educational program. You might want to write about the courses you are taking, about those you want to take, and/or about courses that you think might cause trouble.

PAPER 2   THE PERSON ACROSS FROM ME

Purpose. To tell about the person who is sitting across from you, using both what you see about him or her and what the person tells you about himself or herself.

Paragraph 1. Introduction: Describe this person's physical appearance. Include size, age, clothes, and personal mannerisms: for example, the way he or she moves or speaks.

Paragraph 2. What kind of car does this person drive? Describe it, right down to the seats, the dash, the windshield wipers, and so on. Tell about the way it looks, sounds, smells, and rides.

Paragraph 3. What kind of pet does this person have? Tell everything about this animal.

Paragraph 4. What is the person's best friend like? This may be a friend of the same sex as the person or of the opposite sex.

PAPER 3   NARRATIVE

Purpose. To tell about something that happened to you. Choose an event that was exciting, funny, sad, or important.

Paragraph 1. Introduction: Name the event that you are going to tell about. Then give any background information that the reader needs.

Other Paragraphs. Tell what happened in the order in which it happened. Start a new paragraph each time you start telling about a new part of the event. At the end, be sure that the reader knows why the event was exciting, funny, sad, or important to you.

PAPER 4   DESCRIPTION

Purpose. To describe a car *or* home that you would like to have.

Paragraph 1. Introduction: Say briefly what you would like and why.

Paragraph 2. Tell about the engine of the car *or* about the setting and location of the home that you would like. Give details.

Paragraph 3. Describe the outside of the car *or* the home. Give many details.

Paragraph 4. Tell about the interior of the car *or* home that you want. Give many details.

Paragraph 5. Summarize briefly what you like about the car *or* home.

PAPER 5   FANTASY

Purpose. To tell about what you imagine you would do if you had three wishes that would come true.

Paragraph 1. Introduction: Tell briefly what you would wish for.

Paragraph 2. Name the first wish and tell why you want it or what it would be like. Give details.

Paragraph 3. Name the second wish and tell about it. Give details.

Paragraph 4. Name the third wish and tell about it. Give details.

Paragraph 5. Summarize briefly.

PAPER 6   INSTRUCTION

Purpose. To tell how to make something or do something. Do *not* give a recipe.

Paragraph 1. Introduction: Name what you are going to tell the reader how to do. Let him or her know how you know about it.

Paragraph 2. Preparation: Tell what materials and/or tools are needed and how to get ready to do whatever you are explaining. Be sure not to leave anything out.

Paragraph 3. Step 1: Name the first big step in the process. Then tell in detail how to do it. Be sure that the instructions are complete.

Paragraph 4. Step 2: Name the second big step and tell in detail how to do it.

Other Paragraphs. Repeat this kind of paragraph for as many big steps as there are in doing the process.

Last Paragraph. Tell about finishing the job. This may involve cleaning up, testing, or using the product.

PAPER 7   CAUSE

Purpose. To tell three things that cause something. For instance, give three reasons that you admire someone, or three things that make you angry.

Paragraph 1. Introduction: Tell your reader what you are going to talk about. Name the three causes for your subject.

Paragraph 2. Name the first cause and explain it. Give examples.

Paragraph 3. Name the second cause. Then give details about it to explain it and to show that it is true.

Paragraph 4. Name the third cause and tell about it in detail as you have the others.

Paragraph 5. Summarize briefly.

PAPER 8   EFFECT

Purpose. To tell three things that something causes; for instance, three effects of unemployment, inflation, pollution, bad driving, prosperity, cooperation, or gardening.

Paragraph 1. Introduction: Name your subject and its three effects.

Paragraph 2. Name the first effect. Explain it and give examples.

Paragraph 3. Name the second effect. Explain it and give examples.

Paragraph 4. Name the third effect. Explain it and give examples.

Paragraph 5. Summarize briefly.

PAPER 9   CLASSIFICATION

Purpose. To show three different kinds of something. For instance, you could tell about three different *kinds* of any of the following groups of people: teachers, students, employees, athletes, parents, or children.

Paragraph 1. State what group you are going to tell about and which one of the group's characteristics you are going to classify. For example, if you tell about three different kinds of athletes, you might show how each trains for his or her sport.

Paragraph 2. Name the first kind and show what it is like in relation to the one characteristic. Explain and give examples.

Paragraph 3. Name the second kind and show what it is like in relation to the same characteristic. Explain and give examples.

Paragraph 4. Name the third kind and show what it is like in relation to the same characteristic. Explain and give examples.

Paragraph 5. Summarize briefly.

PAPER 10   COMPARISON OR CONTRAST

Purpose. To show three ways that two things are like each other or different from each other. For example, how are two schools alike? How are two doctors different?

Paragraph 1. Introduction: State what you are comparing. Name the three ways that they are alike or different.

Paragraph 2. Name the first likeness or difference. Tell how it applies to the first thing you are comparing, then how it applies to the second. Give explanations or examples as needed.

Paragraph 3. Name the second likeness or difference. Tell how it applies to the first thing you are comparing, then how it applies to the second. Give explanations or examples as needed.

Paragraph 4. Name the third likeness or difference. Tell how it applies to the first thing you are comparing, then how it applies to the second. Give explanations or examples as needed.

Paragraph 5. Summarize briefly.

PAPER 11   BOOK REPORT ON NONFICTION

Purpose. To report on a nonfiction book that you have read.

Paragraph 1. Introduction: State the title of the book and its author. Tell briefly what it is about.

Paragraph 2. State the author's main idea. Then explain what he or she means and tell how he or she supports this view.

Paragraph 3. State whether you agree or disagree with this main idea. Then support your own opinion with examples.

Paragraph 4. Tell any other ways in which you think the book is good or bad. Use examples to support your opinion.

PAPER 12   BOOK REPORT ON FICTION

Purpose. To report on a novel that you have read.

Paragraph 1. Introduction: State the title and author of the book. Tell briefly what it is about and when and where it takes place.

Paragraph 2. Briefly summarize the plot—that is, what happens in the book.

Paragraph 3. State whether you liked or disliked the book. Give one reason. Then give examples to support your reason.

Other Paragraphs. If you have other reasons for liking or disliking the book, tell about each in a new paragraph and support it with examples.

Index